TAMILNADU
A JOURNEY IN TIME
People, Places and Potpourri

Part- I

George Abraham
Pottamkulam

Notion Press

No.8, 3rd Cross Street
CIT Colony, Mylapore
Chennai, Tamil Nadu – 600004

First Published by Notion Press 2021
Copyright © George Abraham Pottamkulam 2021
All Rights Reserved.

ISBN 978-1-64951-689-3

A Tribute to Another Age

A concise compilation to rediscover a few of the facets and layers of Tamil Nadu's history, cultural heritage and legacy. From the Ancient to the 21st Century, the People, Places and Potpourri that crafted the magnificent mosaic that is our land, Tamil Nadu.

Dedication

This book is dedicated to the following lines...

Porivayininthavithaan poitheerozukk, anerinidraar needuvazvaar.

The Pursuit is for the Truth, so it is the path devoid of falsehood.

Thiruvalluvar -The Tirukkural

Contents

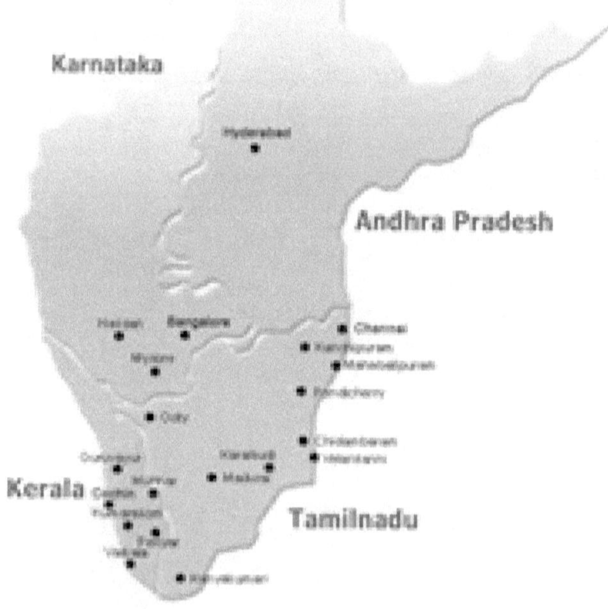

Karnataka
Andhra Pradesh
Kerala
Tamilnadu
Hyderabad
Bangalore
Chennai
Mysore
Ooty
Madurai

Introduction

"This is the Land of one of the oldest living cultures of the world, the Dravidians! They defined culture through their living! A culture which attracted innumerable people to this magical land and live here enmeshed through great teachings and scripted epics that evolved a way of life."

The history of the world has seen men and women born to change the course of our lives through their personalities. We call them role models. Time will honour them as Greats and Legends.

Do men and women of indomitable spirit rise to drive the change and create something new? I believe they rise not just because they want to, but because they feel they have to rise. They belong to a country, caste, creed and community only by birth, but their messages remain universal! Whatever we think of colonialaism now, such men and women transformed the world.

...If your actions inspire others to dream more, learn more, do more and become more, you are a leader.

– John Quincy Adams

In my humble compilation, you will find a galaxy of explorers who were destined to visit our land, become a part of our culture and deeply influence our way of life. They had an impact on our fortunes and misfortunes. Some were born here as proud children of India, as they were, in a way, gentleman adventurers in their own right. They were born in a time when their words were right and their work left a mark, but, perhaps, in a wrong time, a century ago. They all still need mentions as special people - early traders and voyagers, missionaries, great surveyors, planters, conservators and naturalists, great engineers, administrators, law makers, military officers and shikaries - not forgetting the tribals and workers who worked with them in the shadows. Now, slowly they emerge, into the stream of a brighter today. Their works remain a motivation for the future, as are we, the products of a past but not prisoners to it. This book seeks to draw any worthwhile inspiration from the works of the past and correct any mistakes of the future.

Today, we stand at the fork of a trail, as a fingerpost that connects the past to the present and into future. We can join hands to revive these lost tracks of our biodiversity, culture and traditions which have led us to this day, and not be the last generation to tread these gentlemen trails.

In the following pages, we embark on a journey of about three thousand years' history of the evolution of dynasties, trade, missionary work; sprinkles of stories from personal diaries interwoven with anecdotal tales and punctuated with biographies, mostly as book excerpts which will take us back to a long-buried era when West met the Far East. We bring you the modern world as we see it today, as the east reaches out to the West.

By the end of the journey with us, you will be able to arrive at a decision on whether the personalities depicted here were true contributors or consumers. Some will fade into oblivion, some many remain as temporary as tombstones in your mind and a few greats will remain in your hearts forever as 'Living Memorials,' relevant every minute as they stood for freedom, service, enterprise, upliftment and peace. Sadly, today, many of them are misrepresented by those who do not know them in their true motives which kept the fire kindled in them.

"From the Ancient to the 19ᵗʰ Century, the gentlemen who augmented enterprise, battled Religious Bigotry, Social Injustice and Colonial Oppression, Preserved Nature, Freedom Curbs and crafted the magnificent mosaic that is our Nation"

In our county, India, all of us absorb and follow a lot of values from religious epics like Ramayyan and Mahabaratha. In the Ramayyan, when Prabhu Ram became victorius over Ravan and he was returning back for home, he was told by Vibheeshan, "Lord Ram, since you are victorious, you can stake a claim over the Golden city of Lanka."

Lord Ram then turned around and said,

"Janani Janmabhoomshichyaswargadhaabegareyase!"

"My mother land, my mother is so beautiful, and she is greater than all the heavens human beings seek to achieve!"

Symbolic Division

Stretching across nearly the entire width of peninsular India, The Vindhya Range symbolically divides the North and South. South of the Vindhya range lies a triangular-shaped mass of ancient rock, the Deccan Plateau, which slopes gently eastward towards the Bay of Bengal. Godavari, Krishna and the Cauvery, are Southern rivers that originate in the rain-soaked peaks of the Western Ghats.

The Western Ghats Mountain Range or the Sahyadri Range begins South of the *Tapti River,* close to the boundary of Maharashtra and Gujarat. The Western Ghats begin to rise north of Mumbai, running parallel to the coast, until they reach the tip of the peninsula India. Here, they merge with the southernmost portion of the Eastern Ghats, a chain of low interrupted ranges that sweeps northeast in the direction of Chennai.

With an average elevation of 915m, the Western Ghats are covered with tropical, temperate, evergreen and mixed deciduous forests. Waterways and lagoons that characterise Kerala, etch the sedimentary plain of the Malabar Coast.

"If there is one place on the face of earth where all the dreams of living men have found home from the very earliest days when man began the dream of existence, it is India."

– Nobel Laureate Romain Rolland

India has 31 states, 1618 languages, 6400 castes, six religions, 6 ethnic groups, 29 major festivals and one country. Proud to be an Indian!

Destination – South India

Tamil Nadu, Kerala, Karnataka, Goa, Andhra Pradesh, Pudhucherry the Lakshadweep Islands and Andaman and Nicobar Islands comprise South India. Mountain ranges of the Western Ghats, a meandering coastline and a spur into the Eastern Ghats caressed by coral islands, wrap South India in its warm embrace.

With its own language, cuisines, states and distinct customs of the people that vary even within the state, South India is as unique as it is different. The cuisine varies significantly even with every sub-region. Naturally endowed with fertile lowlands, long coastal stretches, dense forests, high mountains and vast plateaus, its architectural grandeur is reflected in the magnificent domes and minars, sprawling temple complexes with beautiful carvings and hand-carved giant statues. The culture of the region is as ancient as civilisation, with temples built by the kings of different dynasties to tell their stories of valour and bravery, a mix of religions and festivals associated with it.

Short History

Many interesting facts reveal themselves in the ancient history of Tamil Nadu. The Dravidian land was ruled by three dynasties, Chola, Pandya and Chera from the 4th Century BC.

The present Thanjavur and Tiruchirapalli districts were ruled upon by the Cholas. Threatening the local people with military strength, Elara, a Chola Prince decided to expand his kingdom, conquering Ceylon in the 2nd century BC.

Devoting much of their time towards learning and establishing trade relations with traders throughout their kingdom, the Pandyas controlled the districts of Madurai, Tirunevely and parts of South Kerala. Ambassador sent by a Pandiyan king in the 1st century BC, was warmly received by Augustus, the Roman Emperor.

The Kanchi Pallavas were in power for 400 years, establishing their supremacy and regal splendour in the South between the 5th and 8th centuries A.D. Having subjugated the Chola domination, they took their armies to Ceylon (Sri Lanka) in the 6th century.

The famous Alvars and Nayanars (sage poets) flourished during the Pallava era and were responsible for the spiritual awakening in the minds of the local populace. The Cholas became a great power in the South in the 9th century A.D. when they defeated the last of the Pallavas.

The Pandyas became dominant in the 13th century. Channels of international trade were established during their rule. The prosperity of Vijayanagar Empire brought about the downfall of the Pandyas.

Soon, Vijayanagar absorbed almostall the territories of the Pandyas. After the disintegration of the Vijayanagar Empire, several petty kings apportioned Tamil Nadu among themselves.

Madras State was renamed as Tamil Nadu in August 1968. As the name suggests, people of Tamil Nadu consider Tamil as a language enriched with all the qualities of an ancient culture and traditions. Among the Dravidian languages, Sanskrit least influences Tamil. The earliest extant literature of the Tamils is called Sangam literature, and it is dated between 500 BC and 200 A.D. Tiruvalluvar's Tirukkural is acclaimed to be the greatest Tamil Classic. Tamil has produced two epics Silappadhikaram and Manimekhalai in the 3rd century and three others, Sivaga Sinthamani, Kundalakesi and Valayapathi, in due time. In the period between 13 and 18 century A.D., the works of Muslim and Christian writers influenced Tamil literature. The Christian influence began with the Portuguese and continued with the Dutch, the French and the British. The Italian priest, Beschi, composed the magnificent poetical work, Tembavani on the life of St. Joseph.

Devanagari-script Bhagavatapurana-Sanskrit British Library-1900

Marina – Madras 1890

A Look Back into the History of Madras

The origin of Madras dates back to a few centuries. Prior to that, small villages existed for well over 1000 years in a cluster of civilisation. Villages around temples were in existence for several centuries, long before the Europeans arrived in India.

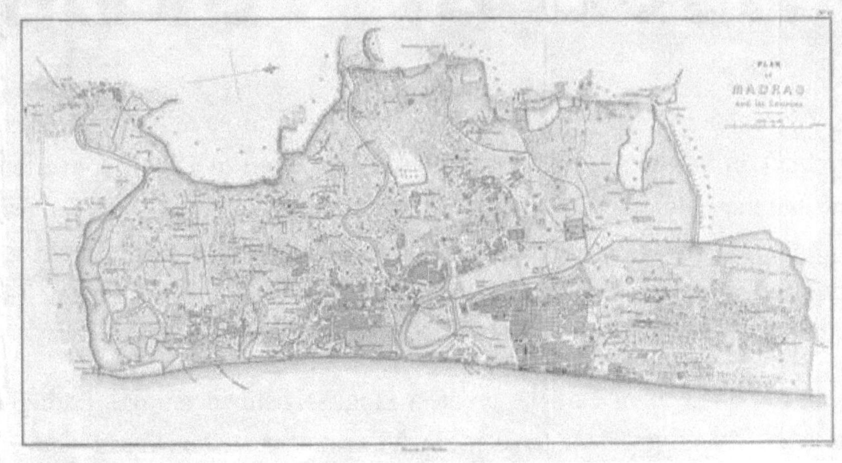

Cholas and Pallavas

During the earlier period, the Kalabhras suppressed Tamil chieftains for several decades. Soon, South India was split into numerous warring kingdoms. The Cholas virtually disappeared, the Cheras prospered through trading and the Kalabhras were overthrown in the late 6th century A.D.

For the next 300 years, the history of South India is resplendent with the fortune of the Chalukyas of Badami, the Pallavas of Kanchi and the Pandyas of Madurai. From their base at Thanjavur, the Cholas spread North and absorbed what was left of the territory of the Pallavas, and made inroads into the South. Music, dance and literature also flourished, and as a result, Tamil culture acquired a more distinct character, enduring in South India long after the Cholas had disappeared from the horizon. Trade wasn't the only thing the Cholas brought to the shores of South-East Asia, but they also introduced their culture as well. Their legacy lives on in Myanmar (Burma), Bali and Cambodia through the dance forms, religion and mythology of the regions.

Muslim Rulers

By 1323 A.D., Muslim rulers had reached Madurai in Tamil Nadu, pushing aside a series of local rulers, including the Hoysalas and Pandyas. Muhammad Tughluq rebuilt the fortifications in Daulatabad in Maharashtra to keep control of Southern India, recalled his army by 1334 in order to wage campaigns elsewhere.

The Vijayanagar Empire has always been thought to have been founded by two chieftain brothers who were captured and taken to Delhi, converted to Islam and then, sent back to the South to serve as governors for the Sultanate. Around 1336 A.D., the brothers reconverted to Hinduism and established a kingdom that eventually covered all the areas of Southern Karnataka, Tamil Nadu and parts of Kerala.

During the reign of one of the greatest kings, Krishnadevaraya, Portuguese chronicler, Domingo Paez arrived in Vijayanagar. After Vasco da Gama arrived in Calicut in 1498, doors were opened to facilitate trade between the Portuguese and Indians. Afonse de Albuquerque reached the shores of India after Vasco da Gama and he established his little kindgom that included Goa. Roman Catholicism was introduced to India by the Portuguese in 1588 A.D. The defeat of the Spanish Armada lay open the sea route to the east for the English and the Dutch.

Francis Day was the first European to reach the shores of Madras. A member of the Masulipatnam council, he undertook a journey down the east coast of South India, looking for a promising place to set court. He founded Madraspatnam and built the Fort of St. George, as the building was finished during The Feast of St. George. A settlement soon began to form around the Fort, and the new town called itself Chennaipatnam. The town adjacent to the the Fort came to be known as Madraspatnarn.

The origin of the name 'Madras' is mired in folklore. Some attribute the name to the small church built by the Portuguese dedicated to the Mother of God - Mae do Deus, whereas others ascribe the name to a local village chieftain Maddarasu. Be that as it may, Madras rose in stature and power with the rise of the British Empire. Many colleges, hospitals and prominent landmarks were established in tune with its rising importance. Towards the end of 19th century, Madras was clearly established as an important hub in South India. Today, Madras is known as Chennai and is the capital of Tamil Nadu, one of South India's largest states.

"Society exists only as a mental concept. In the real world, there are only individuals."

– Oscar Wilde

The Dravidians are the oldest living culture of the world. They defined culture through their living – a culture that attracted innumerable people to this magical land, who lived here surrounded by great teachings, scripting epics that signified a way of life.

The term Dravidian is usually used to refer to the Dravidian speaking populations of South Asia who speak various Dravidian languages such as Telugu, Tamil, Kannada, Malayalam and Tulu. As far as physical features of contemporary Dravidian speakers are concerned, they are usually considered to be Caucasoids or a mixed population of Caucasoids and Veddoids by most of the anthropologists rather than Australoids or Negritos. Modern-day Dravidian speakers can be classified / divided into 6 groups according to their phenotypes.

1. Indo Iranids - Brahuis
2. Indo Melanids – Most of the Tamils
3. Gondids – Gonds and other similar Tribal groups of Central India

Who Were Dravidians in India

According to some claims, the Dravidians originally inhabited the northern part of India and were later pushed to the Southern part of the country by the Aryans. Therefore, Dravidians form about 28% of Indians and reside in

South India, speaking a few prominent Dravidian languages, including Tamil, Malayalam, Telugu, Kannada and Tulu.

The Dravidian language has three subgroups - North Dravidian, Central Dravidian and South Dravidian. In present day India, the states of Andhra Pradesh, Karnataka, Kerala and Tamil Nadu are the significant regions with a Dravidian population with the rest 72% being Aryans, residing in North India.

The different origin of these languages is the reason for different South and North Indian accents. We know very little about the Dravidian people in India, who used to reside in the country before the Aryans invaded Northern India from Iran and Southern Russia.

Some linguists believed that the Dravidian people were well spread across the Indian sub continent and it is because of this that the Indus Valley civilisation (Harappa and MohenjoDaro) is also referred to as a Dravidian civilisation. The debate still exists on whether the Indus Valley civilisation belongs to the Dravidians.

The Dravidian populace residing in present day Central India is tribal people known as Gond. Kannadigaru Dravidians are from Karnataka, northern Kerala, Southern Maharashtra and northwest Tamil Nadu. Kondha Dravidians are from eastern Indian states of Andhra Pradesh and Orissa. Kodava Dravidians are people from Karnataka and Northern Kerala. Besides these, there are Kurukh, Malayali, Tamil, Telugus and Tuluvas people who belong to Dravidians in India.

Dravidians were originally very peace-loving farmers and they were not trained in any kind of warfare. It is believed that when the Aryans invaded India, they pushed the Dravidians to the Southern part. The Aryans who were skilled fighters and prepared with weaponary and chariot racing, forced them to fight back. Dravidians were also a very sophisticated culture and used to worship all forms of life including herbs, and plants. With the coming of the Aryans, the concept of heaven and God came into existence which dramatically changed cultural and religiously identities. Therefore, not much is known about the Dravidians. Only archaeological and linguistic references serve as the main source of information about them.

Dravidian people have dark complexion, dark black hair and eyes and large foreheads. Because of similarities in physical structure, it is also believed that Dravidians had some African ancestral origin. As per these findings and anthropological and genetic data, people migrated from Africa and reached South India via the Southern route about 50,000 years ago. Because of rivers and fertile soil, they stayed in India in large numbers, rather than settling in other parts of the world.

But there are many theories and studies that explain the origin of Dravidians, their link to Africa, Aryan invasion and Dravidian's migration to South India. All theories however put forward one common fact - that the Dravidians were a very classy, hard working and skilled race of people.

The Myth about the Aryans

We read about how Aryans invaded the lands that are present day India and brought their own 'Indian Culture' to India. Some significant studies have shown that this was not the case. An exploration of the way historians came to believe in the 'myth' of the Aryan Theory of Civilisation, is very revealing.

The first millennium BC in northern India has been declared a period of vast historical change. Ample evidence exists from archaeological studies, which has thrown light on this period due to the availability of a significant amount of historical material. The theory of the 'Aryan invasion', as it was called is no longer acceptable due to the recent archaeological work on Harappa and post-Harappan civilisations. This is further corroborated by the linguistic developments made in this area of study

So, what was this myth of the Aryan invasion? From where did it emerge?

The concept of the 'Aryan invasion' was a 19th century invention, created to suit the social and political needs of that period. The 'Indologists', as they were called, established an area of comparative philosophy that gave rise to an idea of a common Indo-European ancestry. The Indo-Aryan was opposed in this scheme of study to the Dravidian. These notions we now know to be false were a result of Colonial interests in India in the 19th century. These were required at the time as a justification and self-explanation of colonial conquest and rule, combined with a need to study the people who were governed. Imperial expansion in India was sought to be justified due to these pseudo-studies done by 19th century academics with an eye to precisely substantiate colonial projects overseas. It became an easy story to tell.

There were once European invaders who came to India and established their culture here. This was in direct contrast to the Dravidians who were gentle people, only fit to be ruled, it was argued. History only repeated itself when the British invaded India, the Indologists said. The British colonialists likened themselves to the glamorized Aryans, and this story was an easy one to sell. So easy infact, that even after more than six decades of independence India regurgitates the same story.

What this goes to show is that the practice involving the foundation of knowledge, the role of academia and intellectuals can also be embedded in politics of power. No writing of history is innocent. The dangers of the Aryan race theory in this case can be measured, when compared to a similar Aryan race theory that evolved in Germany and led to the Holocaust.

The British version, though ostensibly a watered down version of the same, did as much harm when it caused imperial conquest and colonial destruction.

The Literary Heritage of Tamil Nadu

"The Literary Heritage of Tamil Nadu contributed greatly to the Dravidian way of Life which spread light to the neighbouring Southern states of Kerala, Karnataka and Andhra"

Akananuru, (Tamil) a classical Tamil poetic work, is the seventh book in the anthology of Sangam literature (600 BCE - 300 CE), namely *Ettuthokai*. It contains 400 *Akam* (subjective) poems dealing with matters of love and separation.

Other names for *Akananuru* include *Neduntogai* or *Nedunthokai* ("the long anthology"), *Ahappattu*, *Ahananuru* and *Agananuru*.

Authors

As many as 145 poets are said to have contributed to Akananuru collection. Perunthevanaar, who translated the Mahabharatham into Tamil, is one of the authors. Rudrasarman compiled this anthology at the behest of the Pandya king, Ukkiraperuvazhuthi.

Date

It is highly likely that the poems in Akananuru collection were prevalent independently before they were collected and categorised in this present form. The anthology is dated to around the first and the second century CE The poems probably are of a much earlier date. At least, a few poems must belong to 5th century BC to 3rd century BC, depending on the structure of the poems. There were mentions of Nanda and Mauryas in a few poems, which eventually date these poems to 4th to 3rd centuries BC.

Poetic characteristics

This book comes under the *Akam* (subjective) category in its subject matter. Ancient Tamil poems was categorised into the broad categories of *Akam* - Subjective, dealing with matters of the heart and human emotions, and *Puram* - Objective, dealing with the tangibles of life such as war, politics, wealth, etc. The poems of this anthology are of the *Akaval* metre.

In the poems on Akam, the aspects of love of a hero and a heroine are depicted. The story of love is never conceived as a continuous whole. A particular moment of love is captured and described in each poem as the speech of the hero or the lady-companion or somebody else. A young man leading a peaceful life of love and affection with his wife is referred as "A bird with two heads and one soul." Women are always referred as *Mangala Mahilar, Melliyal Mahalir, Seyelai Mahalir* and *Manaiyal* - all of these indicating the soft characterisation and glorifying the household presence of women folk during the Sangam period.

The auspicious time of wedding was considered to be the harvest season. A high standard of moral virtue seems to have prevailed among women of household.

Akananuru contains 401 stanzas and is divided into three sections
Kalintruyanainirai 121 stanzas
Manimidaipavalam 180 stanzas
Nittilakkovai 100 stanzas

English Translations

Bharathidasan University, Tiruchirapalli has published a full translation of all the 400 songs by Professor A. Dakshinamurthy in three Volumes in 1999. This is the first complete English translation of the anthology.

(The heroine's companion sings to her friend at the advent of the rainy season)

The rumbling clouds winged with lightning
Poured amain big drops of rain and augured the rainy season;
Buds with pointed tips have sprouted in the jasmine vines;
The buds of *Illam* and the green trunk *Kondrai* have unfolded soft;
The stags, their black and big horns like twisted iron,
Rushed up towards the pebbled pits filled with water
And leap out jubilantly having slaked their thirst;
The wide expansive Earth is now free
From all agonies of the summer heat
And the forest looks exceedingly sweet;
Behold there O friend of choicest bangles!
Our hero of the hilly track will be coming eftsoon,
Driving fast his ornate chariot drawn by the steeds
With waving plumes and trimmed manes
When the stiffly tugged reins
Will sound like the strumming of *Yal*.
As he drives, he has the chariot bells tied up
So as not to disturb the union of bees
That live on the pollen of the blossoms in the bushes.

He rushes onward thinking all along of your great beauty.

O' friend, whose fragrance is like unto the blossoming *Kantal*

On the mountain, tall and huge, east of Urantai of dinsome festivity!

– Translated by Prof A. Dakshinamurthy

Tolkāppiyam

The *Tolkāppiyam* is a work on the grammar aspect of the Tamil language. It is also the earliest documented work of Tamil literature. Written in the form of noorpaa, or short, formulaic compositions, it comprises of three books – the *Ezhuttadikaram*, the *Solladikaram* and the *Poruladikaram*. Each of these books is further divided into nine chapters each. While the exact date of the work is not known, it has been dated variously between the third century BCE and the 10th century CE, based on linguistic and other evidences. Some modern scholars prefer to date it not as a single entity but in parts or layers. There is also no firm evidence to assign the authorship of this treatise to any one particular author.

Tolkāppiyam deals with orthography, phonology, morphology, semantics, prosody and the subject matter of literature. The Tolkāppiyam classifies Tamil language into *Sentamil* and *Koduntamil*. Classical Tamil, used almost exclusively in literary works, is what the former refers to, while the latter refers to the dialectal Tamil, spoken by the people in various regions of ancient Tamilagam.

Tolkāppiyam categorises alphabets into consonants and vowels by analysing the syllabi. It grammatises the use of words and syntaxes and moves into higher modes of language analysis. The Tolkāppiyam formulated 30 phonemes and three dependent sounds for Tamil.

Etymology of the name

The word Tolkāppiyam is derived from the combination of two words, *Tonmai* and *Kāppiyam*. 'Tonmai' means 'ancient,' whereas 'Kappiam' means literature. Kappiam is derived from the Sanskrit word, Kavyam.

Thi is a derivation of Tolkāppiyam from root words as per the rules defined in Nannūl verse 136.

Date of the Text

Dating of the earliest Tamil grammatical treatise, Tolkāppiyam, has been a very debatable topic and it is still imprecise and uncertain, having seen a wide range of disagreements among scholars in the field. It has been dated variously between 3rd century BCE and the 3rd century CE.

The antediluvian dating stemmed mostly from a descriptive commentary in an 8th-century work called *Iraiyanar Agapporul*, about the existence of three Tamil academies. These have now been rejected as being devoid of any archaeological/linguistic evidence. Currently, there is a disagreement that centres on the divergent dates from the 3rd century BCE or later, with one estimate (by a botanist-author) pegging it as late as the 10th century CE.

Dating it in parts or layers, rather than one single entity is what some scholars prefer and this is estimated to be between the 3rd century BCE and the 5th century CE.

Assigning the authorship of this treatise to any one author is also not possible, since there is no firm evidence to support it.

Thiruvalluvar, the legendary Tamil poet who lived sometime between the fourth and first century BCE. He authored *Thirukkural*, couplets on secular ethics which are as relevant today as they were over 2000 years ago! The *Thirukkural*, is often referred to as *Pothumarai* - The common man's *Veda*.

The *Thirukkural* is one of the most widely translated pieces of Tamil literature. One of the earliest commentaries on the *Thirukkural* was done by a later Tamil poet, Parimelazhagar, in the 12th century CE.

The first translation of the *Thirukkural* in a European language was done in Latin by Constanzo Beschi, a Jesuit missionary in 1730. Beschi too, was a renowned Tamil poet who went by the name Vīramāmunivar.

One of the most popular and commonly quoted translations of the *Thirukkural* was done by G U Pope, an Anglican missionary who took the *Thirukkural* to the western world in 1886. The *Thirukkural* has been translated to more than 30 languages to date.

Tiruvalluvar, Author of Epic, Tirukkural
(Massive Statue at Kanyakumari.)

Tirukkural, or *Kural* as per classic Tamil Sangam literature, comprises 1330 Kurals or couplets, written by the sage Thiruvalluvar.

One of the most important works of the Tamil language, Thirukkural has been given several significant names through the centuries. Tamil marai or Vedas, DeivaNool or Divine Text and Poyyamozhi, a Tamil word that means 'words that never fail' all go to show the significance of this text. Considered to precede Manimekalai and Silapathikaram, Tirukkkural has a mention in both these seminal texts.

Structured into 133 chapters, each with ten couplets, Thirukkural has some total of 1330 couplets. The 133 chapters are grouped into three sections:

Arathupaal or Righteousness
Porutpaal or Wealth
Kamathupaal or Love

A Kural couplet comprises of seven cirs. A cir is a single or a combination of Tamil words. The first line has four cirs and second has three. Thirukkural, for example, is a cir that combines Thiru and Kural. There are 380 verses in Aram, 700 in Porul and 250 in Inbam. The book on ethics, polity and love comprises of 1,330 couplets divided into chapters or *kurals* of ten couplets each.

The Tirukkural has been a very controversial book, with several claims and counter claims as to the source, the exact number of couplets and pertaining to the authorship by Thiruvalluvar. Thiruvalluvar was first mentioned as the author several centuries after the book was written, in a 'praise' song called Garland of Thiruvalluvar in *Thiruvalluva Malai.*

Thirukkural has had several commentaries written about it through the centuries. Manakkudavur has been one of pioneering commentators of this seminal work. Manakkudavar and Pari Perumal, who lived in the 11th century, Kaalingar of the 12th century and Parimelazhagar of the 13th century compiled the earliest recorded commentaries on the Thirukkural.

V. O. Chidambaranar, in 1935, wrote a commentary on the First Part of Tirukkural – Virtue, which was published under a different title. Subsequently, the completed commentary on Tirukkural was published in 2008 as a manuscript of V. O. Chidambaram, compiled by his son, Amar Jothi.

A scholar in Tholkappiyam, Tirukkural and several other significant Tamil literatures, V. O. Chidambaram conducted an in-depth research on Tirukkural, including a meticulous and insightful comparative study of all preceding commentaries. He was able to put forth a new, proven and unparalleled version. His commentary is a very helpful insight into the book and offers precious information to scholars doing research on Tirukkural and Tamil literature in general.

Bottom of Form

"Let a man by patience overcome those who through pride commit excesses,"

– Poet and Saint Thiruvalluvar

Tolstoy was inspired by Thiruvalluvar's philosophy of non-violence and passed it on to Mahatma Gandhi (Left: MK Gandhi; Right: Leo Tolstoy)

In fact, a few realise that *Thirukkural* may have had a big influence on how India got her freedom from Britain in 1947. It is believed that the legendary Russian writer, Leo Tolstoy was deeply inspired by the concept of non-violence found in the *Thirukkural* when he read a German translation of the book. This, in turn, was passed on to Mahatma Gandhi through *A Letter to a Hindu*, when Gandhi, dubbed the 'Father of India's struggle for independence,' sought Tolstoy's guidance.

Tamil literature's Enduring Classics

Tamil's place in the Indian language pantheon is an important one. As an ancient and highly-developed language that evolved independently from Sanskrit and Sanskrit-derived languages, it occupies a special place. The languages of the Dravidian language family, to which Tamil belongs, have time and again, asserted their separate origins and history which is long. After all, among Tamil's more vehement assertions is the fact that it has ancient literature.

Tamil literature goes back to the Sangam Era, named after the assembly (Sangam) of poets based in Madurai. Tradition holds that there were two earlier such sangams, the works of which have been lost. What has come down to the present day, dates to the first and second century C E.

Sangam literature consists of eight anthologies (Ettuthogai) and ten long poems (Pathupattu).

The poetics of these sublime works of poetry are based on the *Tolkappiyam*, which is the earliest Tamil grammar.

At some point after the Sangam period, two epic narratives were written—the *Silappadikaram* (the Tale of an Anklet) by Ilango Adigal and another closely-linked work, the *Manimeghalai* (named after its heroine) by Sattanar.

Tamil literature goes back to the Sangam Era, named after the assembly (Sangam) of poets.

Tradition holds that there were three sangams. The first Sangam 'sat' for 4,440 years and was presided over by the sage Agastya, the legendary progenitor of the Tamil language. His book, the *Akattiyam* was the most important text of this first Sangam. This legendary first work of early Tamil literature has almost entirely been lost except for a few verses that are quoted in commentaries dating back to the medieval period. This first Sangam was convened in a city to the Thenmadurai that was later swallowed by the sea. These narratives continue to be read and studied, and constitute an important component of Tamil culture and literature.

The Story of *Silappadikaram*

The story of *Silappadikaram* (sometimes spelt *Cilappatikaram*) begins in Puhar (Poompuhar), the ancient port town in the northern region of Tamil country. Puhar is no ordinary town. It is the capital of the Chola kingdom and enjoys trade relations with Sri Lanka, Burma and even distant Java.

Ships of all kinds sail in and out of its harbour, and foreigners are forever crowding its markets looking for things to buy. Kovalan, the son of one of Puhar's most prominent and wealthy merchants marries Kannagi (sometimes spelt Kannaki). The young couple set up home and are very much in love before Kovalan deserts his wife entranced as he is by the obvious charms of a dancer, Madhavi. Saddened by Kovalan's action, Kannagi, nevertheless, puts up with the indignity.

Some years later, suspecting Madhavi of infidelity, Kovalan returns to Kannagi, who large-heartedly welcomes him back. In the meantime, Kovalan has frittered away his fortune. The couple then relocates to Madurai, the capital of the Pandya kingdom in a bid to rebuild their life. All that Kovalan and Kannagi have left at capital to begin life anew are a pair of anklets. Kovalan offers one of the anklets to the royal goldsmith for sale. The goldsmith, in turn, implicates Kovalan in the theft of the queen's anklet. Kovalan's wrongful execution which follows soon after drives Kannagi to rage. With her other anklet in hand, Kannagi confronts the king and proves that Kovalan was no thief as the queen's anklet contains pearls whereas hers contained gems.

Devastated, the king dies of remorse and guilt as does his queen. Beset by rage, Kannagi walks out of the palace, wrenches her left breast from her body and hurls it at the city of Madurai, which is then consumed by flames.

On the advice of the guardian deity of Madurai, Kannagi then undertakes a journey to Kodungallur in the Chera kingdom, from where she attains salvation.

Sculpture of Ilango Adigal in Poompuhar Museum|Kasiarunachalam

The Writer

Tradition holds that the writer of *Silappadikaram* is Ilango Adigal (sometimes spelt Ilanko Atigal), the younger brother of the Chera king, Senguttuvan. While one group of historians hold that Senguttuvan lived in the 2nd century CE, others date his reign to a wider window – 2nd to 5th century CE. The story goes that an astrologer predicted that Ilango would reign over the Chera kingdom, which angered Senguttuvan, who was the older son. In deference to Senguttuvan, Ilango renounced all claims to the throne, became a Jain ascetic and later, composed the work.

Senguttuvan himself features in the work when he raises a temple to Kannagi, in the post-Madurai section of the work.

Interestingly, Senguttuvan also features in the *Pathupattu* or the Ten Idylls, an anthology of ten books which is considered the oldest surviving works of Tamil poetry. This is part of Sangam literature.

Some scholars opine that it is probable that like Homer, Ilango Adigal wrote down the oral narratives that were in circulation at that time and the *Silappadikaram* is, therefore, not the work of one, but several writers.

The *Manimeghalai*

The *Manimeghalai* (sometimes spelt *Manimekalai*) by Sattanar (sometimes spelt Cattanar) is a sequel to the Silappadikaram and tells the story of the eponymous daughter of Kovalan and Madhavi. Manimeghalai, like her mother, Madhavi, is a dancer, who gives up her life as a courtesan to become a Buddhist nun when she hears of the death of Kovalan and the doings of Kannagi. The work also features the tragic love story of the Prince Udayakumaran whose love for Manimeghalai is doomed to be unrequited on account of her decision to renounce the world.

A palm leaf manuscript with ancient Tamil text|Wikimedia Commons

The narratives as a peek into history

Silappidakaram consists of three *kaandam* (books) each named after the capitals of the three ancient Tamil kingdoms – Puhar of the Cholas, Madurai of the Pandyas and Vanji of the Cheras.

Statue of Kannagi at Marina Beach, Chennai|Balamurugan Srinivasan

Together, the narratives present a comprehensive picture of early Tamil society with its three princely kingdoms, its merchants, princes and its Hindu, Buddhist and Jain populations, all of whom appear to have coexisted peacefully despite their differences. When Kannagi and Kovalan make the journey from Puhar to Madurai, they also encounter farmers, hunters and pastoralists who live in the countryside away from the main cities and have their own traditions and ways of life.

Unlike the Sanskrit or even the Greek epics, the twin Tamil narratives, sometimes referred to as the *irattaikappiyam*, are unique in that they both have women as protagonists and its associated trials and tribulations. Instead, the narratives place commoners at the centre of the narrative. That the Pandya king dies, consumed as he is by the guilt of his wrongful judgement is also unique, since the tales refuse to place rulers on a higher pedestal. Instead, rulers are shown to be as accountable for their actions as the subjects they govern.

Present Day

The Kodungallur Bhagavathy temple in present day Kerala is closely identified with the tale of Kannagi. Kannagi or Pattini, as she is known, is also present in Sinhalese folklore. Gajabahu, the Sinhalese king is said to have been Senguttuvan's contemporary (some scholars contest this) and present when the Kodungallur temple was consecrated. Several shrines to Pattini are found throughout the island, and she is regarded as a Boddhisattva (an individual on the path to becoming a Buddha). The intertwined early history of the Sinhalese and the Tamils is obvious here, as opposed to more modern day historical narratives that seek to establish that the Sinhalese and Tamils have been two warring communities from time immemorial.

The tale of Kannagi has been made into films and TV serials. A recent English novel, *The Prince* by Samhita Arni was also based on the *Silappadikaram*. A statue of Kannagi adorns the avenue beside the Marina Beach in Chennai and is an evocative reminder of the continued presence of the epics in present day Tamil life.

Cover Image: Kovalan with Madhavi, sculpture in Poompuhar Museum. Photographer- S Sriram

L H I 1

The Kingdoms of the South (3rd BCE – 3rd CE)

Around 15 km from Tamil Nadu's Tiruchirappalli and 45 km from the historic city of Thanjavur, you will find a dam on the Kaveri River that has the most fascinating story. The Kallanai or the Grand Anicut, as it was called, is one of the oldest irrigation works in the world. Said to be built by one of the early Chola kings, Karikala in the 1st-2nd CE, it has been in continuous use for almost 2,000 years.

But the dam (which started as an embankment) is famous not only for its antiquity; the Kallanai is quite an engineering marvel. It not only controlled the annual floods in the region, the irrigation works set in place to divert the flood waters through canals during the time of King Karikala transformed the once semi-arid region south of it into one of the most fertile stretches in the subcontinent. Ancient Sangam poetry celebrates Karikala's success in transforming a wilderness (*kattu*) into a cultivable land (*Nadu*).

Anicut Dam|Wikimedia Commons

Geographically, this stretch went on to become so rich that it catapulted the small local chiefdom that controlled it to fame. It is from here that the early Cholas rose. It is from this region that the later Cholas carried forward the baton of Chola glory. And it is to this event – the building of the embankment – that the later Cholas referred, time and again, to forge a link to the legacy of the heroes of yore.

The period between the 3th BCE and 3rd CE – the so-called Sangam Age – was a period of economic growth and cultural renaissance in the Deep South. And it is the trade, art, culture and literature which thrived during this period that dominates any discussion on the subject. But even as the busy ports overflowing with gold helped give wings to thoughts and verse, this period also saw the emergence of a political system that represented a transformation of its own kind.

Chieftains or *Velirs* mentioned in early Sangam texts gave way to a few who spread out – the *Vendars*. They were the first among equals who went on to create 'kingdoms.' Over the next few hundred years, the southern part of India, i.e. Tamilakam, was carved out between the Cholas, Keralaputras/Cheras and Pandyas, who dominated the landscape and inspired generations (of fellow dynasts) to come.

The modern day cultural divisions of Tamilakam into Tondainadu (centred around Chennai and Kanchipuram), Cholanadu (around Thanjavur and Tiruchirappalli), Pandyanadu (Madurai to Kanyakumari) and Kongunadu (around Coimbatore and Karur), hark back to the ancient world and cover the areas once occupied by the Pallavas, Cholas, Pandyas and Cheras, respectively.

Old political boundaries seem to have been etched into the heart of the region's cultural identity.

Ashoka's Major Rock Edict 2 at Girnar|Wikimedia Commons

Early References

The first 'official' reference to the early kingdoms of the South comes from Mauryan Emperor Ashoka's Major Rock Edict 2 at Girnar, in Gujarat. Here, he refers to the Cholas, Pandyas, Satiyaputra, Keralaputra and Tamrapani (Sri Lanka) as kingdoms on the southern borders of his dominion.

Even earlier, the Greek ambassador in Ashoka's grandfather, Chandragupta Maurya's court, Megasthenes (350 – 290 BCE) mentions a queen who ruled the area deep in the South, extending to the sea in the Pandya country. According to this account in the *Indica*, the kingdom had 365 villages, each of which was expected to meet the needs of the royal household for one day in the year. Megasthenes described the Pandyan queen of the time as 'Pandaia,' a daughter of Heracles (a Greek demi-god said to have come east. Heracles was later also identified as Shiva by some historians).

Sangam literature, which was written over a period of six centuries (3rd BCE – 3rd CE) is, of course, replete with references to various Chola, Chera and Pandya kings and numerous chieftains in between, all mostly at war with each other. In fact, skirmishes, raids and the heroic exploits of kings and princes dominate a large part of the early *puram* poetry of the Sangam Era.

King Kharavela's Hathigumpha inscription|Wikimedia Commons

In Odisha's capital Bhubaneswar, the Udayagiri inscription of Kalinga's King Kharavela, dated to around 2nd BCE - 1st BCE, refers to an expedition he led into the south towards the Krishna River. He is said to have attacked the town of Pithunda, which was ploughed with a plough yoked to asses, in an attempt to desecrate the land. Kharavela claims to have broken up the confederacy of the Tramira (Tamil countries), which had been a threat to Kalinga. The reference to a Tamil confederacy, earlier, even during the time of Chandragupta Maurya (r. *c.* 321–*c.* 297 BCE), indicates that the southern chiefdoms and *vendars* often joined forces to take on attackers from the North.

The Graeco-Roman texts, *The Periplus of the Erythraean Sea* and Pliny's classical work *The Natural History,* also have vivid descriptions of port cities and political capitals in the South, whether Muziris in present day Kerala, Nelcynda in the Kingdom of the Pandyas, or the twin centres of Orthura Regia Sornati identified as Uraiyur and Khaberis identified as Kaveripattinam.

We also know that the Roman Emperor Julian received an embassy from a Pandya ruler as late as 361 CE and a Roman trading centre was located on the Pandya coast at the mouth of the Vaigai River, south-east of Madurai.

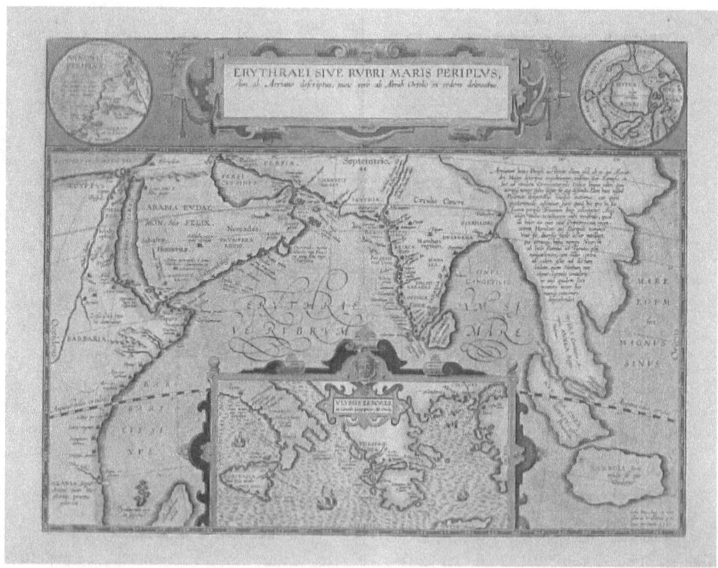

A 1597 map depicting the locations of the Periplus of the Erythraean Sea|Wikimedia Commons

While all these sources help us paint a picture of early political formations in the South, there are numerous archaeological, epigraphic and numismatic clues that are filling the many gaps in early Southern history. Thankfully, the early history of the South coincides with the emergence of Tamil-Brahmi inscriptions that have been found strewn on cave walls and pottery shards from Karur to Korkai.

Also, hundreds of coins from the Sangam Era give a sense of the political and economic authority that the Sangam Cheras, Chola and Pandyas wielded. Over a period of time, you see the coins evolving as well, from crude quadrangle copper coins in the early period (i.e. probably before the Common Era), to circular coins, sometimes in silver, in the later period.

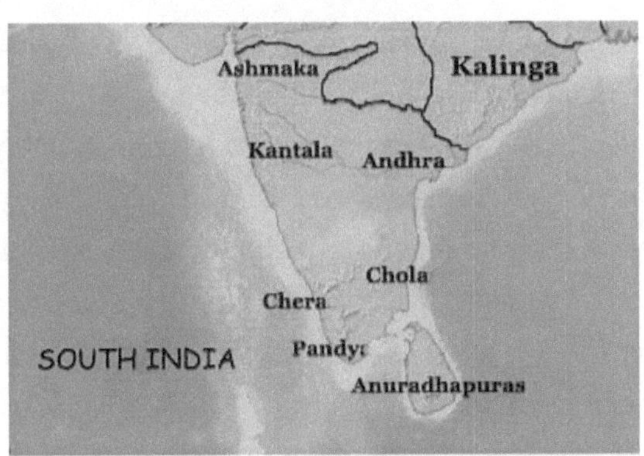

Regions of influence of the Early Chera, Chola and Pandya Kingdoms|Wikimedia Commons

The Rise of the South

One of the most tantalising questions relating to the Early Historic Period of the South remains the one pertaining to the origins of the three 'kingdoms' that dominated the region for centuries – the triad of the Cholas, Pandyas and Cheras.But it is important to note that the political demarcations in early historic Tamilakam were not rigid or well-defined. In fact, Selvakumar believes that it is not until the Pallavas, much later in the 6th CE, that we see the first actual state formation in the South, in the traditional sense. But what is it that helped some chiefs dominate others and muster more regional clout?

The site of Arikamedu near present day Puducherry|Wikimedia Commons

Based on his work in some of the region's most famous archaeological sites, from Arikamedu to Pattanam, Selvakumar believes that by the end of the Megalithic period, there were numerous chiefdoms that occupied land in the deltaic region of Tamilakam. Those who had control over nodal trading towns emerged stronger than the others and gradually expanded their territory. They became local powers and were respected by traders, and over time, they adopted symbols of power such as titles, royal emblems, issuance of coins and the performance of sacrifices.

The Cholas had their capital in Uraiyur and their port in Kaveripattinam. The Cheras were centred first near Kodungallur in Western Kerala and later Karur (around the 1st CE) in Western Tamil Nadu, with their port in Muziris. The Pandyas started out at Korkai and gradually moved up to Madurai.

Apart from this triad of powers, another chiefdom that stood out was that of the Malayamans, who seem to have enjoyed control over the important port site of Arikamedu near present day Puducherry. They also issued coins in copper.

Interestingly, these regional powers managed to always hold on to their core territories. Despite the numerous battles and skirmishes listed in great detail in the Sangam *puram* poems, most of these battles were actually raids for wealth, and not power trips for territory.

The Pandyas

The Pandyas and the Deep South they come from have a special significance in the region's history. It is under them that the great Sangams are said to have taken place ('Sangams' were great meet-ups of poets, steeped in legend and resulted in a huge body of literature, much of which is lost). Another story connects the Pandyas with the origin of political kingdoms in the South. The story goes that, in ancient times, there were three brothers who lived in Korkai, close to the tip of Tamil Nadu and then, a coastal port city. They were called Cheran, Cholan and Pandyan, and they ruled the region together. While Pandyan is said to have remained at home, the other two moved out and founded their own kingdoms.

This may be just folklore, but the Pandyas seem to have started as a coastal chiefdom that rose on the back of the growth of Korkai as a trading centre. *The Periplus of the Erythraean Sea* makes glowing references to the famed pearls from Korkai or 'Colchic,' as it was referred to in Graeco-Roman accounts, and points out that "pearls inferior to the Indian sort are exported in great quantity from the marts of Apologas and Omana." The glory of Korkai and its precious pearls was such that the entire Gulf of Mannar, between South-Eastern India and Western Sri Lanka, was referred to as the 'Colchic Gulf.'

Pottery discovered from the site of Korkai|tnarch.gov.in

Interestingly, the famous Megalithic site of Adichanallur dating back at least 3,800 years and which has yielded as many as 169 clay urns containing human skeletons, is just 15 km from Korkai, reiterating the close connection between Iron Age and Early Historic sites in the South.

Over time, the capital of the Pandyas shifted to Madurai, and the Sangam period work, *Maduraikkanci* by Mankudi Maruthanaar (100 BCE – 100 CE) gives us a rich account of the city with its fortified gates, broad streets, mansions, festivals and vibrant morning markets. In fact, through the Sangam poems, you have references to numerous Pandyan rulers.

The *Silapadikaram* refers to Nedunjeliyan as the ruler in Madurai, who famously orders the death of the heroine Kannaki's husband Kovalam. Nedunjeliyan is said to have died of remorse. Meanwhile, his son and heir, who was the Viceroy of Korkai at the time, according to another poem, is said to have wreaked havoc and terrible vengeance on the goldsmiths of Korkai. We are told he 'sacrificed' 1,000 of them in a single day to appease Kannaki!

Since there is a mention of a Sri Lankan king Gajabahu, who is said to have ruled the island state in the 2nd CE, in the story of Kannaki, the story and hence, Nedunjeliyan is dated to around this time.

Even though the Pandyas moved to Madurai, making it their grand capital, they continued to be closely associated with their roots. The official emblem of the Pandyas was the fish, and they are also referred to as 'Meenavars' in Sangam literature – '*meen*' translating to 'fish'.

There are ample coins from the period of the Sangam Pandyas. They almost always have the symbol of an elephant (commonly found in most coins of the Sangam Cheras, Cholas and Pandyas) and the royal emblem of the fish on the other side. Over a period of time, the fish became more stylized, and this emblem continued to be used even by the medieval Pandyas on their coins.

Statue of King Karikala at Anicut Dam|Wikimedia Commons

The Cholas

While the Pandyas were driven by trade, like the Cheras, because of their powerful ports in Korkai and Muziris, respectively, the Cholas seem to have had a more agrarian core.

Scholars believe that the Cholas were originally known as 'Kozhiyar.' Kozhiyur ('kozhi' means 'hen' or 'chicken') was the name of the settlement of Uraiyur, near present day Tiruchirappalli on the banks of Kaveri River in Tamil Nadu. The term 'kozhi' or 'chozhi,' over time, might have transformed into 'Chola.' Prof Selvakumar believes that the first Cholas must have started out in the Iron Age as village chiefs who gradually expanded their dominion. Through battles and alliances with various other chiefs, they gained control over the entire region of the Kaveri delta country, which came to be named after them as the 'Chola region' – then and now. Today, a whole stretch of India's east coast is called the 'Coramandel' (a British corruption of the word 'Cholamandala') Coast.

The core area of the Cholas was the Kaveri Delta, with Uraiyur as their capital and Kaveripumpattinam or Kaveripattinam as their port. Over time, they extended their dominion to Kanchipuram.

King Karikala was the most significant of the early Chola kings and there are scores of myths and legends around him. They start with a heroic tale of how he got his name. Apparently, he was imprisoned and in the battle that followed, or while trying to escape, his leg was burnt. Hence, the name 'Karikala' – 'the one with a charred leg.'

We know he is credited with the conversion of forest lands into cultivable lands by controlling the waters of the Kaveri through the Kallanai embankment (later dam) at the head of the delta and redistributing them to the south. This was noteworthy, as it not only helped control the annual floods that devastated the region, but it also formed the bulwark of the irrigation system that transformed the land.

Karikala was also known for his military prowess. He is said to have defeated a confederacy of kings at the decisive Battle of Venni that took place around 15 km from present day Thanjavur. He defeated the Chera king, Peruncheralathan, a Pandyan king, and 11 chieftains or *velirs*. A poem in the Sangam text *Purananuru* tells the tale of how the Chera king, who was hurt on his back, is said to have starved himself to death in humiliation. There are references to Karikala also taking the battle to Sri Lanka and bringing back 12,000 slaves from there to work as labourers during a fortification of Kaveripattinam.

But the frequent battles, driven by one-upmanship and greed (raids) could swing either way. There is a reference to another battle, for instance, where another ruler, Talaiyananganattu Cheruvenra Pandiyan, defeated the Cholas and several chiefs including Titiyan, Erumaiyuran and Ezhini, in the Battle of Talayalaganam and seized their 'pagodas,' which were symbols of their authority.

The Cholas had the tiger as their emblem and this is visible across their coins. Interestingly, although we know that Uraiyur was an important trading centre – excavations here have dug up evidence of a thriving textile industry, and historians believe some of the finest muslin of the period came from here –no coins have been found here. Most Chola coins, in fact, most Sangam Era coins, have been found in and around Karur, the Chera capital.

Right: Sangam Chera Portrait Coin with legend 'Makkotai'; Left: Sangam Chera Coin with Bow and Arrow Dr. Suresh Sethuraman

LHI 2

Ancient Nadus of Tamilakam

Tamilakam was divided into 12 socio-geographical regions called Nadu or "country." Each of this Nadu had their own dialect of Tamil:

Thenpandi Nadu

Panri Nadu

Kuda Nadu

Punal Nadu

Puzhi Nadu

Venadu

Aruva Nadu

Kakkanadu

Kuttanadu

Aruva Vadathalai Nadu

Sida (Cheetha) Nadu (NILGIRIS)

Malai Nadu

Tulu Nadu

Tamil speaking lands:

Eela Nadu (Eelam)

Naga Nadu or Yazh Kuthanadu (Jaffna Peninsula)

Vanni Nadu (Vanni region)

OTHERS are trading countries:

Vengi Nadu

Chavaka Nadu (Java)

Kadara Nadu (Kedah)

Kalinga Nadu

Singhala Nadu

Vadugu Nadu

Kannada Nadu (Land of Kannada people)

Erumai Nadu

Telunka Nadu (Land of Telugu people)

Kolla Nadu

Vanka Nadu

Magadha Nadu

Kucala Nadu

Konkana Nadu

Kampocha Nadu (Cambodia)

Palantivu Nadu (Maldives)

Kupaka Nadu

Marattha Nadu

Vatuka Nadu

Tinmaitivu (Andaman and Nicobar Islands)

Ancient Nadus of Tamilagam

Puzhi Nadu -: Eli or Ezhi, was a minor dynastic power that held sway over the region in and around Mount Ezhi (Ezhimala) in present-day Kerala, south India.

Venadu - Venadu is an island village in Nellore district of the Indian state of Andhra Pradesh. It is located in Tada mandal and surrounded by Pulicat Lake.

Aruva nadu - Tondaimandalam also known as Tondai Nadu is a historical region located in the southern part of Andhra Pradesh and northernmost part of Tamil Nadu.

Kakkanad is a major industrial and residential region in the city of Kochi in Kerala, India. It is situated in the eastern part of the city and houses the Cochin Special Economic Zone, Infopark, Smart City and KINFRA Export Promotion Industrial Park.

Kuttanad is a region covering the Alappuzha, Kottayam and Pathanamthitta Districts, in the state of Kerala, India, well known for its vast paddy fields.

Seedhanadu - Nilgiris

Malanadu - The Malabar Coast (also known simply as Malabar) is a region of the southwestern shoreline of the mainland Indian subcontinent.

Tulu Nadu - Tulu Nadu, also called as Tulunaad, is a region on the southwestern coast of India.

South Canara, an erstwhile district and a historical area, encompassing the undivided territory of the contemporary Udupi, Dakshina Kannada, and Kasaragod districts, forms the cultural area of the Tuluver.

Thenpandi Nadu - Thenpandiyanadu of the early Pandyas, Mudikonda Cholamandalam of the Imperial Cholas, Tirunelveli Seemai of the Nayaks.

Punal Nadu (land of floods) - chola kingdom.

Kudanadu - (maybe Kudavasal)

Courtesy Indira Ramachanra

Honouring the Three on the Marina

The reference to G.U. Pope, the English translator in the previous paragraph deserves more insight into the European triumvirate who had a profound influence on the Marina.

Constantius Giuseppe Beschi or Dhairyanthan was the first to reach India and joined the Madurai Mission founded by Jesuit, Roberto de Nobili in 1710. The mission was founded by Nobili soon after his arrival in 1605. Beschi, like de Nobili, adopted a sanyasi's robe, gave up alcohol and meat, and presenting himself as a Brahmin scholar, began to teach to the Tamil folk who were more accepting of an Indian approach. The pioneering European-style of Tamil alphabetical die-creation can be attributed to him, as well as the grammatical rules for written and spoken Tamil which he lay down. He also wrote the *Thonoolvilakkam*, often described as 'a minor Tholkappiam.'

Beschi's most renowned work is his *Themba* – 3615 verses of an epic that he wrote, detailing the life and teachings of Christ. He also studied and translated the Thirukkural in later life and was known as Veeramamunivar, a sobriquet in recognition of his contribution to Tamil literature.

Robert Caldwell was the second of this triumvirate. A Scot from Belfast (N. Ireland), Robert was a Presbyterian, but later became a minister the Anglican Society for Gospel Propagation, and came to Madras in 1838. In 1841, he was put in charge of a mission at 'Tinnevelly' having walked 800 miles from Madras while getting to know the local people. Idaiyangudi, a place 30 miles from Kanniyakumari, became his haven for the next 50 years. He was well-known for his work with Dravidian languages, and is remembered in the Marina even today. His *Comparative Grammar of Dravidian Language* was a monumental work and pioneering study that threw clarity on how all the main South Indian languages – Tamil, Telugu, Malayalam and Kannada – were part of ONE family, a Dravidian family that set itself apart from the Sanskrit and Indo-Aryan languages.

Robert also launched the Dravidian movement, called the 'Tamil renaissance.' He wrote extensively on Dravidian history and ancient civilisations of South India, towards which he conducted 'archaeological digs' at Pazhayay near the River Tamaraparani estuary. His study established the place as a great port of the Pandyas. His interest in South India's history led him to pen lesser-known works outside language studies, 'A Political and General History of the District of Tinnevelly from the earliest Times to 1801.'

The marina's third European is George Uglow Pope. Born in Noca Scotia, Canada on Prince Edward Island, Pope went to England as an infant. When he was only 19, in 1839, he came to Madras and served as Sawyerpuram's missionary, near Tuticorin. It wasn't long when he got involved with literature, working as a scholar to translate Tamil, Telugu and Sanskrit literature. Among

Tamil classics, he translated the Tirukkural, *Naaladiyarand Tiruvachakam*. In 1900, he published his last-mentioned work and wrote, "I date this on my 80th birthday. I find, by reference, that my first Tamil lesson was in 1839. This end, as I suppose, a long life of devotion to Tamil studies. It is not without deep emotion that I thus bring to a close my life's literary work."

Pope makes a reference in his preface to Tirukkural where he writes, "Tamil is a sophisticated, unique language, with a rich vocabulary. It is the mother of all South Indian languages." He taught this at Oxford from 1882, as a Professor of Tamil and Telugu. The Tamil writer, M.P. Somu, found Dr. Pope's tombstone decades later in a corner of the closed Oxford cemetery overgrown by plants. On it was an inscription which read, "This stone has been placed here by his family and by his Tamil friends in South India in loving admiration of his lifelong labours in the cause of Oriental literature and philosophy."

Having contributed extensively to the Tamil language, that warrants their place on the Marina, it is still an Italian and a German that hold claim to the highest pedestal. De Nobili is the one who first introduced the prose style of Tamil literature 100 years before Beschi. Four years before Beschi, Bartholomaeus Ziegenbalg helped in the creation of Tamil typography and it was he who made possible printing of Tamil literature, including his and Beschi's work.

Constantius Beschi and De Nobili

The Italians who loved Tamil.

The Italian who loved Tamil and made the language accessible to everyone by 'removing the sting in literature' and (making) it easy appreciable for the common man is now remembered again after a long time.

The 'Veeramamunivar' Beschi, who is otherwise remembered with just a little 'statue on the Marina,' was a Jesuit who in 1700 arrived in Goa. He further travelled to Avoor, in what later became the Trichinopoly District, mastering several languages such as Sanskrit, Telugu, Persian and Hindustani. Tamil writing is what he is best-known for, however.

While Beschi, Pope and Bishop Caldwell are remembered for their significant contributions towards Tamil literature on the Marina, de Nobili has almost no mention anywhere, not in Madurai, Salem, Jaffna, nor where he lived and worked in Mylapore.

Eric Auzoux, director of the Chennai branch of Alliance Francaise 'rediscovered' De Nobili recently, and there was new research on his life. It may be possible that one day there might be a book remembering de Nobili, the first Christian 'sadhu.'

After arriving in Goa in 1605, De Nobili moved to Madurai in 1606, becoming the first of the Christian-'Brahmins,' a move that earned him his first censure by Rome in 1610. Although taking 13 years to clear his name, De Nobili never found acceptance with the Church, and was always considered a maverick right until his death in Mylapore in 1656. He will always be recognised as the first European Tamil and Sanskrit scholar, although he has no memorial or tombstone to his name anywhere even today. His 21 Tamil books were written after he became blind!

Beschi, who was better remembered, only followed in his predecessor's footsteps.

The First Tamil Imprint

The earliest Tamil imprints were not published from present day Tamil Nadu but from Quilon or Kollam of Kerala.

450 years ago, printing first came to India with the printing of two Christian tracts 1556 and 1557. This was done using a printing machine commandeered by the Portuguese in 1556 when the ship on which it travelled, docked into Goa for victualling. The publications were the experimental Conclusoes and the Doctrina Christam, much better printed. Translated into Malabar (as Tamil was called by the Portugese) by Father Henrique Henriques and Father Manuel de Sa Pedro, a Tamil priest of Tuticorin's Punniyakayal, the latter was printed by Joao de Faria, a builder cum printer in 'Coulam' in October 1578.

Designing the type as an improvisation of the earlier one designed a year earlier by Pedro Luis, a member of Fr Henriques 'Tamil flock,' and Joao Goncalves, a Portuguese blacksmith in Goa, De Faria's 16-page publication was the first publication in any Indian language in the world. It is now in the possession of the Harvard Library in the US.

Produced in the Tranquebar Mission Press sometime between 1715 and 1719, the first nonreligious Tamil books that were printed are said to have been Tamil primers. Not much is known about them, or about what happened to the 92-page Tamil Expositor, what some consider the first non-sectarian Tamil book that was printed. Making its appearance in 1811, this collection of Tamil idioms must have been printed at a mission press since private printing presses had not yet begun business at the time.

Founded in 1812 but taking off in 1820, it was the College of Fort St. George that takes the credit for printing nonreligious books in South Indian languages. Under the guidance of Tamil Pandit Chidambara Pandaram and Telugu Pandit K. Gurumurthy Sastri, the College's press produced grammars, dictionaries and scientific texts continuously. Its efforts were ably supplemented by the 1819 founded Madras School Book Society and hugely encouraged by Governor Sir Thomas Munro from 1820.

While book printing paved the way, journals soon followed suit. The Tamil magazine first appeared in 1831. It was published by the Religious Tract Society and set the pace for future books, but did not last very long. Two decades later, Rajavritti Bodhini appeared from a press of the same name. It comprised of news and articles that first appeared in English language papers.

Rajavritti Bodhiniwas challenged the same year, and overtaken by Dina Varthamani, whose publisher was the Rev. P. Percival. The superior quality of articles warranted their anthology being brought out as a book, Vinodha Rasa Manjari.

Percival was a Sanskrit scholar himself. He headed the Department of Sanskrit and Vernacular Literature at Presidency College from 1856 and worked with Arumuga Navalar on a Tamil dictionary. He became the first full-time Registrar of the University of Madras in 1929.

The Beach Promenade in 1910 G U Pope

"The most important thing is to try and inspire people so that they can be great in whatever they want to do."

– Kobe Bryant

The Madras Presidency

The Madras Presidency, officially the Presidency of Fort St. George and also known as Madras Province, was an administrative subdivision of British India. The presidency included much of southern India, including the Malabar region of North Kerala, present day Indian State of Tamil Nadu, Coastal Andhra and Rayalseema regions of Andhra Pradesh, Lakshadweep Islands,

Ganjam, Malkangiri, Koraput, Rayagada, Nabarangapur and Gajapati districts of southern Odisha and the Bellary, Dakshin Kannada, and Udupi districts of Karnataka at its largest extent. The presidency had its summer capital at Ootacamund and winter capital at Madras.

In 1639, the village of Madraspatnam was purchased by the English East India Company and the Agency of Fort St. George was built a year later. This was a precursor to the Madras Presidency, although Company factories at Machilipatnam and Armagon already existed since the early 1600's.

Upgraded to a Presidency in 1652, the agency went back once more to its previous avatar in 1655. In 1684, it was re-elevated to a Presidency with the appointment of Elihu Yale as president. The Pitt's India Act provisions pronounced Madras as one of three provinces set up by the East India Company in 1785. Thereafter, the term 'Governor' applied to the head of the area rather than 'President,' who in turn, became a subordinate to the Governor-General in Calcutta, the title of which would persist until 1947.

The governor held judicial, legislative and executive powers, and was ably assisted by a Council whose constitution was modified by reforms enacted in 1861, 1909, 1919 and 1935. Elections were regularly held in Madras up until the Second World War broke out in 1939. Comprising 22 districts by 1908, each headed by a District Collector, the province was further sub-divided into taluks, firqas and villages being the smallest administrative unit.

Following the Montague-Chelmsford reforms of 1919, Madras was British India's first province to implement a diarchy system, with a Governor ruling alongside a prime minister. In the early part of the 20th century, Madras was the home to many significant contributors of the Indian independence movement.

A Look Back at Madras's Founders

References made below regarding the founding of Madras – or present day Chennai, elaborate on two different contributors to the foundation of the city.

In the first reference, Nanditha Krishna, in her little book, spoke about the Varahishwarar Temple in Damal of Kanchipuram Disrict. Her great-

great-grandmother, Rangammal, aka Pattamal, who was the mother of C.P. Ramaswami Aiyer, was from Damal and herein laid her interest in the temple. Rangammal's parents, Venkatasubba and Savitri Ammal, were large landowners. Damal, Damar or Damarla was derived from the names of Venkatappa and Ayyappa of the Velugotti family. They granted the east india company a plot of 'no man's land' measuring three square miles, where Andrew Cogan and Francis Day built a functional stockade which they named Fort St George. Venkatappa and Ayyappa's father, was Chennappa Nayak. He was a general of the Vijayanagara ruler, Venkata II (1586-1640) as per Nanditha, while they were governors of the 'provinces' of Wandiwash and Poonamallee.

Damal is a small place that lies about 85 km south-west of Madras and 14 km north-west of Kanchi, with NH-46 cutting through the village. It was first mentioned on Pallava copper plates dating to c.556 CE. Kanchipuram, at the time, belonged to the Damarkottamor province. Damal is also mentioned in all subsequent Chola, Pandya and Vijayanagara records. Eventually, the village passed into the hands of the Nawabs of Arcot, who in the latter half of the 18th century, ceded it to the British. Damal is a village mainly of Nayakar that reflects the Vijayanagar influence. It is a fertile area where rice, millet, groundnut, gingelly and sugarcane grow and thrive.

In the second reference, the founding of Madras was shared by Michael Herridge, former Deputy High Commissioner of the UK in South India. His hobby, genealogy, occupies him through his retirement, and he has collected data on how the city was founded.

The book titled 'The Origins of Francis Day, Founder of Fort St George (Madras), was compiled by his possible descendant, James Day. Besides stating whatever he knows in Madras about Francis Day, James Day also offers several new bits of information. (From an article in the Genealogists' Magazine.)

Appointed as a Factor of the East India Company in 1632, Francis Day earned an annual salary of £30, which was increased by £5 annually for seven years. In 1639, it was said of him while he was in charge of Armagon, "On the Coromandel Coast, there is not one able servant left, unless it is Francis Day."

Deducing facts from several incomplete records available at the time, James Day thinks that Francis Day was likely the grandson of William Day, the Bishop of Winchester in 1595 and who served in Eton and St. George's Chapel, Windsor previously. This was the same place where Prince Charles was recently betrothed to Camilla Parker Bowles. The son of William Day of Bray, the Bishop's eldest son, and Helen Wentworth, the daughter of an Elizabethan parliamentarian, Francis was the fourth of their six sons probably born in 1605 and most likely went to Eton.

James Day continues his narration on the basis of insufficient information and thinks that Francis Day described as a 'cloth worker' married Chelsea Elizabeth Matson, the daughter of a farmer on July 5, 1630, and this is the same Francis Day of Madras. This assiduous genealogical research also had other findings which indicate that Francis went back to England in 1646, became Mayor of Walling Oxfordshire in 1664 or 1665 and died in Great Haseley in 1673. He had real estate interests in War grave and Kilhaim Berkshire and in Wallingford. His son, Francis and several other 'Day' generations, served the East India Company in India, with the family connection probably lasting more than over 200 years.

Early beginnings Fort St George, Madras, circa 1860

They visit their temples regularly and draw the morning kolam outside their doors, even in the new flat-style living they've adapted to. The

The Villages of Madras

Triplicane was one of the earliest land acquisitions, rented from the Sultan of Golconda in 1676, while Egmore Purasawalkam and Tondiarpet, were leased from the Emperor Aurangzeb in 1693. These were the first villages that John Company moved into from Fort St. George, the site of which had been granted to the Company on August 21, 1639. The Company acquired these four rented villages in 1720, and in time, they came to be known as the 'Old Towns.'

In 1708, Nawab Daud Khan, described as the "Nabob of the Cornattta and Chingee Countrys" and representing the Mughals' Subedar of the Deccan granted Tiruvottriyur, Nungambakkam, Vyasarpadi, Ennor; and Sathangadu in what became known as the five 'New Villages.'

When the Nawab of Arcot celebrated his accession to the throne, five more villages were added, which were gifted to the British in return for his families' protection during 'blood' feuds. These villages were Vepery, Perambur, Pudupakkam, Ernavore (near Tiruvottriyur) and Sadayankuppam. Nathaniel Higginson, Thomas Pitt and Richard Benyon were the Governors who received these three bits of territorial largesse respectively. With Santhome and Mylapore becoming a part of Fort St. George in 1749-1750 during the Governorship of Thomas Saunders, as a part of the spoils of the Anglo-French wars in Europe at the time, Madras began to move towards the Age of Expansionism to the Age of Trade. It was also the start of its journey towards becoming the sprawling metropolis of today.

"In 2021, Madras Turned 382 Years as East India Company Purchased the Village of Madraspatanam in 1639 and Established the Agency of Fort St George as Precursor of Madras Presidency."

Founders' Day, Madras

For many years now, August 22nd has been celebrated as 'Founders Day' in Madras, often marked by a commemorative week of participatory celebrations by the city. Historians are divided on whether it shouldn't in fact be July 22nd, and with context to that is narrated the tale below.

In 1565, after the Battle of Talikota, the defeated Vijayanagar kingdom moved its headquarters to Chandragiri from where the erstwhile emperor ruled his abbreviated Southern kingdom through several governors — many of them local chieftains — titled Naiks.

Naik-governed territories, included Madurai, Thanjavur, Gingee and, closer to the subject of this story, Poonamallee. Damarla Venkatadri (aka Venkatappa and Venkatapathi) Naik, described as the 'Lord General of the Carnatica' and 'Grand Vizier of the Emperor,' was in charge of Tondaimandalam — an area marked in the east by the coast from Pulicat to just north of San Thome and stretching westwards to a little beyond Wandiwash, his capital. His brother, Aiyappa, was put in charge of the coast by Venkatadri, and had his headquarters in Poonamallee. It was with Aiyappa Naik that Beri Thimmappa, *dubash* to Francis Day, an East India Company subsidiary in Armagon (now Durgarayapatnam, near Nellore), initially negotiated to grant a piece of land on this stretch of coast that could help Day move from the non-profitable Armagon.

Headquartered at Machilipatnam, the East India Company on the Coromandel Coast was where Thomas Ivie arrived on July 22nd to take charge as agent, having been authorised by Day to go and find a new settlement. When Ivie arrived in Machilipatnam, he found that Andrew Cogan had already arrived there on July 19th to take charge as agent. The confusion was eventually sorted out in Cogan's favour on September 3rd. Day, who arrived there a few days earlier to participate in the voting process that elected Cogan, handed over his report to Cogan in person. This is where the confusion on dates begins.

Dated '27th July, 1639,' the report was handed over to Cogan and stated that, "The firman granted Mr. Day privileges in Madraspatam by the Nague Damela Vintutedra." The firman was dated '22nd July 1639,' and this is where the first reference to 'Madraspatam' was first found in the British records. A closer reading of Day's report reveals his detailed statement, "I had your consent to make a voyage to the Nague and therefore, set sail for those parts on 23rd July and arrived the 27th."

Considering these dates, Day could not have received a grant dated 'July 22nd.' As Col Henry Davison Love, a meticulous recorder of early Madras history, says, "July is probably a slip for August." In agreement with this view, the catalysts of the Madras Day and Madras Week celebrations decided to stick with August 22nd as Founders' Day. Every time they meet, they wonder what can be done to have the founders – Beri Thimappa, Francis Day and Andrew Cogan - remembered forever in the city.

Henry Davison Love's, three-volume monumental history of Madras from 1640-1800 is the Bible for all modern researchers after Madras's early history.

According to him, "The Naik's grant, erroneously styled a *Farman* which was probably drafted by Day, was delivered (to Andrew Cogan) at Masulipatam on September 3, 1639. Three copies exist, all of them endorsed by Cogan. Only the last bears the date of 22nd July, 1639, where July is probably a slip for August, since Day did not reach Madras until 27th July."

The explanation to Day's July 27th arrival offers further indication that August 22nd is the more likely date. Thomas Ivie, who was sent from Bantam to Java to take charge of Masulipatnam, arrived at his new post on July 22nd. On the way, he stopped at Armagom now (Durgarayapatnam) where Francis Day was chief. On the way south, Day authorised him to sail South and negotiate for new coastal settlements

Day wrote in his subsequent report to Ivie of the visit and the orders he received at Masulipatnam, "Yours of the 19th July departure… I had your consent to make a voyage to the Nague, therefore set sail for those parts the 23th July and arrived on the 27th …This letter, curiously dated July 27th was written in Armagom again says, "July appears to be an error for August."

This report, with which was enclosed the farman was delivered to Andrew Cogan on September 3, 1639 by day who had "Arrived at masulipatnam a few days before, (probably around august 27th) Cogan himself had arrived in Masulipatam on august 17th from Surat via Goa and Golconda, and found Ivie in charge. The dispute that ensued was concluded when the factors, Day included, voted that Cogan be recognised as agent.

On September 5th, Cogan and his men, with Clive (awaiting his return to Bantam) and a signatory, resolved that Day had to be sent back to Madraspatnam and prolong negotiations with the Nague until instructions came from Bantam to set up the new factory. The correspondence was confirmed in a report to the Company in London in a letter dated October 29th in which it is stated "And on August last, the said Francis Day, having dispatch what he was sent about, came from this place, and shewes (show) what he had done."

Madras – The Famous Names and Architecture

Gentlemen Administrator: Francis Day

Francis Day (1605–1673) was an English colonial administrator, associated with the East India Company. He served as a factor of the Company's factory at Masulipatnam from 1632 to 1639. In 1639, he negotiated the purchase of a strip of land South of the Dutch factory at Pulicat from the Raja of Chandragiri, where the town of Madras was built. He served as the second Agent of Madras from 1643 to 1644. Along with Andrew Cogan, he is regarded as the founder of Madras.

Early Life

Francis Day was born to William Day of Bray and his wife Helen Wentworth, the daughter of a member of the House of Commons. He is believed to be the grandson of William Day, who was appointed Bishop of Winchester in 1595. Francis completed his education from Eton College and joined the services of the East India Company in 1632.

Purchase of Madras

In 1637, Francis Day, then a member of the Masulipatnam Council and Chief of the Armagon Factory, undertook a voyage of exploration down the Coromandel Coast, as far as Pondicherry. At that time, the Coromandel Coast was ruled by the Raja of Chandragiri through a local chief or Nayak, Damarla Venkatappa Nayak, who ruled the coast from Pulicat up to Santhome. He had his seat at Wandiwash and his brother, Ayyappa Nayak resided at Poonamallee.

It is widely presumed that Ayyappa Nayak was the one who wooed the English to choose the area comprising the modern day Georgetown for settlement. Day and his superior, Andrew Cogan, investigated the proposed site and examined trading possibilities. The results were favourable and Day secured a grant offering the village of Madraspatnam to the English for a period of two years. The Grant was dated August 1639, and after obtaining the approval of the Factory at Masulipatnam and the Presidency of Bantam (in Java), the settlement of Madraspatnam was begun.

Day also had other reasons to choose Madras for a factory – the availability of cotton, and at a much cheaper rate, as attested to by the prosperous Portuguese settlement of San Tôme. The nearness of the Portuguese, who could be counted upon as neutral spectators if not active supporters in times of war, particularly influenced the English in their choice. The land allocated under the Grant also lay upon an island between the Adyar and Cooum rivers, a factor of safety important in those turbulent times.

Day was, however, sorely criticised by captains of men-of-war, for his choice of the location of the fort, due to immense difficulties in anchoring ships in Madras Roads. This meant that at various important junctures in the Carnatic Wars, the powerful English fleet was rendered useless, having to weigh anchor and move out to sea at low tide. Merchantmen too found the same flaw, though for different reasons – they would have to wait until high tide to bring goods and passengers ashore or risk wetting them in the *Majula* boats used as ferries between the Fort and Madras Roads.

The chief difficulty, as usual with the English in those days, was lack of money. At last, in February 1640, Day and Cogan accompanied by a few factors and writers, a garrison of about 25 European soldiers and a few other European artificers, besides a Hindu powder-maker by name Naga Battan, proceeded to Madras and started the English factory. They reached Madraspatnam on 20 February; and this date is important because it marks the first actual settlement of the English at the place.

Within the first walls of Fort St. George lived the Europeans of early Madras, surrounded by Indian settlers outside them in Chennapatnam. In the light of this, if April 23rd gets officially celebrated as Fort St. George Day, the least we could hope is for a couple of nearby roads to be named after Andrew Cogan, Francis Day and Beri Thimmappa who laid a path for it to unfold.

Victoria Hall

Fort St George 1910 Fort St George (or historically, White Town) is the name of the first English (later British) fortress in India, founded in 1644 in the coastal city of Madras, or modern day Chennai. The construction of the fort was an impetus for increased trading activity and further settlements, in hitherto uninhabited land. Thus, it is perfectly feasible to deduce that the city grew around the fortress. The fort is one of 163 notified areas (megalithic sites) in the state of Tamil Nadu.

Having entered India around 1600 for trading activities, the East India Company began licensed trade at Surat, its initial trade bastion. However, with Malaccan Straits being the hub of trading activity, it was necessary for them to secure trade lines and commercial interests in the spice trade. This they did by purchasing coastal land originally called Chennirayarpattinam or Chennapatnam, from a Vijayanagar chieftain Damerla Chennappa Nayak, who was based in Chandragiri, where the construction of a harbour and fort began. The fort was completed on 23 April 1644, coinciding with St George's Day, celebrated in honour of the patron saint of England.

Christened as Fort St George, it faced the sea and some fishing villages, and soon became the hub of merchant activity. It gave birth to a new settlement area called George Town (historically referred to as Black Town), growing to envelop villages which eventually led to the formation of Madras city.

The fort also helped fortify English rule over the Carnatic, keep kings of Arcot and Srirangapatanam, including Pondicherry-based French forces at bay. A stronghold six-metre high wall, the Fort has withstood a number of assaults in the 18th century. The French briefly took possession from 1746 to 1749, but then, was restored to Great Britain under the Treaty of Aix-la-Chapelle, ending in the War of the Austrian Succession.

Early British traders in madras (Chennai) Fort St George, Madras, on the Coromandel Coast, 1754; painting by Jan Van Ryne

Serving as one of the administrative headquarters for Tamil Nadu's legislative assembly, the Fort still houses a garrison of troops which are in transit to South India and the Andaman. The Fort Museum contains many British Raj relics, including portraits of many Madras Governors. The fort is maintained and administered by the Archaeological Survey of India as a ticketed monument. St Mary's Church is the oldest Anglican Church, East of Suez and also the oldest British building in India. It was built between 1678 and 1680. Its graveyard tombstones are the oldest English tombstones in India. The ancient prayer house solemnised the marriages of Robert Clive and Governor Elihu Yale, who later became the first benefactor of United States Yale University. It is popularly known as the **'Westminster Abbey of the East.'**

Architects: William Dixon, Edward Foule

Burials: Sir Thomas Munro, 1ˢᵗ Baronet, George Pigot, Baron Pigot, LordVere Hobart.

Hobart Fort Museum

Completed in 1795, the Fort Museum that first housed Madras Bank's office has many exhibits from the English period. The Public Exchange Hall upstairs was used for public meetings, lottery draws and occasional entertainment. Everything from weapons, coins, medals, uniforms and other artefacts from England, Scotland, France and India, dating back to the colonial period is displayed at the museum. Clive's and Cornwallis' original letters make for a fascinating read. The place also has a set of quaint period uniforms on display. However, the piece de resistance is a large statue of Lord Cornwallis.

Wellesley House is a modern building whose first floor includes the Banquet Hall, displayed with paintings of the Governor of the Fort and the regime's other high officials. Tipu's canons decorate the ramparts of the museum. The 14.5 feet statue stands near the entrance stairway in the museum. Created by Charles Bank in England, the statue which was brought to India has a pedestal carved with a scene depicting Tipu's emissary handing over the ruler's two sons as hostage in lieu of a ransom he was unable to pay to the British. Wellesley House takes its name from Richard Wellesley, Governor-General of India, and brother of the Duke of Wellington.Hobart Fort's flag staff made of teakwood is the tallest in the country at 150 feet. It currently houses the Tamil Nadu legislative assembly and other official buildings.

Pipe Organs of St Mary's Church

The only time the parishioners of St. Mary's church have ever seen it so packed was during the splendid restoration of its 1894 pipe organ. The sounds of it were coaxed out by Dr. Richard Marlow of Trinity College, Cambridge who S. Paul, the regular organ player since 1959 reiterated that he had never heard in all these years since the restoration. For a tone-deaf music heretic like me, neither the sonority nor the sweetness made the slightest bit of difference; for I kept thinking about the organs that had roused the congregations here for over three centuries.

St. Mary's got its first organ in 1687; just seven years after the church had been consecrated. The Fort Council, headed by Governor William Gyfford, presented it to what was then the Governor's Church. The circumstances of the purchase were fortuitous. The records state, "Capt. Weltden having offered an Organ to Sale for Pagodas 70, which is below prime cost, it is ordered to be bought and paid for." Weltden was the master of the Curtana, an East Indiaman that had called at Madras.

In 1746, when the French Occupied Fort St. George, the church "hath been dishonoured and profaned excessively." This included its looting with part of the booty taken to Pondicherry including this organ. Eyre Coote was to bring it back to St. Mary's in 1761, after he had reduced Pondicherry to rubble.

Meanwhile, during the uneasy peace the British and the French tried to maintain between 1749 and 1760, the Ministers and Churchwardens of St. Mary's decided to order a Mr. Bridge to build a new organ and ship it out from London. He quoted £300 and the price was accepted. The church, however, requested the Government meet at least a part of the cost as well as arrange for free passage from London for an organist. No records exist of how that appeal was answered nor about what happened when Coote brought back the 1746 organ from Pondicherry.

In 1791, the Government refused another request from the Church, for a grant to re-erect the original brought back from Pondicherry. The Government mentioned 'lapse of time' as the reason for refusal.

The next organ the church got was in 1859, when Sir Adam Hay donated an organ that had belonged to his son, Capt. John Hay, Military Secretary to Governor Lord Harris. This organ has been replaced by the present organ, which was ordered from Hill and Sons, London, for £340. When it arrived, the Hay organ was sold to a church in George Town for Rs.500.

Hills and Sons were the outstanding organ builders in 19th-century Britain. Their pipe organs are to be found wherever the Union Jack was planted. When St. Mary's decided to buy an organ, it went for the best in Victorian England.

The cost for making a totally handcrafted pipe organ like the St. Mary's one would now be about £80,000 (nearly Rs.700, 000), according to Christopher Gray, who restored it as well as improved a few others in Madras.

Gray had come out at the urging of Randall Giles, an American who was spending some time in Madras helping the Church of South India develop a music tradition with Carnatic difference. Giles had seen a report prepared by Clive Johnson an American musicologist, who had holidayed in Madras and found the organs in the city in grave disrepair. He had reported in 2002 that the St. Mary's organ was working only at about 60 per cent of its capacity. Five years earlier, a German father and son team, Adolph Jurgen and Legraf had spent six weeks in Madras thoroughly cleaning and tuning the instrument), but obviously, that was not enough.

The organ, however, is not a Western invention as was discovered in the New Oxford Companion to Music. It apparently was invented by an engineer, Kresibios, in Alexandria c. 246 BCE, as per my reference. "The Church which up till the 8th century was rigidly opposed to any kind of instrumental music in worship, revised its views and from the middle of the 9th century, church organs and organists became increasingly accepted," it states.

Trade to Establishing an Empire

"In the middle of the seventeenth century, Asia still had a far more important place in the world than Europe," so wrote J. Pirenne in his 'History of the Universe,' published in Paris in 1950. He added, "The riches of Asia were incomparably greater than those of the European states. Her industrial techniques showed a subtlety and a tradition that the European handicrafts lacked. There weren't any newer methods used by Western traders that Asians had to envy. In matters of credit, transfer of funds, insurance, and cartels, neither India and Persia, nor China had anything to learn from Europe."

(Quoted in Auguste Toussaint's 'History of the Indian Ocean') The British East India Company made its presence felt in India in the 17th century, during the height of power of the Mughal Empire. Instead of selling their own goods here, the British found it more profitable to sell Indian goods in Europe. The early days were hard. There was competition from other Europeans, as well as other trade routes (the Red Sea route through Egypt, the Persian Gulf Route through Iraq, and the Northern Caravan Route through Afghanistan, Persia and Turkey). Thus, the early British Traders were in no position to dictate terms, and trade concessions were hard won.

However, eventually and with perseverance, the Company slowly established trading bases wherever it could along either side of the lengthy Indian coastline. As the East India Company slowly changed in character from a purely trading concern to a political-military-economic machine, it was these trading bases that formed the nucleus of British settlements, and it was here that the first British buildings came up. In keeping with the nature of the Company, the first buildings were warehouses, barracks and living quarters protected by a fort. The earliest British forts followed Portuguese and French variations of the Italian Renaissance's model of an ideal city and its defences.

In the forts at Madras and Calcutta, the French military engineer Vauban's influence is apparent. Regular polygonal geometry and salient triangular bastions with recessed flanks at each angle maximised all-round cover and minimised vulnerability by offering overlapping fields of fire. Ditches and earthworks between the main ring of bastions and lower, outlying areas increased defensive capability. The area surrounding the fort was cleared of all obstacles so as to remove any cover for attackers. These first forts at Madras, Bombay and Calcutta were the principal seats from where the Company oversaw its affairs. Features common to them all include double walls and angular bastions for artillery to dominate the approach. The fortifications also took advantage of natural features like the sea and rivers for defence.

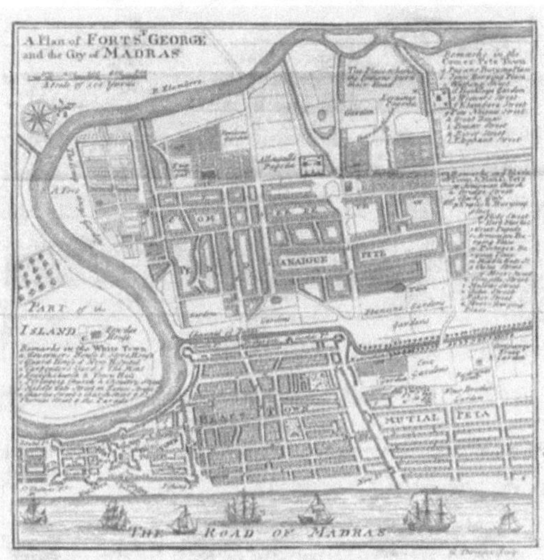

Plan, Madras City, showing Fort St. George in lower left

Around the forts, the first signs of segregation were already apparent – the European and Indian communities lived in separate settlements with very distinct characters. In the case of Fort St. George, Madras, the main fortifications surrounded the warehouses and other military buildings, and the so-called 'white town' had another ring of fortification separating it from the 'black town.'

Although Fort St. George Madras was one of the first British outposts, it fell to the French in 1745, and again in 1758, before it was finally retaken by the British. The French were also weakened by their losses in Europe and were slowly abandoning India to the British.

In addition to warehouses within the fort walls, there was also the need for arsenals, barracks and residential accommodation for the British. A church, too, was a necessity. The first English church in India was thus St. Mary's at Madras fort, founded in 1678.

Gallery inside Fort Museum at Fort St George Chennai

International Museum Day, May 18th, was celebrated in Madras with the renovated Fort Museum hoping it will now draw bigger crowds. A particularly popular destination with foreign tourists, its new look should make it a more attractive stop on a visitor's itinerary. Only, it needs time for history buffs to enjoy its offerings, and well-trained guides to tell the stories of many of the exhibits, as well as of the building itself.

The Fort Museum, which first opened its doors to the public in February 1948, is one of Fort St. George's historic landmarks, a symbol, in its earlier avatars of the growth of mercantilism in Madras. Once the house of a free merchant named Robert Hughes, the building was acquired in 1787 by another free merchant, Peter Massey Cassin, who renovated it and made it a club of sorts where the towns free merchants — those independent of the East India Company — could regularly meet. Using the profits of lotteries, Cassin completed a part of the renovation by 1790 and opened it to the merchants.

Two years later, the Exchange Coffee Tavern was opened on the first floor of the building, where the portrait gallery is today. Here, merchants would sip Madeira or coffee, while signals from the tower on the roof, which housed the city's first lighthouse by 1796, enquired about cargos on ships the prices that were quoted. Bids were signalled back the same way, by those interrupting their coffee and conversation, until eventually deals were struck.

By 1795, renovation was over and the building's exterior looked as it does today. On the ground floor were offices for rent and the banking facilities provided by the Bank of Madras, which, in time, became one of the three major founding institutions of the Imperial Bank, now State Bank of India. The Tavern had, by the time the renovation was completed, become a part of what was to be known as the Public Exchange Hall, the domain of merchants, brokers and ships' captains.

Today, the tavern is my favourite place in the Museum. In the gallery is a very significant picture of that of Navab Muhammad Ali who ceded the Carnatic (the eastern half of what was to become the Madras Presidency) to the British and his friend, Major Stringer Lawrence also called the 'Father of the Indian Army' The Hall or 'Long Room' as it was called by its users, has been embellished with gubernatorial and other portraits. It was a room also used for public meetings, lottery drawings and entertainments. Among the places in the ground floor were auction rooms, upmarket shops and a public subscription library. When Governor Edward Clive decided he wanted the free merchants out of the Fort, the building lapsed into disuse before Governor Thomas Munro, in 1826, rented it out to government offices. In 1861, it became the Officers' Mess of the regiment headquartered in the fort.

Governor Lord Connemara ordered the purchase of the building in 1882, by which time, its ownership included a few Indian shareholders. The building, bought for Rs. 61,000 from the Madras Exchange Company, continued, thereafter, to be used as an Officers Mess until the last British Regiment marched out of the Fort. It was converted into a museum on suggestion of Col. D.M. Reid of the Madras Guards to keep alive the British era in Madras. Today, it has over 3,500 documents, artefacts and paintings. Among them are the oldest British portraits in the city, that of of King George and Queen Charlotte, dating to 1761.

The Peregrinating Statue

When the 3rd Baron Cornwallis of Linton, an eighth-generation descendant of the 1st Marquess and 2nd Earl Cornwallis, who is well-known in India, visited Madras recently, I wondered what he thought of the scene depicted on the circular base of the statue of his forefather in the Fort Museum. I was also wondering about what he thought of all the shifts the statue had made before it found this niche under the stairs that keeps it virtually out of sight. I didn't intercept him after the tour he took of the city to look at the Cornwallis sites, but the authorised history of the Cornwallis family, he presented to me the day before the tour probably reflects his views.

Most people who visit the Fort Museum briefly peer up at the 14 feet tall, Thomas Banks statue of the imperially robed, regally postured Governor-General of India, scarcely wondering who he was. It is almost certain that none of them paused to look at the scene just below eye level. A brass relief narration on it tells of a story of fame or infamy, depending on the viewer's viewpoint. It narrates Tippu Sultan handing over two of his sons to Lord Cornwallis in 1793 as hostages after the Third Mysore War. As per British records, it was a statue erected at the time by 'the citizens of Madras to commemorate Cornwallis's military achievements in 1800.' Today, most people will agree that holding children hostage until reparation for the ravages of war were paid is highly unacceptable.

According to the Cornwallis Family History, Cornwallis assured Tippu's negotiators that "as he had only one son himself, he experienced the affection of a parent in more than an ordinary degree, but even that child could not be received by him with greater tenderness than would Tippu's."

The two boys who, according to Tippu's spokesman, "must now look up to your Lordship as their father," were, however, not returned to Mysore until May 1794, after every penny of the nearly £8 million 'indemnity' had been paid.

During their two-year stay in Madras, looked after by John Doveton, Madras society fêted them, with European Society 'displaying' them at many a ball.

When Madras Society decided to honour Cornwallis, it erected the statue under a cupola at the junction of what is now Cenotaph Road and Mount Road in Teynampet, also at the time the southern boundary of the Great Choultry Plain. In 1906 it was moved to the Parade Ground in the Fort which became the 'Cornwallis Square,' and then, in 1925 to a new larger cupola in front of Bentinck's Building, also called the Collectorate. The statue which was moved in 1928 to the reading hall of the Connemara Public Library was finally relocated in 1950 to the Fort Museum.

The Cornwallis tracing their descendants to a Richard of Cornwall, nephew of Richard the Lion Heart in 1225, also now called 'Men of Kent.' The Indian connection starts with Charles, the 1st Marquess Cornwallis. Despite his surrender at Yorktown, virtually sealing the fate of the British in what became the United States; Cornwallis continued to find favour in Britain, being made Governor-General of India in 1786. He acclimatised himself for India, and prepared himself to live in the country by spending May to August of 1786 in Madras. By the time he left India in 1793, he had fought the Third Mysore War with a degree of success, but did not have a 'happy success' in Calcutta implementing land reforms not winning Indian approval on both counts.

Nevertheless, he was sworn in as Governor-General of India a second time in 1798 but was then sent as Viceroy to Ireland. He next led the British team to France to negotiate a peace settlement with Napolean. And in 1805, at age 66, he was appointed Governor-General of India for a third time. Six months after his arrival in India, he died in Ghazipur near Benares. He was buried there, in accordance with his wishes, 'Where the tree falls, let it lie.'

A curious aspect of Charles Cornwallis's career is the fact that Pitt saw him as his troubleshooter: "Pitt regarded him as an infallible cure for all ills," wrote one historian. Another stated, "Lord Cornwallis was Mr. Pitt's invaluable refuge in every Indian difficulty." Yet, Cornwallis, for all his energy, leadership qualities and tactical brilliance, could be slow and ponderous, "lack mental staying power," and commit "foolish blunders."

The present Lord Cornwallis, who has been visiting India every ten years for the last 50 years, descends from the female line, the 1st Marquess' male line and the Marquessate having died out in the fourth generation. The new Baronetcy commenced in 1927 with Fiennes Stanley Wykeham, who adopted the Cornwallis name, his grandmother having been a Cornwallis. His grandson, the present Baron Fiennes Cornwallis, is a dedicated Masonic leader, just like all Cornwallis's, was visiting various Masonic Lodges in India. He was in Madras, to visit one of the Oldest Lodges in the Country.

Monument to Cornwallis at Fort St. George Chennai

Marble Statue - Charles Cornwallis, 1st Marquees KG

Charles Cornwallis, 1st Marquees Cornwallis KG Fort Museum Fort-St. George Chennai the Third Governor-General of India, Charles Earl Cornwallis (1738-1805) held office between 1786 and 1793.

He reformed the British East India Company administration and carried out important revenue, land and legal reforms. The statue of Lord Cornwalis is the piece de resistance at the Fort Museum.

This 14.5 feet tall statue was carved and erected by Thomas Banks in 1800, and financed by public funds.

The 14.5 feet marble statue was carved in Britain and was brought to India via sea. It was erected in 1799 by Thomas Banks at Fort Square. Later, it was taken and kept inside the Fort Museum.

The 'Ionic Rotunda' shown in this picture still stands as a monument at Fort Square (near Fort Museum) in Fort St. George, Chennai.

An antique photograph by Frederick Fiebig (year1851) shows the erection of statue of Charles, Earl Cornwallis (1738-1805) – (the third Governor-General of India and held office between 1786 and 1793), beneath this Ionic Rotunda.

The Clive House is situated, behind St. Mary's Church, on Charles Street within Fort St. George. The building was erected in the early eighteenth century by an Armenian merchant named Nazar Jacob.

The Clive of Madras

When Christie's annual sale of Indian treasures opened recently, the primary focus will be on several items from the Clive-Farr collection in Powys Castle, Wales. The centrepiece is a 25 cm round jade flask with a tall narrow neck. It is intricately-decorated with bands of emeralds and studded with ruby flowers, all in pure gold. The flask was expected to fetch close to £2 million! Other items from the Clive collection being auctioned are a blue enamelled hood – embellished with sapphires (£50-80,000), a dagger with age encrusted handle (£35-50,000) and a jade bowl and fly whisk with black agate handle, inset with rubies (£5-8000).

Robert Clive acquired his wealth long after he began his career in Madras. As a 19-year old boy, he arrived in the capital of the East India Company settlements on May 31, 1744, as a lowly writer on £5 per annum wages. The writer's quarters were where the Grand Arsenal later came up, then becoming Admiralty House and later, which became known as Clive House. The Archaeological Survey of India, which has its Regional Office there, is now busy restoring the building, and it shouldn't be long before it opens to the public.

Clive was no soldier when he arrived in India. So unaccustomed to a pistol was he, that he almost killed himself more than once when he attempted but failed to do it in in his writers' quarters. It wasn't long when he became a soldier in Cuddlore in 1746 – to where he fled from the French - both by circumstance and on the order of Major Stringer Lawrence, the Father of the Indian Army. There, he found his true vocation on the battlefield. His first victory on the field was at the siege of Arcot, where Clive found himself drawing the attention of French besiegers in a diversionary move planned by Lawrence. Other victories in the triangular plain of Arcot, Cuddalore and Trichinopoly followed. In 1749, when the French Surrendered Madras to the British after a three-year occupation, Clive returned to the town, not as a writer but as a hero honoured with the title 'Bahadur.' His reward was the Stewardship of Fort St. George and being, in that role, in charge of the Commissariat, it is no surprise that Clive took his first real step towards becoming a 'nabob.'

While in Madras, on February 18, 1753 he married Margaret Maskelyne at St. Mary's Church in the Fort officiated by early Protestant Missionary Rev Fabricius. Clive moved with his wife into what was known as 'The Great House in Charles Street.' This was built by an Armenian merchant around 1700 and was rented out to Robert Clive by Aga Shawmier Sultan in 1752. When Clive left for Britain in 1754, the house was taken over by the Government for the sessions of the Courts of Admiralty and became known as Admiralty House in 1755.

Returning to India as Deputy Governor of Madras but based in Fort St. David, Cuddalore, Clive looked forward to French skirmishes during the ongoing Carnatic Wars. When Calcutta fell to Nawab Suraj-ul-Dowlah, Clive was sent with an expeditionary force from Madras to the rescue. There followed the Battle of Plassey, and the commissions he made as Steward of Fort St. George began to seem small changed thereafter. It was the Mughal treasures, estimated at being over £200,000 in the late 1750s, plus a fortune in cash he acquired that laid the foundations for Powys Castle and the Barony of Plassey. Peace, however, was something Clive couldn't handle, and he never found a useful way to spend his wealth. He was happiest in the battlefield, and when one didn't come his way, he attempted to take his life. He was successful in 1774 — using an overdose of opium and not a pistol, dying at the age of only 49.

Sir Thomas Munro, 1st Baronet,

Munros of Madras

Major-general Sir Thomas Munro, 1st Baronet KCB (27 May 1761 – 6 July 1827) was a Scottish soldier and colonial administrator. He was an East India Company Army officer and a statesman.

Lineage

Munro was born in Glasgow on 27 May 1761 to the merchant, Alexander Munro. Thomas' grandfather was a tailor, who prospered by successful investments in American tobacco. After working as a bank clerk, Alexander Munro joined the family's prosperous tobacco business, but was ruined by the collapse of the tobacco trade during the American Revolutionary War. Thomas was also a direct descendant of George Munro, 10th Baron of Foulis (d.1452), chief of the Highland Clan Munro.

Education and sport

Thomas was educated at the University of Glasgow. While at school, he was distinguished for a singular openness of temper, a mild and generous disposition, with great personal courage and presence of mind. Being naturally of a robust frame of body, he surpassed all his school fellows in athletic exercises, and was particularly eminent as a boxer. He at first intended to enter his father's business, but in 1779 was appointed to an infantry cadetship in Madras.

Military career

He served with his regiment during the hard-fought war against Haidar Ali (1780–1783), serving under his older and distant relation Major Sir Hector Munro, 8th of Novar. Thomas also later, served alongside a younger distant relation, John Munro, 9th of Teaninich. Thomas served again with his regiment in the first campaign against Tipu Sultan (1790–1792). He was then chosen as one of four military officers to administer the Baramahal, part of the territory acquired from Tipu, where he remained for seven years learning the principles of revenue survey and assessment, which he afterwards applied throughout the presidency of Madras.

After the final downfall of Tipu in 1799, he spent a short time restoring order in Kanara; and then for another seven years (1800–1807) was placed in charge of the northern districts ceded by the Nizam of Hyderabad, where he introduced the *ryotwari* system of land revenue.

After a long furlough in Britain, during which he gave valuable evidence upon matters connected with the renewal of the British East India Company's charter, Munro returned to Madras in 1814 with special instructions to reform the judicial and police systems.

He was appointed as brigadier-general during the outbreak of the Pindari War in 1817, to command the reserve division that would hope to reduce the Southern territories of the Peshwa. Of his bravery during this conquest, Lord Canning said in the House of Commons,

He went into the field with not more than five or six hundred men, of whom a very small proportion were Europeans. Nine forts were surrendered to him or taken by assault on his way, and at the end of a silent and scarcely-observed progress, he emerged leaving everything secure and tranquil behind him.

In 1819, Munro was appointed a Knight Commander of the Order of the Bath (KCB).

Governor of Madras

In 1820, he was appointed governor of Madras, where he founded systems of revenue assessment and general administration which substantially persisted into the twentieth century. He is regarded as the father of the 'Ryotwari system.' His official minutes, published by Sir A. Arbuthnot, form a manual of experience and advice for the modern civilian. Munro was created a Baronet, of Lindertis in the County, in 1825.

Incident in Mantralaya (Andhra Pradesh)

Mantralaya village in Andhra Pradesh is a place where the 'Brindavan' of famous 'Dvaita' saint 'Raghavendra Swami' is located. When Sir Thomas Munro was the collector of Bellary in 1800, the Madras Government ordered him to procure the entire income from the Math and Manthralaya village. When the revenue officials were unable to comply with this order, Sir Thomas Munro visited the Math for investigation. He removed his hat and shoes and entered the sacred precincts. Sri Raghavendraswamy emerged from the Vrindavan and conversed with him for some time, about the resumption of endowment. The Saint was visible and audible only to Munro, who received *Manthraksha* (God's blessing). The Collector went back and wrote an order in favour of the Math and the village. This notification was published in the Madras Government Gazette in Chapter XI, page 213, with the caption "Manchali Adoni Taluka." This order is still preserved in Fort St. George and Manthralayam. Sir Thomas Munro was Scottish by birth and Hindu at heart. At Sri Venkateswara temple in Tirumala (AP State,) he instituted the offering of pongal each day to the deity in a vessel known as the Munro Gangalam.

Sir Munro died of cholera on 6 July 1827 while on tour in the ceded districts, where his name is preserved by more than one memorial. An equestrian statue of him, by Francis Legatt Chantrey, stands in Madras city. At his behest, a Committee of public instruction was formed in 1826, which eventually led to the formation of Presidency College.

Rajaji and Munro

Among the historical treasures I received during these past few weeks, was one of Satyamevajayate, a four-volume, 2000-page collection of Rajaji's writings between 1956 and 1966. The first edition of this work was published in two volumes (1956-61 and 1962-66) by Bharathan Publications. This collection of wisdom and rare foresight has been out of print for nearly 40 years and has now been reprinted by The Catalyst Trust, Tiruvanmiyur. In this, the Rajaji accurately and analytically predicted the fall of Communism, the necessity for liberalisation of the Indian economy and the strong opposition that Congress would have to face.

Every one of the nearly 800 or more articles that Rajaji had written during those years of Swarajya, as the voice of his Swathantra party, opposed the Congress. For today, I'm drawn to a tribute paid to a 19th century Scot who, according to a recent edition of the Sunday Hindu Magazine, is still revered in parts of Andhra Pradesh. His picture worshipped alongside those of Hanuman and Rama and Sir I Cuddapah. This is a portrait of Thomas Munro — the same Governor depicted in the statue in the middle of Madras's Island. There was a time, in what we call ceded districts, when Munrolappa was not an uncommon local name. I don't know whether, in more recent times, it is still given to children in these districts, but his worship in a temple which was both blessed and doomed only confirms that he is still not forgotten.

Rajaji too remembered him all his life. As is seen in his collection, a tribute he wrote in 1961 he says, "I am in love with Sir Thomas Munro who lived and died two centuries ago. Whenever any young Civil Servant came to me for blessings or when I spoke to them, I advised them to read about Sir Thomas M, who was the ideal administrator."

Of Munro, who spent 47 of his years in the Madras Presidency, Rajaji went on to say, "(He) was of those exceptionally good and great men who came from Britain to India and left a record of service which anyone can be proud of. He was unpopular with his fellow officials and other British residents because of his sympathy with the people of the land and his admiration of some of their qualities. He was an initiator of peace. It was his work in this direction and his just and wise administrations that have made a household name in South India."

I too have for long been an admirer of Munro, for what he did for the Southern settlements, for education and for the development of Madras. But more than anything else, for the way he saw a future for India different to what the waning company envisaged. Rajaji quotes one of these statements in his article, addressed to the Company Court of Directors, which reads,

"Your rule is alien, and it can never be popular. You have much to bring to your subjects, but you cannot turn India into England or Scotland. Work through, not in spite of, native systems and native ways, with a prejudice in their favour rather than against them; and then, in the fullness of time, your subjects can frame and maintain a worthy Government for themselves. Get out and take the glory of the achievement and the sense of having done your duty as the chief reward for your exertions."

An equestrian statue of Sir Thomas Munro was carved by Francis Legatt Chantrey, stands majestically near Gymkhana, (Island Grounds), Chennai.

James Achilles Kirkpatrick

The Philanderer of Madras

Madras had a couple of headline-grabbing authors with tales of love in the Hyderabad court and a passion for photography in the courts of 19th century Punjab. Authors like William Darymple have a written a couple of splendid books – some are one a smooth read, the other a visual and anecdotal treat –

but it is the exhaustive research over the years revealed in both that I envy. It is that research that not only enriched the books but also gave me the opportunity to record the Madras connection for both

Dalrymple's 'White Mughals' might be all about the great love James Achilles Kirkpatrick and that 'most excellent among women,' Khair-un-Nissa shared in the 18th century, especially at a time when there were many more such interracial romances or relationships. To me, Kirkpatrick's Madras connections are as fascinating, particularly as so much about them have been left unsaid. In fact, the book begins in the woods of Government House, Madras with Lord Clive (II) trying to learn from two of his Hyderabad spies the truth about the scandal that resident Kirkpatrick was causing.

James Achilles was the second son of a philandering colonel of the Madras Cavalry, also a James but better known as 'The Handsome Colonel.' Col. James, paused long enough between his flings to marry Katherine Munro in St. Mary's in the Fort in 1762. She was the eldest daughter of the late Dr. Andrew Munro of Charles Street Surgeon of Fort St. George (1742-1756) and in charge of the fifth edition of its first hospital. In it, intoxication, gaming and boxing were rampant among those who chose not to leave with Dr. Munro s favourite dispensation, 'hysterickdrafts!'

Born in Madras on August 22, 1764 and baptised in St. Mary's, James Achilles lost his mother when he was 18 months old and was taken to England three years later, when his father went back. It was as a 15-year-old that James Achilles returned to Madras in 1779, the handsome Colonel having bought him a cadetship in the Madras Army. It was in that Army that James Achilles saw service for the next 14 years, 'without in anyway distinguishing himself' except for being at the siege of Seringapatam in the Third Mysore War, during which, he was attacked and severely wounded by his orderly. He established house with an Indian woman and sired a son, whom he took back to England in 1791 to live with his father and acquired a rare fluency in Indian languages. He was to describe himself in the Madras Courier 'as an officer who from his proficiency in the Persian and Hindoostanee tongues, and conversancy in the manner and customs of the race of men by whom these languages are spoken, had contracted a certain degree of partiality towards them.' These foretold of things to come.

James Achilles' illegitimate half-brother William — the result of another of the handsome Colonel's conquests — was appointed Resident (Ambassador, but, in time, a post with almost Viceregal powers) in Hyderabad in 1793-1794. Four years later, Governor-General Richard Wellesley, struck by William's language skills, appointed him his ADC. In 1800, he was made military secretary and chief political adviser. The appointment was further sweetened with James Achilles being appointed Resident in Hyderabad. The die was cast for honours when he got the better of the French, for love, when he espied Khair-un-Nissa, and for doubts, when his loyalty became suspect.

As Wellesley commandeered a regiment in Madras, he had honed his soldiering in Fort St. George and on the march to Mysore, before displaying his promise at Assaye in the Deccan.

City's First English Women

I had read recently that an Elizabeth Marsh was one of the very few Englishwomen in 1770's Madras, but I still wondered who the first one to arrive in Madras was, braving the surf and the masula boats.

Meanwhile, checking my sources, the first name I came across was Elizabeth Bland, who in 1655, together with her husband Thomas, accused the Agent (then the Chief of Council) Henry Greenhill, of "heinous crimes" including being "accessory to this wicked deed" of "making away with a child which she was gone for 5 months." It was found that she and her husband were falsely accusing the agent because he had refused to lend her money, and in turn, had demanded the money Thomas Bland owed him. Elizabeth Bland herself confessed to accusing Agent Greenhill, as part of a blackmail plan.

Next there is, Ascentia Dawes, presumably the sister or wife of William Dawes, a Civil Servant who became a Councillor and who died during the first coup in Fort St. George. Ascentia Dawes is heard of in 1665, accused of the murder of her servant girl. First found guilty of murder, "though not in manner mention or form," she was later acquitted, but will always be remembered for being the first accused in India to face a trial by jury.

Another name of this period is that of Elizabeth Clarke, the wife of Thomas Clarke Jnr., one of the earliest European settlers in Madras. Certainly, he was working for the Company by 1643, four years after the founding of the city. In time, he became interpreter and Portuguese writer for the Council, and bought a house at what is now the southern end of Broadway. He died in 1683, and in 1686, his widow was requesting the Council for compensation for their first house that had been pulled down to make way for fortifications. That same year, she married Niccolo Manucci, a doctor who was best-known for his writings on the Mughal court. Manucci, through this marriage, acquired the Clarkes' house and it became a Madras landmark as Manucci's Gardens.

Whether Elizabeth Clarke was on the scene or not in the 1640s – thus pre-dating Elizabeth Bland – I have not been able to ascertain. But the English would not have counted her as one of theirs – she was the daughter of a Harling married to a Pereyra. And Pereyra would have been a 'Portugee' or a mestizo.

Footnote: The early records are full of the name Elizabeth. Good Queen Bess had apparently not been forgotten even a couple of centuries later to judge by the popularity of the name in Olde Madras.

Thomas Pitt. Detail of a print after an oil painting by Sir Godfrey Kneller

Chronicler of Madras

Thomas Pitt (5 July 1653 – 28 April 1726), born at Blandford Forum, Dorset, to the Reverend John Pitt, a Church of England cleric, and rector of Blandford St Mary, and Sarah Jay, was an English merchant involved in trade with India.

Thomas Pitt, or 'Pirate Pitt' to many, was Governor of Madras from 1698 to 1709. Beginning his career in the East as an 'interloper' (an independent trader banned by the East India Company), he was once described by the Directors as "a desperate fellow, and one that, we fear, will not stop at doing any mischief that lies in his power." Yet, when they changed their mind, he had the longest stint of any Governor of Madras, "a period which proved to be the Golden Age of Madras in respect of the development of trade and increasing of wealth."

The Pitt story is a fascinating one and has not really been told in objective detail. But that's not my story today. My tale for the day is about one of Pitt's more significant contributions to the nascent city.

Although never been dated accurately, Pitt's Map of Madras has been stated to be the first accurate map of any city in India, being published c. 1711 after a survey that he ordered. The only original engraving of the map known to be in existence is in Oxford's famed Bodleian Library. And it is from the internal evidence in the map that it becomes apparent that the survey probably began in 1707 and the map included details that date up to 1711.

The map names streets inside and outside of the Fort; it shows significant private properties and places of worship. The most striking feature of White Town (Fort St George) is the exact shape of the inner fort wherein was Governor's 'Castle.' It is centred in the east in a square enclosed by four walls and protected by triangular bastions in the corners. To the South-East of the inner fort's neighbour is the St Mary's Church and close to the Eastern walls, is the Town Hall, clearly depicted as a domed building that Presidency College later day dome might well have drawn inspiration from.

South of the Fort is the island with Pitt's tree-lined Great Walk clearly seen. North of the Fort is the first 'Black Town,' even then developed on a gridiron pattern and protected on three sides by walls and on the fourth by the sea.

Almost in the centre of 'Black Town' is 'The Great Pagoda' (the Chennakesava Perumal Temple), about where the southern edge of today's High Court campus is. Also marked are 'The English Burying Place' (whose vestiges still remain in a corner of the Law College campus) and 'The Armenian Church,' across from where Handloom House now is.

Across from Black Town's northern wall is 'Muthial Peta,' which developed as the New Black Town (George Town) in the 1750s. But the gridiron pattern was already in place, as the map shows. The street names here are rather different from todays: Mud Point Street, Comatee Street, Malabars Street, Chitee Street and Fisher Street are marked. Prominently indicated is Rodrigues Tomb. Separated from Black Town and Muthial Peta by 'The Cannall of the Pedda' and 'Gardens' (fields and groves) is 'Comer Pete or Peddanaigue Pete,' already grid-ironed but with a different set of street names from today. What is in place are 'Allingalls Pagoda' (Ekambareswarar Temple) and 'Loraine's Pagoda' (Bairagimadam Temple).

South of Peddanigue Pete and nestling in a curve of the Elambore River (now Buckingham Canal) and across from The Island is 'The Company's Garden,' Pitt's rest-and-recreation 'country seat.' There's a small fort on the south, a walled enclosure north of it and a mansion on the east with a tree-lined walk/drive leading to it. What a magnificent picture of 70-year-old Madras this 300-year-old map offers!

THE PITT DIAMOND

Pitt is most famous for his purchase of a 410 carat (82 g) uncut diamond acquired from an Indian merchant named Jamchand in Madras in 1701. The merchant had purchased the diamond from an English sea captain, who had, in fact, stolen the diamond from a servant of Abul Hasan Qutb Shah. According to another version, the servant found the diamond in one of the Golkonda mines on the Krishna River and had concealed it inside a large wound in his leg, which he had suffered from as he fled the Siege of Golconda.

Pitt bought the diamond for 48,000 pagodas or £20,400 and sent it back to England in 1702 with his eldest son. For two years from 1704–1706, the jeweller Harris laboured in London to hew a 141 carat (28.2 g) cushion brilliant from the rough stone. Several secondary stones were produced from the cut that were sold to Peter the Great of Russia. After many attempts to sell it to various European royals, including Louis XIV of France, Pitt and his sons went with the diamond to Calais in 1717. With John Law acting as agent, it was sold that year to the French régent, Philippe II, Duke of Orléans for £135,000, becoming one of the crown jewels of France. Today, "Le Régent" as it came to be known, remains in the French Royal Treasury at the Louvre, where it has been on display since 1887.

Pitt owned a piece of land called a copyhold, and whoever laid hands on it was entitled to Pitt's most valuable possession after his death. If Pitt hadn't sold the diamond, it would have been confiscated as a heriot.

According to a story that rings truer, the diamond was found in 1701 on the banks of the river Krishna by a miner working for a lessee. The stone, 410 carats before it was cut, as it was later assessed, was smuggled out by the finder in the bandages he wrapped around his leg to protect a self-inflicted wound. Putting together the various stories about the smuggling, this sounds like the most plausible reconstruction of events.

The miner, described as a slave but probably what we would call bonded labour, escaped to the Coast and sought passage to Madras from an English skipper to whom he spoke of his escape with a diamond — presumably offering some of its proceeds for his passage to freedom. What happened to the miner thereafter is not known, but the uncut stone turned up with Jamchand, perhaps the biggest diamond dealer in the South. As the story goes, he bought it from the ship's captain for £1000.

Pitt himself later recorded his negotiations with Jamchand — who was introduced to him by a free merchant, Samuel Glover, and came accompanied by Venkata Chetti, one of the town's leading Indian merchants during every visit in the course of the protracted negotiations. The bargaining in December 1701 began with Jamchand asking for 200,000 pagodas and Pitt offering 30,000. (It was about 2.33 pagodas to the pound sterling at the time). Finally — and I skip all Pitt's details of the hard bargaining that went on over a couple of months — Pitt bought the diamond for 48,000 pagodas "believing it must prove a pennyworth if it proved good." Pitt cites Governor Richard Benyon as being a witness of sorts to the purchase. Glover, who expected to benefit from the transaction, did not receive the 3000 pagodas Jamchand had promised him as the diamond merchant had not been "pleased with Pitt's transactions in the matter." Nevertheless, Jamchand and Pitt continued to do business with each other till the former Governor left for England.

The diamond was sent by Pitt to England with his son Robert, a free merchant in Madras as soon as the deal was finalised in 1702. Till Robert reached England and his father received word of his safe arrival, Thomas Pitt was a much-worried man, particularly as the bill of lading mentioned the diamond's value at only 6500 pagodas.

In London, the diamond was cut and polished at a cost of £5000, but the chippings and dust from the cutting fetched Pitt about £7500. In 1717, he sold the diamond, which had been cut to about 137 carats, to the Duke of Orléans, who was the Régent during the minority of Louis XV of France, for £135,000 — and the Pitt family became rich enough to fuel its political ambitions. The brokerage for the negotiations cost each party £5000.

In 1791, when the French Crown jewels were inventoried and valued, what was now the Régent Diamond was priced at £480,000. A year later it had been stolen, together with the greater part of the French Crown Jewels. An anonymous letter led to their being found in a ditch in an alley off the Champs Elysees.

The 'Régent' was later pledged by Napoleon to the Dutch Government to raise funds for his ambitions, then redeemed and returned to the French Treasury, where it has remained — a long way from Madras.

Indo-Saracenic Architecture

Ma. Se's sketches of the city that was Connemara Library; Victoria Public Hall and the statue of Munro.

Indo-Saracenic Architecture is one of the most distinctive architectural styles in the city, especially since it was pioneered there itself. An amalgamation of European, Indian and Islamic styles of architecture, it combined the pinnacles of Gothic architecture, the Chhatris of Indian architecture and the minarets of Islamic architecture. Indo-Saracenic is a breathtaking combination of Western and Eastern sensibilities. These buildings were built during the British Raj era of India in the late 19th century, and thus, reflect Victorian styles that were in vogue back in Europe, while taking styles of religious or royal Indian and Islamic architecture and putting it into a nonreligious context. The vast majority of these buildings are a rich brick red, though they sometimes can be white. Notable examples of Indo-Saracenic architecture include the Chennai Central Station, the Chennai Government Museum, the Ripon Building and the Madras High Court.

The Victoria Memorial Hall and Technical Institute, while not technically in the Indo-Saracenic style, was designed by Henry Irwin, a British architect who also designed the Government Museum, as well as numerous other notable buildings.

Egmore Museum, established in 1851, is located in Egmore, Chennai. Known as the Madras Museum, the museum is the second oldest museum in India, the first being the Indian Museum at Kolkata started in 1814. It is also one of the largest museums in South Asia. It is particularly rich in archaeological and numismatic collections. It has the largest collection of Roman antiquities outside Europe. Many of the buildings within the Museum campus are over 100 years old. Among them, the colossal Museum Theatre is one of the most impressive. The National Art Gallery is also present in the museum premises. Built in Indo-Saracenic style, it houses rare works of artists like Raja Ravi Varma - The Celebrated Painter from The Mavelikara Palace in close relation with Travancore Royalty.

Ripon Building, San Thome Cathedral and Madras High Court.

National Art Gallery; Amir Mahal; Chepauk Palace; and Senate House.

A Home of its own

Robert Fellows Chisholm

The resurrected Senate House, the first of the University of Madras at 80% complete, stands as a glorious example of classical restoration. The Great Hall in the Vice Chancellor's room of the northern wing and the most ornate of the smaller hall on the first floor of the southern wing are truly areas of great beauty. Once the domes are complete, there won't be a building in the state to match it in splendour and it will again be one of the great Sarcenic buildings of India, living up to what it has been called even when it was in disrepair, 'the work of a genius'.Together with the Presidency College,PWD and Revenue Board building –the last being the Northern extension of Chepauk Palace — it was designed, supervised, decorated and furnished by Robert Fellowes Chisholm of Britain when he arrived in Madras from Calcutta in 1865. Before he left India in 1902, apart from changing the Madras skyline, had become renowned for creating the Lakshmi Vilas Palace and Museum, Baroda; Trivandrum's Napier Museum, the Lawrence School, Ooty; and Rangoon's Anglican Cathedral. He truly is one of the great figures in the history of post-1800 architecture in south India.

A view of the Senate House, and Presidency College

Chisholm in Chepauk

The Nawab of Carnatic, Muhammad Ali was refused permission to build his palace in Fort St. George, and so, on a suggestion, he built Chepauk Palace not far from the Fort's guns. Work on it was completed in 1768. By 1770, its 117 acres stretched from Pycroft's Road to the Cooum and from the beach - which in those days reached upto what is now KamarajSalai - to Bell's Road. Much of Robert Fellows Chisholm's early work, which he came from Calcutta to supervise, was raised in this campus after it had been bought by the Government of Madras in auction in 1859 for Rs.5,80,000. The Government ousted the Nawabs from the premises in 1855 on specious grounds and, therefore, the auction was simply a eyewash.

Be that as it may, Chisholm raised that symbol of imperialism around 1866-67 in the palace grounds, a tower that linked the two halves of the palace. To this day, I'm still confused about which half is the Khalsa Mahal and which the Humayun Mahal and Darbar Hall, with all descriptions proving beyond my interpretation. Getting back to Chisholm at Chepauk, he also helped design the RWD building around the same time as the tower. He then started working on two other buildings whose designs not only won him prizes in open competition but also brought him to Madras. Work on the Presidency College building began in 1867 and completed in 1870 and work on Senate House, Chisholm's masterpiece, started in 1869 and was completed in 1873. In between, he did something less Indo-Saracenic – designing the first pavilion of Madras Cricket Club in 1866. When a cyclone wrecked it in 1888, Henry Irwin designed the famous old pavilion in 1891 that survived until the 1980s as a cricketing landmark.

Chisholm built many more landmarks in Madras in the years that followed, but that complex of buildings around Chepauk Palace will always remain a memorial to his genius. And what a memorial they must have been when they formed a regal Indo-Saracenic cluster whose view was unimpeded by all the hotch potch of buildings and trees that have come up around them and hide the view!

"Success is not doing more. It's in doing the right thing,"

– **Sadhguru**

Vastrakala

The Tapestry-maker from France

Vastrakala is a small Madras-based business house that restores upholstery of furniture in the Royal House of Orange, or the Dutch royal family by re-creating 18th century oriental embroidery. A creative studio rather than a manufacturing unit, Vastrakala, also known as the House of Jean François Lesage, have embroidered furnishings for Windsor Palace, the office of the French President and renowned names like Stephen Spielberg, Naomi Campbell and Claudia Schiffer.

Jean François was 28 when he decided, seven years ago, that it was time to settle down after years of dabbling with the art of South Asia, both as an art auctioneer as well as a traveller in search of exotica. He then decided to do what he should have done a decade earlier, and that was to get into the embroidery business. The House of Lesages, successors to the House of Michonet since 1924, was founded by the Lesanges cousins in 1868. It is the best-known atelier of embroidery in the haute couture world. The world of high fashion, however, didn't interest Jean François the way it did his grandfather, Albert or father, François. The House of Les might have embellished the dresses of emperors and kings, film stars and the wealthy, but Jean François didn't have his heart set on joining it, and so, he moved on. He did not accept the world of embroidery as his, until he began looking at buildings and interiors in South Asia and saw their rich embellishments with embroidery. Vastrakala was born out of this, founded by him with Patrick Savouret and Malavika Rao.

Today, Vastrakala encompasses an extended family of over 125 skilled artisans who work together. The business is equally divided between bespoke orders and quality work for the international marketplace. The number of artisans keep increasing, as Vastrakala trains more skilled craftsmen to produce work of great quality, always trying to push them. The training takes time, and Vastrakala is content to grow organically and slowly.

Meanwhile, Jean François' love affair with buildings had him first open his atelier in the old Buchi Babu house. His dreams of restoring the building died when it was sold. Now, Vastrakala creates embroidery against the backdrop of another 'not-quite-so-old' house. Jean François still harbours dreams of the day he can buy a grand old house in Madras, which he can restore and create magic with his embroidery complementing the home as well as showing each other off.

Courtesy Madras Miscellany – S. Muthaih The Hindu

Rippon Buildings

Rippon Buildings is a fine example of the neoclassical style of architecture - a combination of Gothic, Iconic and Corinthian. An all-white structure, it is located near the Chennai Central Railway Station.

History

Commissioned in 1913, Ripon Building was built by Loganatha Mudaliar and took four years to build at a cost of ₹750,000, including a sum of ₹550,000 paid to Mudaliar. Named after Lord Ripon, Governor-General of British India and the Father of local self-government, the foundation stone was laid by Earl of Minto, the then Viceroy and Governor-General of India on 12 December 1909. The Municipal Corporation of Madras, after functioning from several other places including Errabalu Chetty Street, settled in the Ripon building in 1913, with P. L. Moore as its President at the time of the inauguration. The inaugural function was attended by over 3,000 of the city's elite. A rectangular building, it is 85 metres (279 ft) in length and 32 metres (105 ft) in width, with

43 metres (141 ft) central tower containing a clock 2.5 m (8.2 ft) in diameter. The first of its three floors have approximately 2,800 m^2 (30,139 sq ft) of space. Constructed with stock bricks, the walls are set and plastered with lime mortar, and the roof is supported with teak wood joists. The original flooring of the ground floor was Cuddapah slate that has been replaced with marble. One of the main attractions of the building is the Westminster Quarter chiming clock. This was installed by Oakes and Co. in 1913. The clock has a mechanical key system, which is wound every day. The building has four bells, which were cast by Gillet and Johnston in 1913. The Ripon Building is the seat of the Chennai Corporation (Madras Corporation) in Chennai (Madras), Tamil Nadu.

Madras Courier was the first newspaper to be established in the Madras Presidency, British India. First published on October 12, 1785, it was the leading newspaper of its time. Selling for a princely sum of one rupee, it thrived for three decades.

The Raj Bhavan in Guindy.

A story that began with the foundationless 'Castle' for the British surrounded by four walls — a staid complex grandiosely called Fort St. George in 1640 — went ahead with the people who were originally Agents becoming Presidents, then Governors in 1661. In 1693, they moved the 'Castle' eastwards to new premises called Fort House, which became the core of today's Secretariat.

The tale continues with the Governors using Admiralty House in the Fort — now called Clive House — as their town house. The house in Chepauk — later known as Government House in Government Estate, and recently pulled down to build the new Assembly and Secretariat — became their country house. The Chepauk house, acquired in 1753, became the Government House in 1800. When Governor Thomas Munro wasn't satisfied with the Government House and its spacious surroundings giving him the peace he required to concentrate on work, he persuaded the council in 1821 to acquire Guindy Lodge which was mortgaged to the Government Bank. This property - which until 1946 was the new country house - became Raj Bhavan after Independence.

"Live your beliefs and you can turn the world around."

– Henry David Thoreau

Born: 9 December 1870, Ranipet **Died:** 24 May 1960, India

Full name: Ida Sophia Scudder

Nationality: American **Parents:** John Scudder Jr.

Education: Weill Cornell Medical College

Dr. Ida Sophia Scudder was a third-generation American medical missionary in India. She dedicated her life to the plight of Indian women and the fight against bubonic plague, cholera and leprosy. In 1918, she started one of Asia's foremost teaching hospitals, the Christian Medical College & Hospital, Vellore, India

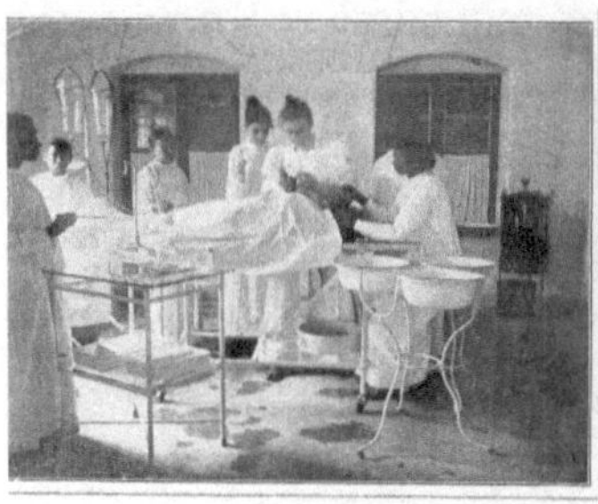

Ida Scudder Quotes

"God will provide," "Once you start, I am sure everything will fall into place. It always has."

"Only those who can see the invisible can achieve the impossible,"

Ida S. Scudder with Mahatma Gandhi, 1928

The 4 generations of scudder family served in India as medical Missionaries.

Ida Scudder with her parents

One day in 1953, aged 82, she was at "Hilltop", her bungalow at Kodaikanal, and opened a stack of letters and telegrams. Her name is a famous one in India. A letter once reached her addressed simply, "Dr. Ida, India." But the mail was heavier than usual because friends around the world were congratulating her on winning the Elizabeth Blackwell Citation from the New York Eye and Ear Infirmary, as one of 1952's five outstanding women doctors.

Road side clinic

A fundraiser with a piano recital by Canadian, Stephane Lemetin and dinner at Le Royal Meridian on December 4th, commemorates one of the biggest memorial to an individual whose name has all but been forgotten outside North Arcot District and in medical circles. The inauguration of this seven-storey memorial, marks the most fitting tribute to the woman it is being named after, for it will be devoted to those medical services that were closest to her heart. Led by her work for mother and child, she gave up the dream of marrying a millionaire in America to toil in a parched district of Madras Presidency. Perhaps, the only memorial left is to rename Vellore 'Idavelle' after the woman who founded a one-bed clinic on January 1, 1900 and saw it grow into an institution serving thousands over the years and sending forth hundreds of doctors and nurses to serve all over India and abroad.

'Idavelle'

Reminded about the centenary of that founding, I scanned once again a treasured review copy of mine, of Dr. Ida, by Dorothy Clarke Wilson, published in 1959. The review brought to life the huge, tennis-enjoying Nebraskan woman with the distinctive white hair, hurtling after a tennis ball. Once again, I am reminded of one-room beginnings, of what is now the Vellore Christian Medial College and Hospital.

Even as I read once again the tale of the three calls in the night that her father, Dr. John could not answer and which neither could she, for she was still dreaming of returning to America and not of becoming the woman doctor that was needed that night. As I read the book 'Roadside' of a tale that began in a bullock-cart, offering treatment to patients who gathered along a long dirt road, and even as I read of the campaigns in America and the faith and hope that raised, brick by brick, several institutions in one campus in a country Americans knew as only being the back of beyond, this re-reading brought into greater focus other names, less remembered, without whom the Vellore medical saga would not have been possible.

It was in 1819 that Dr. John Scudder, the first medical missionary from America sailed for India. Over the next 150 years, he and 41 other members of his family were to contribute over 1000 years of service to India! There was always the Scudder family around Ida Scudder in her darkest moments at Vellore, where she struggled to develop one of Asia's leading medical institutions of the time.

Courtesy Late S Mutiah

Sister Anna Jacob is 100 years young and was one of the early nurses trained by CMC founder Dr. Ida Scudder

"When love and skill work together, expect a masterpiece."

– John Ruskin

Ravi Varma amidst the Masons

There was a rather delightful cartoon I saw the other day. It featured a child looking rather upset after his birthday party and queried, "Appa, how come I get to celebrate my birthday for one day while Chennai gets to celebrate it for one week?"

Indeed, Madras' celebrations went on for two weeks for what might have been the last of the celebratory occasions, put together by the Freemasons to remember the founding of the city.

That was my first visit to the Freemasons' Hall on Commander-in-Chief Road, and I found its interior rather splendid after some meticulously executed restoration. But more than the restoration which reflected that the City, in parts, is at last catching on to the idea of wanting to care for its living heritage. I was happy to make two discoveries during my visit. One was a Ravi Varma portrait adding one more to the few Ravi Varma originals in the city that I know of — and the other that the Masons have long had a connection with

St. George's School and Orphanage – an ancient organisation – having had a representative on the School's Board of Management.

There's quite a treasure trove of antiquities in the Hall, ranging from portraits in oils and photographs of the Grand Masters, who have headed the organisation in South India from the 1780s, to the antique Master's chairs, other furniture and the ornamentation in the three temples that the Hall houses, all carefully preserved. Among those portraits was one of Lord Ampthill, Governor of Madras 1901-1906. Ampthill, the son of the diplomat Lord Odo Russell, was the Private Secretary of Joseph Chamberlain, a major figure in late 19th century British politics and father of Neville Chamberlain, a later Prime Minister. Joseph Chamberlain of Birmingham, who was President, Board of Trade and later, Colonial Secretary, was best-known for his advocacy of the British Empire becoming a united trading block.

Lord Ampthill acted as Viceroy in 1904, when Lord Curzon was on Home Leave. I, however, remember Ampthill for having been an enthusiastic patron of Raja Ravi Varma, that great artist who might be considered the father of Modern Indian Art. To find Ampthill painted by Ravi Varma was, therefore, a most happy discovery.

It was in 1873 that Ravi Varma came to the art world's attention when he was awarded the First Prize for his 'Nair Lady at her Toilet,' at the Madras Fine Arts exhibition. Prizes followed more prizes in the Madras exhibitions that came thereafter — and so did the patronage of the Governors of Madras. In the 1904 exhibition, when his exhibits were not for competition, Ravi Varma put up a striking portrait of Lady Ampthill. The next year he exhibited at the Madras show, the portrait of Lord Ampthill in his Masonic regalia. The Governor invited him to accompany him and the Prince of Wales (later to become King George V) to Mysore and paint the highlight of a visit where royalty entertained royalty. One of the most memorable pictures that came out of that tour was the impressions of *Mysore Khedda*.

Ravi Varma died in October 1906, and by then, Lord Ampthill had retired to England, but he wrote from there to Varma's son,

"A gentler, courteous nature I have never known, and added to that, there were the lofty ideas and pure motives which inspired the art to which he devoted so much resultant benefit to Indian life. It would be difficult to ever estimate the influence for good which your father's paintings, widely popularised as they were, had among all kinds and conditions of your countrymen. They spread a refined taste in art, and they must have done much to influence religious thoughts."

Indeed, recognition of the artist's influence has been an area of much focus in the last few years, judging by the several books on Raja Ravi Varma that have been coming out.

Lord Ampthill in Full Masonic Regali by Raja Ravi Varma

The adjacent painting to that of Ampthill in the Freemasons' Hall is that of a Sir Archibald Campbell. A civilian in his 30's, Campbell who was also a Grand Master, retired as Chief Secretary of Madras.

Encouraged by Lady Campbell, the Rev. Wilhelm Gericke founded the Female Orphans' Asylum in 1787. This was followed by the Male Orphans' Asylum headed by Dr. Andrew Bell, who introduced the *gurukulam* system of education, which he later introduced as the Madras System of Education in

Britain with fair success. The two orphanages were run separately in what is now known as the Egmore Redoubt, a small fort to the rear of the now Egmore Railway Station. In 1871-72, the two orphanages were merged together with St. Mary's Charity School - which grew out of the school for orphans founded in St. Mary's in the 1680s – to become the Civil Orphans' Asylum. In 1904, the Asylum moved into Conway Gardens, opposite which the Pachaiyappa's College now stands. In 1954, it took the name by which it is known today - St. George's Orphanage and Higher Secondary School. Given its roots, this is the oldest Western-style school in the country. As part of its contribution to underprivileged society, the Masons have long had a role to play in this school.

Tamil iyer couple c. 1945; the wife is wearing a Madras style sari. Brahmins

Affuent chettiar family heirs

Wedding Cermony

The Trade History of 18th Century

The Madras Merchants

Thomas Parry (1768–1824) was a Welsh merchant. The third son of Edward Parry and Anne Vaughan, of Leighton Hall near Welshpool, he was instrumental in realising the potential for business and commerce in India. Parry came to Chennai, as a part of British India in the late 1780s and set up a modest business of piece goods and banking. The business he set up continued to grow and Parry became a household name in Chennai. Parry set up the *EID Parry Company* in 1787, the corporate headquarters of which stand at Parry's Corner, in a well-known central business district of Madras.

Parry Limited, the public company headquartered in Chennai, South India has been in business for more than 225 years. It has many firsts to its credit, including the manufacturing of fertilisers (1906) for the first time in the Indian subcontinent. The company is currently engaged in the manufacture and marketing of sugar and bioproducts. Parry's is the oldest surviving mercantile name in Chennai.

Chronicling the Parry's Story

EID Parry is one of the oldest business entities of the Indian subcontinent and was founded by Thomas Parry, a Welshman who came to India in the late 1780s. On 17th July 1788, he started a business of banking and piece goods.

By 1819, a partnership firm named "Parry and Dare" Company was founded by Thomas Parry and John William Dare. Parry's Corner, one of the most prominent central business districts of Chennai, derives its name from Parry. Over a period of time, the business established by Parry continued to grow, and its flagship company EID Parry emerged.

In 1908 Parry and Company set up 'The Pottery' unit in Ranipettai. Over the years, this was named as "Parryware."

'Parry and Company Limited' and 'East India Distilleries and Sugars Limited' were merged to form EID Parry India Limited. In its more than 200-year existence, this house remained active and operated many businesses.

The Murugappa Group took over EID Parry in 1981 from financial and public institutions such as Life Insurance Corporation of India, United Assurance Co and Unit Trust of India.

Parry and Co. sugar refineries at Samalkota, c. 1914

Dare House at Parry's Corner

John Binny

Binny and Company Binny and Co. is the shipping, textile, banking and insurance firm based in the city of Chennai, India. It is one of the oldest business firms in Chennai city.

History

Binny and Co. was founded in Madras by John Binny as a general, clearing and forwarding agency in 1797. Initially, the company functioned from a building then known as Amir Bagh on Mount Road, where the headquarters of the Indian Overseas Bank is now located. The company then moved to a house a few blocks away, where Hotel Taj Connemara is now situated. The firm moved to its present headquarters in Armenian Street in 1812. With the passage of time, Binny and Co. entered the banking and insurance sectors.

John Binny set up a partnership with one Mr. Denison and renamed the company as Binny and Denison in 1800. Binny and Co. were the landing agents for the British India Steam Navigation Company and had a fleet of 35 barges and 30 lighters to transport men and goods from ships to land. They also ran a motor bus service for land transportation. Binny and Co. was one of the founding members of the Madras Chamber of Commerce and Industry.

Binny and Co. set up the Buckingham Mills in 1876 followed by the Carnatic Mills in 1881.[3] Both were merged to form the Buckingham and Carnatic

Mills in 1920.[3] The Bangalore Cotton, Silk and Woollen Mills was set up in Bangalore in 1884. The Buckingham and Carnatic Mills was the most long-lasting among the company's many ventures.

Decline Binny and Co. suffered heavily from the crash of Arbuthnot Bank on 22 October 1906. India's Independence on 15 August 1947, further crippled the fortunes of the company. The Buckingham and Carnatic Mills, the company's only venture that was still successful, began to decline by the 1970s. The mills closed down their operations in 1996 and the mills were sold out in 2001.

A Forgotten 200-year-old Binny and Company

The ABP of Madras's commerce and the contributors of its phenomenal growth are Arbuthnot, Binny and Parry. The oldest of them, Parry's is still going strong. Binny's, the second oldest, is an institution that I hope will pull itself out of the morass that started with the floods of the 1980s. Arbuthnot's survives only in the names of other companies it helped to found, like Gillanders Arbuthnot.

Binny's, in the unfortunate state it now finds itself, is sadly unable to celebrate its 200th birthday when the New Year dawns. Perhaps, the best celebration of that anniversary year will be some answers to help revive a grand old company that was responsible for the development of much of North Madras. That development came when a trading firm became a managing agency and helped lay the foundations of major industry in Madras with the Buckingham and the Carnatic Mills.

The trading activities began with the arrival, in 1797 Madras of an 18-year-old Scot named John Binny, who entered the service of the Nawab of the Carnatic as a doctor! F de Souza, who recorded it says, "Who his patients were, whether he killed or cured, or conducted even a single operation we have no knowledge." But what is known is that he might have done some business on the side, particularly in private banking, especially considering the times. What is certain is that the partnership concerns of Binny and Dennison went into business in 1800. This is when the story of Binny and Co., founded by John 'Deaf' Binny, begins. Binny's home was where the Hotel Connemara came up.

A 200-year-old Chapter Ends

The headline, 'Decks cleared for VRS disbursement at Binny', and the announcement that a rehabilitation scheme for the ancient company had been cleared by a financial agency, marks the end of a chapter in the life of one of the three surviving Indian corporate houses with roots in the 18th century. The good news is that the name Binny Ltd. will survive, and remain in the textile business. The sad news is that its spinning and weaving operations will move to suburban Singaperumalkoil, near Maraimalainagar. The future of 'Buckingham' and 'Carnatic Mills' properties where the city's industrialisation began, and to which North Madras owes its growth, is rather uncertain. I only hope that many of the Mills' buildings, homes and clubhouse, all deserving of being listed as heritage properties, survive any future plans.

There has also been the same uncertainty about Binny's headquarters building in Armenian Street, and I hope that this historic site too, where the Binny story began, does not fall prey to development. Of the Arbuthnot's, Binny's and Parry's who first developed Madras on a substantial scale, it was the Binny's from Scotland who were the first to arrive in Old Madras, making their mark here as early as 1682. It was Charles Binny, however, who arrived in 1669 and entered the service of the Nawab of the Carnatic, forging the links between both families. He was followed by kin who also served the Nawab. John 'Deaf' Binny arrived in 1797 to follow the family tradition. Two years later, deciding that serving the Nawab of the Carnatic and lending money to 'His Highness' held no future at a time when the scandal of the Carnatic Debts was causing a furore in the British Parliament, John Binny decided to establish an agency house in his rented home in Armenian Street.

No sooner had Binny's become Binny and Dennison in 1800, John Binny moved into a house and property that had been a part of Amir Bagh (where the Indian Overseas Bank is now headquartered). Binny paid Rs. 28, 000 for this garden house on the site of which the Hotel Connemara was later developed. Binny and Dennison bought the Armenian Street home in 1804 for Rs. 35,000. As Binny Ltd. was established in 1814, the rest of the property was bought in bits and pieces for less than Rs. 15,000 over the next 55 years, mainly from emigrating Armenian merchants.

Binny's foray into the Madras industry took another ten years. It was spurred by Governor Lord Napier's statement in 1869, "India is not a preserve of Manchester, and the Government and people of England would repudiate a calculated neglect of the industrial capacities of this country." For one reason or another, it took this thought time to percolate into the general thinking and implementation. It wasn't until 1876 before the Buckingham Mill Co. Ltd. was registered. A garden house in Vyasarpadi, Eddystone Lodge, and the adjacent Stephenson property were both purchased for less than Rs. 20, 000 and the mill buildings built to Robert Chisholm's design by Parthasarady Naick. The mill went on-stream as a spinning unit in 1878 with a complement of 300 employees. With the demand for textiles increasing, Buckingham added weaving to its capacity in 1893. Meanwhile, the Carnatic Mill Co. Ltd. had been floated in 1881 and had started as a spinning and weaving unit in 1884, across the Otteri Nullah from the Buckingham Mills. Together, the two made drill, particularly khaki drill, world-famous.

With the largest khaki dyeing plant in the world, Binny's ensured that khaki became synonymous with the Company's name. A significant memory in the troubled times of today is that khaki was used by the Guides or Indian border scouts in the Northwest Frontier region in 1848, after the First Afghan War, and grew in popularity thereafter.

While it has never really been spelt out who at Binny's acted on Lord Napier's suggestion and made Buckingham and Carnatic happen, two names appear frequently in the affairs of the two companies when it was founded - Charles Ainslie and Clement Simpson, both being biblically bearded. But what is especially significant for that time, is that from the start, both mill companies had Indians on their Boards - P. Somosoonthram Chetty, Abdulla Badsha Saheb, Ismail Sait, Abdul Rahman Sait and Abdollah Abooboukir. The fall of the House of Arbuthnot on October 22, 1906 changed the close-to-the-soil way Binny's had developed. The crash almost sank Binny, and only a takeover by

James Mackay, later the first Lord Inchcape, George Mackenzie and Duncan Mackinnon of B.I. Steam Navigation revived the fortunes of the Company.

Boyson of Binny

Two years after its founding, i.e. in 1886, the Gymkhana club got its first businessman (or boxwallah as men of that ilk were known) in the Hon. John Alexander Boyson.

The Boysons had a long association with Madras. JA's father, JR Boyson had been solicitor to the Government of Madras and then in 1863, become one of the founders of the National Bank of India (later a part of Grindlays and now Standard Chartered Bank). The local agents for the bank were Binny and Co, who's Managing Partner; RO Campbell was also one of the Directors of the bank, besides being President of the Bank of Madras.

Campbell and the Boysons were related by marriage, and it is perhaps no wonder that JA joined Binny. When Campbell retired from Binny in 1871, JA succeeded to his share in the partnership. He was to be with the firm for a record 50 plus years.

It was during JA's (or Boyson as we shall now refer to him) tenure as one of the senior partners that Binny got into the yarn business, an area in which it will forever be remembered. The Buckingham Mills came up in 1876 and the Carnatic Mills in 1881. In between, in 1877, the Bangalore Steam Woollen

Mills were set up. In 1882, this became the Bangalore Woollen, Cotton and Silk Mills Co. Limited. In 1903, Binny went into coal mining, and in 1905, it became the local agent for Burmah-Shell, setting up a vast storage facility at Royapuram. This was to be a convenient target for the German ship, Emden, in 1914. Under Boyson, Binny pioneered the introduction of electricity and trams into Madras.

But all was not rosy. It was also during Boyson's tenure that Binny experienced two of its greatest crises. The first was its disastrous venture into sugar, begun in 1897, thanks to a desire on the part of Boyson and his junior GL Chambers to rival Parry. The Deccan Sugar and Abkhari Company were set up and were soon bleeding money hand over fist. By 1902, Binny was in dire straits. It was left to Parry to step in and buy the loss-making unit from Binny. Boyson, who had left Madras by then for London, with a view to managing the office there prior to retirement, had to come back. Chambers had conveniently gone off on a cruise, and someone had to hold the fort.

And then, in 1906 came the Arbuthnot Crash, which saw the going bust of one of the biggest business houses of the city. Arbuthnots, which had also been into banking, just like Binny and Parry, went down with the savings of several thousand depositors. Confidence in British business houses was at an all-time low and soon, there was a run on Binny. Boyson was the man on-the-spot, and he worked at lightning speed.

Maintaining continuous telegraphic contact with London, Boyson and his partner, CB Simpson, first tried organising a local guarantee put together between the Chartered Bank, the National Bank, the Mercantile Bank, Best and Co and Wilson and Co. When this failed, he turned to British India Steam Navigation, one of whose directors was James Lyle Mackay, later Lord Inchcape and founder of the Inchcape group of companies. Negotiations followed and the Inchcape group agreed to acquire and restructure Binny.

Following this, on 31st October 1906, the old firm of Binny and Co went into voluntary liquidation. And on 16th November, it resurrected, now as a private limited firm under the Inchcape group. Boyson's partnership in the old firm was now worthless, and he was practically ruined. But being a Scot, he cannily managed to make himself and Simpson the Madras managers of the new firm at 3500 pounds a year plus 20% of the net profits. He prospered thereafter. In 1911, he became the only Director in India for Binny. He was knighted in 1914, and that year, returned to England where he remained a Director at the London office until his death in 1926. His son, John Charles Boyson, became a Director of Binny in Madras and remained one until 1934.

Boyson was active in Madras society. He was Chairman of the Madras Chamber of Commerce in 1889-90 and also 1893-94. He fought for the laying of a broad-gauge Madras-Vijayawada railway line, which eventually came to fruition. He was a Director on the Board of the Bank of Madras and an active member of the Madras Musical Association, founded in 1864 and still going strong. Boyson was also evidently an active clubman for he presided over the Madras Club the same year that he was overlord at the Gymkhana.

Sir Alexander John Arbuthnot KCSI

Born 11 October 1822 – 10 June 1907

Arbuthnot served in Madras (now Chennai) as the director of Public Instruction (1855). A key force in the incorporation of Madras University (1857), he served as the Vice Chancellor from 1971 to 1972 and was also the chief secretary to the Madras Government (1862–67). He was a member of the Legislative Council (1867–72), a member of the Madras Executive Council, served on the Viceroy's Executive Council (1875–80) and was acting Governor of Madras,

India, for about three months, from 19 February 1872 to 15 May 1872. He later served as a member of the Council of the Secretary of State for India from 1888 to 1893.

Arbuthnot was honoured by the Crown with the titles of Knight Commander of the Most Exalted Order of the Star of India (1873) and Companion of The Most Eminent Order of the Indian Empire (CIE).

The less-known branch of the Arbuthnot family is the Civil and Military branch, which contributed enormously to South Indian development. A member of this branch was Alexander Arbuthnot, who went on to become Chief Secretary and Acting Governor of Madras, and then, played a wider role in Indian affairs. He believed as much in a healthy mind as he did in a healthy body, and in 1857, was responsible for the establishment of the University of Madras. Nowhere in the University is this founding father and subsequent Vice Chancellor remembered as anything more than a name in a list. It was in 1858 that he delivered the first-ever convocation address to its graduates.

Invited in 1868 to deliver a convocation address again, he concluded with the words, "If I were called upon to name the greatest man who has lived and died in the 19th century, my choice would fall on one who laboured long and nobly in the profession (teaching) which I am now urging on your attention. No one, who in the piety and purity of his life, in the earnestness and simplicity of his character, in the largeness and liberality of his views, in the solidity of his learning, in the reverence for all that was great and good, in his abhorrence of all that was mean and petty, combined in himself more of the real characteristics of greatness than are to be found in any other man of his time, the great and good Dr. Arnold."

The street where Arbuthnot and Co. had its office, and on whose foundations rose the Indian Bank headquarters, is now named Arbuthnot Street which refers to the business house. Surely Alexander Arbuthnot, founder of the University of Madras and pioneer of cricket and rugby in South India, who has nothing to remember him by, needs greater mention? Perhaps, Bell's Road or a road near the University becoming Alexander Arbuthnot Road might not have to just remain a dream.

The Arbuthnot Family Tree

There were two branches of the Arbuthnot family who made a mark in Madras. The Arbuthnot branch of the family, which founded the ABP of Madras commerce and industry, was rather younger than Parry's or Binny's but in a short span of time, became the biggest company in South India and a pioneer in the industry. Sadly, mismanagement, living life big and fast, and undoubtedly a bit of lining of their own pockets by a couple of directors — one of whom went to jail and another committed suicide — led in 1906 to the worst financial crash in South Indian history. The losses suffered by thousands, many of them small depositors who had put in their life's savings, led to one of the finest hours of *The Hindu*, whose criticism of Arbuthnot was the loudest and the most hard-hitting. It was almost strident when it spoke of the business of Arbuthnot and Co. being "a swindle of the vilest description, decoying innumerable innocent men and women into investing in its rapacious maw…"

Sir George Gough Arbuthnot

Arbuthnot and Co was a mercantile bank, based in Madras, India. It was founded as Francis Latour and Co in the late 18th century, then became Arbuthnot De Monte and Co. and failed spectacularly on 22 October 1906.

In the last quarter of 1906, Madras was hit by the worst financial crisis the city was ever to suffer. Of the three best-known British commercial names in 19th century Madras, one crashed, a second had to be resurrected by a distress sale; and the third had to be bailed out by a benevolent benefactor. The agency house to close shop, Arbuthnot's, was considered the soundest of the three. Parry's (now EID Parry), may have been the earliest of them and Binny and Co.'s founders may have had the oldest associations with Madras, but it was Arbuthnot and Co., established in 1810, that was the city's strongest commercial organisation in the 19th Century. When it fell, thousands lost their savings, and the good name of British stability was severely rocked.

Arbuthnot and Co. had two partners at the time of its failure, Sir George Gough Arbuthnot and J.M. Young, a salaried partner who seems to have had no voice in the running of the firm. The firm entered into an arrangement with Patrick Macfadyen, who operated P Macfadyen and Co. which was effectively Arbuthnot's London branch. Macfadyen engaged in market speculation, in the process losing huge amounts of the firm's money. Prior to its collapse, Arbuthnot's employed between 11,000 and 12,000 people, had 7,000 creditors and £1,000,000 in liabilities. It was ascertained that the liabilities of Macfadyen's were £400,000 and there were 1,000 creditors. It was agreed by the English trustee in bankruptcy and the official assignee in Madras, that the assets of the two insolvent firms were to be treated as one and the same business with all creditors entitled to partake in the pooled assets.

Macfadyen committed suicide by throwing himself under a train in 1906, and both firms had to close their doors. Both Macfadyen and Arbuthnot were consistently over-optimistic concerning their market speculations. Arbuthnot was tried for the fraudulent activities the collapse revealed and received a sentence of '18 months' rigorous imprisonment.'

A key figure in the case was the Madras lawyer, V. Krishnaswamy Iyer, who went on to organise a group of Chettiars that founded Indian Bank in 1907.

Dr. Champakaraman Pillai

The Forgotten Freedom Fighter and Explorer

I think it will do justice to provide details on this gentleman from Trivandrum (I have heard many a Tamilian clamour – he is not a Malayali, he is Tamilian) for he was at the forefront in the fight for Indian Independence, even before Gandhiji, NSC Bose and many other luminaries stepped in and wrote their names in the records of history. I don't think many in Trivandrum or Kerala will recall this character, oh alas! Most of India would not know the man behind the usage of the term 'Jai Hind,' that we hear uttered every now and then.

Dr. Chempakaraman Pillai (Born 15Th September 1891 – Died 13 May 1934) was born in Trivandrum to police constable (One relative mentions that his father was the Travancore royal physician) Chinnaswamy Pillai and Nagammal of the Vellala community. Pillai was greatly influenced by Bal Gangadhar Tilak and his journal 'Kesari,' and when Tilak was arrested and sentenced to transportation, Pillai pledged lifelong dedication to the cause of India's liberation. It was at this time that Pillai came into contact with an Englishman Strickland. With the latter's help, he left India and went to Italy when he was 17 years old. Even from his younger days, there was spirit of revolution in his blood. His thirst for freedom was so great, that during his student days in Maharaja's College, Trivandrum, he greeted all his friends with 'Jai Hind', a term coined by him.

In the course of his short life abroad, he was to meet many famous and infamous people, including Gandhiji, Nehru, ACN Nambiar, Motilal and Jawaharlal Nehru, MN Roy, Chatto, NSC Bose, Kaiser, Hindenberg, Hitler and many others in the Nazi party.

He even served aboard the Emden during its voyage, and was probably involved in its shelling of Madras living his last years in Germany, dying before the World War. All through this period, he worked for India's freedom, though ending up choosing the wrong route and some wrong friends in the process. Some even say that he was the inspiration behind NSC Bose.

His Overseas Trip and Scholarship

He sailed out in 1908 (probably staying two years in Ceylon in exile as some put it) with Strickland, studied in Italy and Switzerland before proceeding to Germany which would then become his home for the rest of his life. He was proficient in English, French, German and other languages, and spearheaded the fight against the British from Germany. He reached Italy and was able to study in the Berlin School of Languages there, and also enrolled for engineering studies. He continued education in Switzerland and finished it in Germany, securing doctorates in Engineering and Economics. An engineer armed with a dual doctorate (some have mentioned wrongly that he was a Doctor of Medicine, and as Emden's surgeon) in Political Science and Economics, he found employment in the German foreign office.

Anti-British Activities

As a student in Berlin, he formed the Aid India International Committee that campaigned for India's liberation. When World War I (1914-1918) broke out, he established the Indian Independence Committee and the Indian Voluntary Corps. He also set up an army camp at Mesopotamia from where he established secret contacts with Indian nationalist leaders. Dr. Chempakaraman Pillai then helped set up an organisation called International Pro-India Committee at Zurich before the outbreak of the World War I. During the war Dr. Chempakaraman Pillai intensified his revolutionary activities. By 1914 Pillai had organised and created a revolution movement in Zurich (with the support of the German Counsel for his activities). The other members of his group were Chatto, Prabhakar and Hafiz, later joined by Har Dayal and Thara Chandar Das. All these people reached Berlin either through USA or Switzerland, two neutral states.

Responding to "Fourteen Points" of the then President of the United States, Woodrow Wilson, and Chempakaraman came up with an Eight Point proposal for Indian independence. His proposal demanded the French and the Portuguese also to leave the country.

Chempakaraman launched *Pro-India*, a monthly published in German and English from Zurich, Switzerland, through which he highlighted the glorious past of India. Another institution founded by him at Berlin was the "Orient Club."

Post World War I After the war, Chempak became a Member of the nationalist party of Germany. Champakraman Pillai was not pro-Nazi as some said, but was apparently murdered (poisoned or beaten to death) by Hitler's goons. In the Pan German Nationalist party, he was the only non-white man to have the honour and with his shiny black complexion, was proud of the distinction. Having met Kaiser Wilhelm and claiming close friendship with two important Generals, Hindenberg and Ludendorf, he was considered something of a dandy with perfect drawing room manners. Pillai was then active in the German Fatherland Party. In later years in Berlin, where he died, he remained one of the very few Indians in Germany. After the world war, when Hitler came to power, Dr. Chempakaraman Pillai developed a working relationship with Hitler with a hope of getting military assistance to end the British rule in India.

Although he had a friendly relation with Hitler, he could not tolerate a derogatory remark made by the latter against India. This led to discordance between them and an enraged Hitler ordered the confiscation of Chempakaraman Pillai's property. This incident hurt him deeply, and it turned out to be the cause of his death on May 13, 1934. By 1930's he had become upset with Hitler's attitude about Indians, comments about colour and other principles, especially those expressed in speeches and his book. Hitler had stated that Indians deserved to be ruled by the British, and stated that they were not Aryans due to the colour. Finally, he chose to protest, in 1931, writing a complaint to him with a deadline for an answer.

While many say the letter was addressed to the Fuhrer, it was actually sent to the secretary. The reply of apology apparently came one day later than Pillai required. Pillai first wanted to send the letter dated December 10th 1931 directly to Hitler, after listening to his words at the press conference in Hotel Kaiserhof on Dec 1931, but then changed his mind and sent it to the Reich Chancellor.

His Secret Name

Many of the Indians were on the English secret service watch lists. They were all entrusted with special tasks, and Pillai worked under the assumed German East African name of Abdullah Bin Manzur.

Swadeshi Movement

In 1924, Dr. Chempakaraman Pillai organised the first exhibition of Indian Swadeshi goods at the international fair held at Leipzig.

Free Government of India 1915

He had the privilege of being the Prime Minister of the Provisional Government of India set up in Afghanistan in December 1915, with Raja Mahendra Pratap of Kabul as President. However, the defeat of the Germans in the war shattered the hopes of the revolutionaries. On the other hand, some documents list him actually as Foreign Minister.

Pillai and the INA

Pillai was the forerunner of Rash Behari Bose and Subhas Chandra Bose in organising an Indian Army abroa, to strike against the enemies at home. In 1933, Dr. Chempakaraman Pillai met Subhash Chandra Bose, and they jointly conceived the idea of Azad Hind.

Marriage to Lakshmi

In 1933, Pillai met Lakshmi Bai from Manipur living in Berlin, and they decided to get married. After a short married life, Pillai fell ill due to apparent poisoning, and went to Italy for treatment. They came back to Germany, but he died on May 28th, 1934. The body was cremated by Lakshmi Bai. Immediately before his death, he asked his wife to sprinkle his ashes in "Nanjilnadu" (Kanyakumari district) and the Karamana River in Thiruvananthapuram. His wish was fulfilled in September 1966.

These were her words on her husband's final journey, *"My husband's ashes have been kept in the drawing room of my flat in Bombay, awaiting the honour commensurate with the bold, noble and self-sacrificing life led by Dr. Pillai for the sake of his motherland. When he was alive, he had taken a vow that he would return to the land of his birth in a powerful warship flying the flag of the Indian Republic. But cruel fate willed otherwise, and he died an untimely death, on foreign soil of suspected slow poisoning. He died a crushed and wounded man in the service of his country, though he was the only man in Germany who had the moral courage to challenge Adolf Hitler when the latter made disparaging remarks about India. It was because of this that both he and I suffered numerous troubles and difficulties in Germany, including the loss of our flat and belongings.*

Now that India is free, independent and a republic, it is time that it carried out the cherished desire of Dr. Pillai as a mark of respect to the memory of a man who gave all his time, energy and thought for the liberation of his country. I feel it would be a most significant and noble gesture on the part of the Government, if his ashes are taken from Bombay in a warship of the Indian Navy to Cochin, the biggest port in Kerala and the land of his birth and where he once landed during World War I from the German Naval Ship, Emden.

For the past 30 years, I have preserved the ashes as the symbol of the patriot who gave his all and who gained nothing. I have lived a lonely life and I only want the dream of Dr. Pillai to be honoured with me accompanying the ashes.

When the country becomes independent, it is not possible to forget those who made it possible. Dr. Pillai was the greatest of revolutionaries, who really carried the torch of freedom to other countries."

After independence, she wanted to keep the memory of Dr. Pillai alive and to spread his views. She was also supported by a nephew of Dr. Pillai to petition the Government of Tamil Nadu, in order to rename Fort St. George to Fort Chembakaraman, but that did not seem to have gone well with the government. They erected a statue there (as you can see in the picture).

Sethu Seshan, the grand-nephew of Dr. Chembakaraman Pillai adds a final note to the Chembakaraman Pillai saga by retelling the story of the doctor's 'last journey.' She says that Lakshmi Bai travelled with her husband's ashes from Bombay to Trivandrum aboard INS Delhi some years after Independence, immersing them in the River Karamana during a Government-sponsored function. The doctor in Emden was finally laid to rest — in Kerala.

Curiously, Lakshmi Bai confirms the visit of Pillai to Cochin on the Emden. That Emden called on Cochin is clear and is well-documented in the book Ruby Daniel of Cochin (a very interesting story of German sailors landing up for supper in a Jewish house in Cochin and the men folk of Cochin forcing the Germans to eat with their hands). Lakshmi Bai died in Bombay in 1972. Famous ornithologist, the late Salim Ali recalled, "Pillai was an excellent cook and gave us delicious Indian meals prepared from ersatz masalas."

Pillai figures in famed ornithologist Salim Ali's autobiography, 'The Fall of a Sparrow.' Salim Ali spent 1929-30 in Germany, during which time in August 1929, he ran into Chempakaraman Pillai who, he says, was *'one of the prominent Indians settled in Berlin since before and all through World War I.'*

Pillai, a 'fugitive' from India, was a member of what called itself the Provisional Government of India. This revolutionary group was recognised as a sort of fashion by the Kaiser. In fact, Salim Ali writes, "Pillai claimed to have had frequent meetings with the Kaiser during the progress of the War in Europe to apprise him of the subversive propaganda (anti-British) conducted vicariously by the Provisional Government in India." I wonder whether the story of the Emden and Pillai was part of this propaganda, a hero-building exercise. The President of the Provisional Government was Raja Mahendra Pratap from the United Provinces, a sincere but naive idealist. Pillai, on the other hand, according to Salim Ali, was "a more practical and pragmatic revolutionary."

Emden and Pillai

To summarise the landing of the Emden in Kochi, although the war had been going on for eight weeks, Müller found the city of Madras lit up like a carnival. Already aware of reports of German atrocities on the Western Front, he took pains to angle his 25 salvos of 130 shells against the fuel tanks with a minimum of error. As a result, only five people were killed and 12 injured in the destruction of 346,000 gallons of fuel worth about 8,000 pounds. Although the destruction was less than it might have been, its psychological effect on the British was devastating. For days, trains were packed with people fleeing before the 'mystery ship' could return, the economy of the city was affected for weeks, the raid was the talk of the bazaars for months, and the word 'Emden' took its place in the Madras dialect of the Tamil language to signify 'an enterprising and ingenious person.'

While I was writing this, I wondered for long, '*How would Hitler have addressed Chempakaraman Pillai?*'

Well, he obviously did as he gave Pillai an apology of sorts for his demeaning comments about Indians in Mein Kempf,

"They are people incapable of governing themselves," he said.

This is something to think about I guess. Herr Schampak, maybe?

The following lines that Ganesan (he learnt it in his childhood) once used, repeatedly spun around in my mind, "*Emden vitta gundu, adhil erindha tank rendu.*"

This entire amazing story was unravelled as I mused about my days in Madras in the early 80's, the walk to Marina beach up the Pycroft's road and the Presidency College on the shore. Then, I remembered the shell on the High court wall and Emden, the German ship. I thought I would research a bit more of that story, and it was thus that this amazing tale came to light. I had not the slightest clue until then, a history book or patriotism class had taken me there before, but just vestiges of a ship.

Even today, people in North Kerala call dark stout guys 'Yumunden' without knowing that the origin of the name was the hulking WW1 German frigate, SMS Emden. SMS Emden's story is well covered on Wikipedia. But we will focus on the day it steamed into Madras Harbour.

EMDEN'S STORMING OF MADRAS HARBOUR

Late at night on September 22, 1914, Emden quietly approached the city of Madras on the east side of the Indian peninsula. Once within range, Emden opened fire on many large *Burmah-Shell* fuel oil tanks that the British kept near the city. After firing 130 shells, the oil tanks were burning and the city was in a panic. Although the raid did little damage, it was a severe blow to British morale, and thousands of people fled Madras, thinking that Emden might be planning another attack. Emden then sailed southwards down the East Coast of Ceylon (Sri Lanka), causing panic among the British. Sri Lankan mothers frightened their children with the Emden bogeyman, and to this day, a particularly obnoxious person is referred to as an Emden. Emden supplied new words to many South Indian Languages. Malayalam word 'Emandan' meaning 'a big and powerful thing,' or 'as big as Emden' were derived from Emden following its successful attack on Madras Port.

A classic war adventure, Emden's story has many a book written on it. In the end, 78 (some say 60) British ships were required to run her down. The adventures of the ship are chronicled in the book 'Last Corsair.' I thought the story ended there, but it hadn't!

Incredible as it may seem, the Emden had a very strong Malayali and Tamil connection. I was amazed when I stumbled upon this. Well, to sum it up in a simple line – this anti-imperialist attack was apparently directed by the Emden's engineer, Chempakaraman Pillai, assisting the captain Helmut Von Mueller.

S Muthaiah states, "Fanciful legends abound of his (Pillai) being Mueller's second-in-command, of his directing the firing on specific targets in and around

Madras Harbour, and of his rowing ashore at Cochin to greet his family and admirers! Authentic records of the voyage of the Emden do not corroborate any of this, but they do speak of his work aboard the cruiser and his post war attempts to gather an anti-British group of Indians in Germany, which became a forerunner to the Indian National Army. His volunteer force – another legend has it – was the inspiration for Netaji Subash Chandra Bose's 'Indian National Army.'"

Pillai was among the ones who first gave the slogan of 'Jai Hind' to the people of India and to the many Indians abroad who were struggling for the cause of Indian Independence. He had the privilege of being the Prime Minister of the Provisional Government of India set up in Afghanistan in December 1915. However, the defeat of the Germans in the war shattered the hopes of the revolutionaries

Dr. Chembakaraman Pillai died in Germany in 1934 and his wife, Lakshmi Bai, who is said to have suffered at the hands of the Nazis herself, returned to India and lived and died in Bombay. The most intriguing part of the Chembakaraman story is the mystery of his missing papers. J. V. Swamy, a nephew of the doctor, claims that shortly before Lakshmi Bai's death, the Bombay Police visited her flat and took away 17 boxes containing her husband's papers.

The story does not end here too for the Emden. After many a success, Emden had to be destroyed. The ship's crew were well aware that their time was up. They were finally chased and cornered by as many as 60-80 allied ships and the ship was finally sunk. Von Mueller's report has an interesting tale to tell on how this happened.

When Von Müller's party landed at the Cocos Islands, it managed to steal the 97-tonne copra schooner 'Ayesha' and sailed to Penang. From here, they made their way to Istanbul, which I believe, is another fascinating story. They survived numerous threats to make it to the Arabian Peninsula, where they travel by camel caravan and survived an attack by Bedouin tribesman before reaching safe haven in Istanbul. There was so much behind that Emden attack on Madras – a luminary called Chembakaraman Pillai, Hitler, Imperialism, the ship SMS Emden and the British…What an adventurous story!

A Note on Pillai's Last Days RKN has written a short story 'Emden' which is among his collection of short stories 'Old and New.'

How Oil Came to Madras

One of the most fascinating stories on the sidelines of the Port story is the arrival of oil in Madras. The first phase in the development of the Port ended in 1895, and within a decade of this, the first motor cars had begun to roll off the ships that called at Madras. The first automobile dealer was Addison and Co and in 1901, AJ Yorke - a Director of Parry - became the first owner of a car in the city. He drove in it every day from Ben's Gardens (present day Boat Club Road) to his office in Parry's Corner. First Line Beach was therefore an early witness to the automobile, and this needed petrol.

Shell Oil Ads

However, almost a decade before petrol, Chennai got to see 'kerosene' for the first time. This was thanks to Best and Co, one of the giants of First Line Beach. Founded by Andrews Van Dunlop Best in 1879, the company was initially into shipping and trading, business lines in which it made an early fortune. In 1893, thanks to improved port facilities, Best and Co. by then agents in Madras for the London-based Marcus Samuel and Co., began importing by sea, kerosene in tankers.

Marcus Samuel had made their name in selling trinkets and curios of which their sea-shells were most popular. When they diversified into kerosene, they marketed it under the Shell brand. It was a Shell tanker that first came to Madras in 1893 and emptied its contents directly into a bulk-storage facility put up by Best and Co. on the sand opposite the High Court.

But the credit for first bringing kerosene to the city belongs in reality to an Indian. This was Haji Sir Ismail Sait, a rich Cutchi Memon businessman of South India, who is today remembered in a hospital named after him in Bangalore. He ran the English Warehouse in Madras and Bangalore, which retailed everything from toys to mining equipment. Haji Sir Ismail was on the Board of Binny's Carnatic Mill Co. Ltd in 1881 and was even then importing kerosene oil from America in cans and selling them through Spencer and Co. By the 1890s, he had developed a system of branches and depots upcountry and was firmly entrenched in the trade. In Madras, Haji Sir Ismail pioneered the sale of kerosene through carts, a system that survived well into the 1970s.

'Best' studied Haji Sir Ismail's methods and given their financial muscle, went on to make a name for them in kerosene. In 1897, Samuel and Co. formed the Shell Transport and Trading Company with Best as their Indian agents. In 1907, Shell merged with the Royal Dutch Petroleum Company. Four years earlier, the latter had built its oil storage facility opposite the High Court with Arbuthnot and Co, another First Line Beach major, as its agent. In 1906, Arbuthnot's collapsed and Best and Company became the agents for Royal Dutch.

Meanwhile, oil from Burmah arrived in Madras in 1903, with Binny as the agents for the Burmah Oil Co. Limited. By 1905, they too had their storage facilities fronting the High Court. The signing up of Binny's with Burmah Oil was not to the liking of Haji Sir Ismail, and he had to be placated, given that he was a powerful Director on Board. The commission from the sale of Burmah Oil was split on a 3:5 bases between Haji Sir Ismail and Binny. But Binny's interest in oil was short-lived. In 1906, it gave up the agency to Shaw Wallace.

High Court Dome

The building of oil storage facilities on the beach, fronting the High Court was no easy task. There was no road on the beach and as the Fort was controlled by the military (as it still is). Special permission was obtained, and a tramline was laid to transport construction material. But by 1910, there were at least three giant oil tanks on the beachfront. These were to be easy targets for the German ship the Emden, when it came cruising down the Madras shoreline in 1914.

The First World War had begun that year, and on 22nd September, the Emden found itself near Madras, technically enemy territory, as this was a British colony. The light from the High Court's top dome, which also served as the city's lighthouse streamed out and provided easy guidance. At 9.30 P.M, Captain Karl Von Müller gave orders to fire and the Emden shelled the Madras coastline. The Burmah Oil tanks were easy targets, and burst into flames. A merchant ship was sunk in the harbour, and shells landed in George Town and also the compound of the High Court. When British guns began firing in retaliation at 10 P.M, the Emden left unscathed.

The oil tankers burnt for three days. The city was gripped by an unprecedented panic. Thousands fled, and properties were sold at rock-bottom prices. In Germany, a jubilant Kaiser Wilhelm II decreed that the crew of the ship could add the word Emden to their names. In Madras, the word came to mean a ruffian or a bully, and continues to remain so. A plaque on the High Court wall commemorates the shelling by the Emden even now. Some unexploded shells are kept in the Fort Museum.

By the time the war ended, the Port had expanded, and the oil tanks were moved to Royapuram, where they stand even today. By then, motor cars and public transport vehicles had begun to ply in large numbers. Motor oils were sold in cans, with *Chester* and *Monkey* brands being popular. Then, in 1927, Royal Dutch and Burmah Oil merged to form Burmah-Shell. They had their offices in the buildings of Best and Co. Shell Motor Oil became the preferred brand of petrol. In the early 1930s, Madras got its first petrol bunk, run by Shell. This was near the Mount Road roundtana, where the Annadurai statue stands today.

The Mother of all 'Chambers of Commerce' in South India

On 29th September this year, the Madras Chamber of Commerce and Industry held its 176th Chamber Day. It marked the end of a year-long quartoseptcentennial celebration of one of the oldest Chambers of Commerce in the country. The Calcutta Chamber was the first, founded in 1833, but it folded up a few years later, only to reborn in 1853 as the Bengal Chamber of Commerce. The Bombay Chamber is, therefore, technically the oldest surviving today, founded as it were on 23rd September 1836. A week later, on September 29th was born the Madras Chamber of Commerce.

A group of businessmen, who were all English, met at Binny's offices on Armenian Street and resolved to found Madras Presidency's Chamber of Commerce. Prominent among them were representatives of Arbuthnot's, Binny and Parry (represented by Dare himself) who were the three leading business establishments of the Presidency at the time. With the coming to an end of East India Company's monopoly over Indian trade three years previously, free merchants who for long flourished but were not recognised by the Government finally came into their own. With the three Presidencies often at loggerheads with each other over scarce resources, poor infrastructure and a race for prosperity, it was necessary for the commercial entities of each region to band together and convey their concerns to the Government. In the case of Madras, there was also the necessity to fight for the development of the region itself, for with Calcutta being the imperial capital and Bombay fast emerging as the commercial capital, Madras was nowhere in the picture and most neglected.

Shortly after its formation, the Chamber sent a request for official recognition to the Governor, Sir Frederick Adam. The official sanction came forthwith, but with the astute observation that no Indians were on board. This was corrected by the induction of two Armenians and an Indian – G Sidhaloo Chetty, who was into the businesses of coir, port handling and textiles. A street named after him survives even today in the Choolai area. The Chamber, however, remained dominated by the British right until the 1960s.

Shortly after inception, the Chamber began its fight for infrastructure, most of which would be considered basic amenities today. The first of these was the fight for better roads. The Presidency, which at that time, stretched from Orissa to Cape Comorin (Kanyakumari), was a vast territory and the poor quality of roads meant that areas closer to Bengal and Bombay Presidencies preferred to use the better infrastructure there, thereby benefitting Calcutta and Bombay cities respectively. This was particularly true of coal mines, which were in the east and the cotton growing belt, which was in the west. The Chamber, therefore, began petitioning the local Government for better roads and in 1850. A Road Commission was appointed by the Government to look into the prevailing conditions. The report appalled everyone, and from then on, road works began, which by the end of the 19th century, spanned a network of 25,000 miles. This naturally had a positive impact on trade. Similarly, the Chamber became a great champion of the Railways, warmly supporting the establishment of an extensive rail network in the region. Thanks to its help, the two principal railway companies of the South, the Madras Railway Company (later merged with other entities to form the Madras and Southern Mahratta Railway) and the South Indian Railway company became very profitable ventures. When these two were merged post independence, they formed the nucleus of the Southern Railways, one of the best-run divisions of the Indian Railways today.

Similarly, the Chamber fought hard for the establishment of post and telegraph services in the entire region. Beginning with 1785, a postal system had been introduced, which was developing slowly. The Chamber, from 1836 onwards, repeatedly gave suggestions to the Governments of the day on how to streamline operations and pass on the benefits to the end user. It also spearheaded the move to build a head post office for the region, and this was completed in 1884, a landmark wonder in the Indo-Saracenic style of architecture and still a dominating presence on the Chennai skyline. In the 1930s, air facilities in the South were pioneered by the Chamber too, with its member's W M Browning (of Burmah-Shell) and Sir Gerald Hodgson (of Parry) helping in the founding of the Madras Flying Club, and later, the establishment of airport facilities.

Interestingly, the Chamber was the only one to protest the imposition of income tax when it was first implemented in the country in 1859, largely as a measure to generate revenues to offset the losses incurred during the mutiny. Henry Nelson (of Parry) was the Chairman, and he spearheaded the spirited fight against the hated tax. In this fight, he was greatly supported by two journalists of the Madras Times – Charles Lawson and Henry Cornish. They were to later found *The Madras Mail* in 1868, which became the mouthpiece of the Chamber. When the Madras Mail shifted offices to First Line Beach, the Chamber, which until then had operated from the offices of Arbuthnot and Co. and for a short while at Dare House, became a long-standing tenant of the Mail. The editors of the Madras Mail, from Sir Charles Lawson onwards were to be Secretaries of the Chamber, a tradition that continued untnil the Mail was acquired in the 1920s by Spencer's and shifted offices to Mount Road.

Spencer's and other giants on Mount Road were unlike the 'industrial outfits' on First Line Beach – which included Parry and Binny a couple of roads away, Best and Co, Gordon Woodroffe et al. These were considered traders, and they had a rival organisation – the Madras Traders Association. It was, therefore, no longer possible for the Madras Mail to wholeheartedly champion the Chamber as it had done earlier.

At a time when most Indian exports were commodities, the Chamber played an important role in the improvement of output from fields and plantations. It was active in the cultivation of cotton for which demand from England appeared limitless, particularly after the outbreak of the American Civil War, which cut off supply of the American variety. The Chamber studied various means of mechanisation of ginning, cleaning and weaving, and also experimented with schemes to cultivate American cotton on Indian soil. The efforts met with partial success, but they did ensure that South India was put firmly on the cotton map of the world.

The Madras Port

The Chamber's greatest success was its role in ensuring that Madras got a port of international standards. This may not sound so great today, but for over 200 years – from 1639 onwards – it was the general opinion of those familiar with the sea, that Madras was not a place that could ever have a good port. The sea was very rough close to the coast, and there were cyclones at all times of the year, causing untold damage to the ships that berthed at the edge of the city. Consequently, all ships dropped anchor two miles into the sea, and goods and passengers were offloaded onto Catamarans, which then rowed them ashore. Loss of life and goods was heavy in this last two-mile journey, and the boatmen, knowing full well that they controlled the lifeline to the city, were a law unto themselves.

It was the Chamber that began a campaign for the construction of a proper harbour on the coast of Madras. Several proposals were put forward, and most foundered on either poor technology or the want of funds. There were great debates on how the angry surf could be tamed, and several theories abounded. In 1859, work began on the construction of a pier, with the Chairman of the Madras Chamber being one of the honoured threesome entrusted with inaugurating the works. The other two, who were part of the inauguration, were the Governor and the Commander-in-Chief. The construction proceeded in fits and starts, but was all washed away in a cyclone of 1872, which was unprecedented in its violence.

Work was stopped and a fresh proposal, this time including the construction of an eastern breakwater to contain the surf and provide a smooth-water enclosure, was made. Work on this began in 1875, and despite a severe cyclone in 1881, progressed and by 1886, the city had a harbour of sorts. There was anxiety all along that the cost of the project would be passed on to the shipping lines that operated along the Coromandel Coast. There was opposition from vested interests in Calcutta, who feared that the Madras Port would be a serious threat to their own facility. The Chamber had to allay all these fears, and when the harbour was eventually completed, it was rewarded for its efforts by a good representation in the Port Trust. This was to continue long after independence, when political considerations changed equations, and the Chamber, sadly, lost its representation.

The new port was not without its problems, and one of these was the rapid silting up of the eastern opening, resulting in continuous dredging operations. In 1904, the Port Trust got a new and dynamic Chairman, Francis JE Spring, the Secretary of the Railway Board formerly. He began putting into action a massive re-engineering programme. Spring made the Chamber his ally in this project, and over a period of ten years, the eastern entrance was closed, a north-eastern opening was created, and several key modifications were made, including the construction of dry and wet docks. When completed, the Madras Port was truly world-class, and trade boomed. The city was to never look back after that. During the Second World War, it was practically the only English stronghold on the entire Eastern sector, with most of the ports in the Far East, having fallen to the Japanese. The Madras Port played a very vital role in the shipment of war supplies, and that, in many ways, contributed to the making of the city. All this would not have been possible without the Madras Chamber championing a port.

It was while the battle on the Port was in progress that the Chamber celebrated its golden jubilee, with Governor Lord Connemara presiding over the dinner held at The Madras Club. A special citation was presented to Lawson on the occasion, recognising his valuable services. By then, the Chamber was also represented on the Madras Legislative Council, and its voice was truly heard at the highest echelons of power. The new century, however, brought several new challenges in its wake.

The Palayakat Brand

It is Deepavali day as I write this, and my mind goes back to Deepavalis long ago, when the male household staff would strut around in their new white shirts and starched checked *Palayakat* sarongs that Mother had shopped for - with me dragged in tow - at Moulana's or Palayakat on Colombo's Main Street. It was many years later that I learnt that the sarongs had been introduced to Ceylon by the Portuguese, but popularised by the Dutch and that they derived their name — that had become almost generic — from Pulicat, one of whose many local versions was Palaya Kadu. It was around the same time that I learnt they were also called Madras Checks, under which name they had become internationally known.

Over many years of research, I've found it increasingly difficult to access material based on Portuguese records. Dutch records, especially those based on their trade, have always been easier to find, and that's where I had learnt that as early as 1603, the Dutch exported to Java (Banten/Bantam) and to the Moluccas (Amboina), the Spice Islands, 28 varieties of cloth from Durgarayapattinam (Armagon), Pulicat, San Thomé and Nagapattinam. By 1612, Pulicat was being described as 'the left arm of Dutch trade in Asia and the Moluccas the right'. It was said that without the textiles of Pulicat, the spice trade of the Moluccas would die!

Textiles were also exported from Porto Novo, Nagore, Tranquebar, Devanampattinam (Old Cuddalore) and Pondicherry, but the second major export port of the Dutch was Nagapattinam from 1845, with supplies coming from Salem and Tanjore. This was a trade that thrived not only on exports to Java and the Moluccas, but from there to the Malay Peninsula and Sumatra and other island sultanates in the archipelago. The trade was so successful that it was able to withstand the challenge of cloth woven by the Javanese from 1684.

The Javanese specialised in creating decorative patterns on the cloth using the batik technique, whereas the textiles of the Coromandel favoured check patterns, large and small, as well as stripes. The Dutch tried to get the Pulicat weavers to adopt the batik patterns and techniques, but the quality of the output was poor, and so, checks it was again — and the Dutch found a market still available for Coromandel textiles. It was around 1700 that the Dutch began to expand that market with exports to Europe.

Textiles exported by the Dutch in the early 1690s were worth about a million florins. This doubled by 1700. But the supply remained short of demand — even when the Dutch invested over 3 million florins on the Coromandel Coast and in Salem and Tanjore in the early 1700s to ensure supplies.

The investments were made with local merchants, mostly Telugu Chetties in Pulicat, Tamil Chetties in Nagapattinam and Marakkayar all along the coast. The first Chief Merchant of the Dutch in Pulicat was Achyuthappa Chetti, and he was followed by his brother, Chinnana Chetti and then, Lakshmi Chetti. Agents and kinsfolk of many of these Chetties and Marakkayar settled in Banten, Makassar (Malacca), Aceh in Sumatra from the 1670s, and even in Colombo. To this day, their descendants have retained their identities in these places. The Dutch also recruited several Chetties to serve as accountants (Kanakapulles) in Java and Ceylon.

Old Landmark Names of Chennai

Chellaram's and Savoy

I was delighted to get a letter which brought back memories of old D'Angelis and Bosotto's by referring to the address: Room 41, Third Floor and Old Bosotto Building. Reader H. Kripal writes that after Klein and Peyerl sold their premises to Venkatapathi Naidu, the photographers shifted to Narasingapuram Street, before moving further down Mount Road.

The reader also goes on to point out that the 'Venkatapathi Naidu Building' was once rented to Idanmul Lekhraj and, then, for a long time, in fact, until a couple of years ago, to Kishenchand Chellaram, whose shop was a landmark at Round Tana.

Kisenchand Chellaram was the son of Chellaram Gianchand, whose name survives in a shop on Wallajah Road. Chellaram Gianchand also owned the New Elphinstone, which Western India Theatres rented until 1959, when they bought the property.

Reader R.E. Smith says that the Savoy ownership in Ooty was transferred by D'Angelis to his daughter in 1925. She had for long helped her father in running the place, but had disappointed him when she married the hotel's Italian chef. She sold the hotel to Spencer's in 1943 after she married again. She married a third time to Mr. Penn, who owned a brewery in Bangalore, where she remained for years. She left India in the mid-1960s. But by then, the brewery had become nucleus of the U.B. Group.

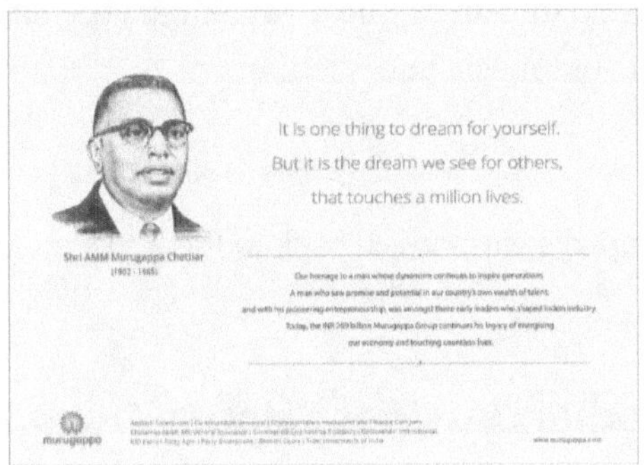

The Murugappa Group

Founded in 1900, the **Murugappa** Group is one of India's leading business conglomerates, founded, managed and largely owned by the Murugappa family. The group has 28 businesses, including 11 listed companies actively trading in NSE and BSE. Headquartered in Chennai, the major companies of the group include Carborundum Universal Ltd, Cholamandalam Investment and Finance Company Ltd., Cholamandalam MS General Insurance Company Ltd., Coromandel International Ltd., Coromandel Engineering Company Ltd., EID Parry (India) Ltd., Parry Agro Industries Ltd., Tube Investments of India Limited, and Wendt (India) Ltd.

Active in several segments including Abrasives, Auto Components, Cycles, Sugar, Farm Inputs, Fertilisers, Plantations, Bioproducts and Nutraceuticals, the Group has forged strong alliances with leading international companies like Groupechimiquetunisien, Foskor, Cargill, Mitsui Sumitomo, Morgan Crucible and Sociedad Química y Minera de Chile (SQM). The Group has a wide geographical presence, spanning 13 states in India and five continents across the globe.

Brands like BSA, Hercules, Ballmaster, Ajax, Parry's, Chola, Gromor and Paramfos are from the Murugappa stable. The organisation has a workforce of over 32,000 employees.

1901– 1910

The foundation for this group was laid by Dewan Bahadur A M Murugappa Chettiar who established a money-lending and banking business in 1900.

Having first been set up in Burma, (now Myanmar) the business then spread to Malaysia, Sri Lanka, Indonesia and Vietnam.

1921 - 1930

In the 1930's, Murugappa's was moved back to India to start all over again from the scratch.

A Rare South Indian Business House Does Things the Difficult Way

It was during the first years of World War II that the three sons of Dewan Bahadur Murugappa Chettiar decided to move out of traditional Chettiar businesses and establish various industries, no matter how small. They began with steel furniture and sandpaper, both of which prospered during the War. When India became independent, they saw a country not only in need of industrialisation but a population in need of affordable consumer products. The youngest brother, A.M.M. Arunachalam, A.M.M. to all, thought bicycles would be a good thing to be in, if a brand name like Raleigh or Hercules came with the vehicles. He remembered the failure of a kinsman, S.A.A. Annamalai, who pioneered bicycle manufacturing in India nearly two decades earlier but could not compete with the established imported brands.

Sir Arcot Ramaswami Mudaliar, a friend of the family and an international statesman, helped forge the link with Hercules. When A.M.M. first suggested the brand to Sir Ramaswami, his eldest brother, Murugappa, he did not realise the significance of the Hercules connection. As per A.M.M.'s biography, on looking back, they "never realised that Hercules which was owned by Tube Investments was an industrial giant in Britain, and a tie-up with any of its firms would be so meaningful in the future. 'We were truly babes in the industrial woods at the time,' laughed A.M.M. That fortuitous request for a partnership led to much bigger things for the A.M.M. family, but at the time, they had no clue as to how the future would unfold."

One thing the Murugappa group held close was forging a friendship with Sir Ivan Stedeford, Chairman of TI and a Brit. He was the one who agreed to less than 50 percent investment sought by the A.M.M. Family in the initial discussions, who in those days, were very eager for any assistance if a project was big, providing assistance as knowhow and engineering fees, rather than cash. Once TI Cycles got underway, he was the most helpful and contributed through substantial investment becoming known as the Tl Group before attaining sustainability and taking on the family name. This enduring friendship and contribution is remembered in the model suburban hospital developed in Ambattur. Opened by Sir Ivan in 1966, it is called the Sir Ivan Stedeford Hospital. The nearby higher secondary school established by the family remembers another person who helped the growth of the Murugappa Group. It is named as Sir Ramaswami Mudaliar H.S. School, and these two institutions are a testimony to their starlwarts' contribution.

Dr. A. Lakshmanaswami Mudaliar Vice Chancellor of Madras University with A.M.M Murugappa Chettiar.

A.M.M. Murugappa Chettiar with Pandit Nehru.

A. Vellayan is the Executive Chairman of the Murugappa Corporate Board. He is also the Chairman of EID Parry (India) Limited and Coromandel International Ltd. He is also on the board of Kanoria Chemicals Ltd. He holds a diploma in Industrial Administration from the University of Aston, UK and a master's degree in Business Studies from the University of Warwick Business School, UK

A. Vellayan

Murugappa group

WW Ladden – Making British Indian

In town recently was Kay Harvey from Canada, daughter of WW Ladden who studied in the Nilgiris. She mentioned about a European corporate group which decided to become Indian some years before Independence, forming Amalgamations Ltd. in 1938. Her father who was the Chairman, chose S. Anantharamakrishnan as his successor.

Ladden had been an ambulance driver during World War I, and won a Military Medal. After being decommissioned, he worked as a Swiss industrialist's chauffeur. This was when he first heard about Sir Alexander MacDougall of Simpson's. Ladden later became a partner in a small garage in London which looked after MacDougall's car. When his partner ran off with the company's money, Ladden was facing ruin. MacDougall, who happened to come in to pick up his car one day, heard the story. Liking what he had seen of the way Ladden had handled his business in the garage, he asked him on the spur of the moment whether he would like to come out to India. This brought Ladden to

Madras in 1924, when he became General Manager of Simpson's. By 1930, he was Managing Director, and that year, recruited J, who was auditing the Group for Fraser and Ross, as the Group's Company Secretary. When Amalgamations Ltd. was floated as the holding company, J was on the Board.

Mayor of Madras in 1933, then Sheriff of the city and a State Legislator, Ladden was one of the leading public figures in Madras from the 1930s through to the 1950s. There was no reason for him to give way to anyone. Yet, in 1953, he invited J to become Chairman of the Group and agreed to serve as his Vice Chairman. Ladden remained a Director of the Group until the early 1960s.

In this day and age, when HRD is made out to be a science by Human Resources Managers, what made Ladden pick Anantharamakrishnan from a team of auditing clerks and give him his head?

When MacDougall did this with Ladden, J.V.R Rao remembered that Ladden picked him in a similar fashion. Rao had gone to MacDougall for a letter of recommendation for a Madras Southern Mahratta Railway post. In the room with MacDougall was Ladden when Rao mentioned his qualifications.

Suddenly, Ladden spoke up when hearing Rao, "Why the hell should we give him a certificate to join the railways? Why doesn't he try our company?"

Rao murmured uncertainly, "But what will I do?"

Ladden replied, "Find out when you join. Try us for three months."

Stunned, Rao forsook the security of a railway job for a hire and mercantile one, went on to head Addison's and become Simpson's Director.

It was this uncanny ability to pick the right men that Ladden brought to Amalgamations. And how it paid off!

The Legend Legacy of Shri. S. Anantharamakrishnan

Popularly known as 'J,' Shri. S. Anantharamakrishnan was a man who nurtured a dream of a self-sufficient, prosperous and industrialised India. With his vision for India's industrial future, he inspired the pioneering of industries and spearheaded the thirst for the world's finest technologies. He generated the momentum for mechanisation of Indian farming and the dieselisation of the Indian road transport industry. J's brainchild, the Amalgamations Group, is today at the forefront as one of India's largest light engineering conglomerates. He continues to inspire and motivate the Amalgamations Group that has gone from strength to strength.

Shri S. Anantharamakrishnan Founder Amalgamations Group

'We need to set our sights high, to be satisfied with nothing less than the best, and to commit ourselves totally and unreservedly to participate in the struggle to build a more liveable world.' — LEONARD CHESHIRE

Gentleman Soldier and Humanitarian: LEONARD CHESHIRE

Born 1917 – Died 1992

Leonard Cheshire was born in 1917, and like many young men and women, signed up to fight for his country in WW II. He married Sue Ryder in 1959, and they made their home in the Suffolk village of Cavendish, although both spent much of the year away, visiting their humanitarian projects around the world. Leonard was admitted to the Order of Merit in 1981 and made a life peer in the House of Lords in 1991. He took the title Baron Cheshire of Woodhall in the County of Lincolnshire, in memory of his time serving at RAF Woodhall Spa. Leonard died from the effects of motor neuron disease on 31 July 1992, at the age of 74.

"In war, Leonard Cheshire was a hero. In peace, he served his nation no less well." — SIR JOHN MAJOR

"A shining example of what a human being can achieve in a lifetime of dedication." — HM THE QUEen Elizabeth II

There were a few more decorated war heroes in the last century than Leonard Cheshire. But of him it has also been said, "There cannot be many men who have received their countries highest award for wartime bravery, but who are remembered primarily for humanitarian service."

Indeed, Cheshire is best remembered today for the Cheshire Homes movement he launched in 1948. One of those homes, the Chennai Cheshire Home, a couple of days ago launched the celebrations of its 50th year with a unique art event in which a painting by the Governor of Tamil Nadu, Sardar Surjit Singh Barnala, hung alongside the paintings of some of the young artists who live in the home.

Cheshire, who proudly wore the Victoria Cross, the Distinguished Flying Cross and the Distinguished Service Order with two bars, succeeded Guy Gibson (who, it is said, had a Bangalore background) as commander of the legendary Royal Air Force No.617 (bomber) Squadron, better known as the 'Dam busters.' In 1943, when he was just 25, he became the youngest Group Captain in the service. Later, for his post war humanitarian activities, he was made a peer of the realm and given the Order of Merit.

A daredevil when he was young, Cheshire was to become more responsible as a bomber pilot and squadron commander, but he never lost the habit of putting himself in danger whenever he flew. One of his legendary bits of daring was to fly his Mosquito in slow figures-of-eight over a target - that filled the sky with anti-aircraft fire and swarms of fighters — in order to give the rest of his squadron a mark to aim at.

Cheshire was a changed man after he had flown as the official British observer with the flight that dropped the atom bomb on Nagasaki. In 1948, the change heightened when he nursed a terminally ill friend. The numbers of such friends grew — and 'Nurse' Cheshire launched the Cheshire Homes for the disabled and ailing homeless. When he died in 1992, his wife, Sue Ryder, who had been a Special Operations Executive famed for her work behind German lines in Poland, took over the Cheshire Foundation. Today, the Foundation runs 200 homes in over 50 countries; 22 of them in India.

An Indian Guide

The Madras Home was started in December 1958, with Mary Clubvala Jadhavas its driving spirit. She touched several social services organisations. The Guild of Service, the School of Social Work, the YWCA, the Indian Red Cross, the Bharat Scouts and Guides, the Indian Council for Social Welfare, the Women's Indian Association, the Seva Samajam Boys' and Girls' Homes, the Bala Vihar, the Juvenile Bureau and numerous other organisations owe much to her; in some cases, their beginnings. In fact, she was a member of nearly 150 social welfare organisations! In 1956, she was appointed the first woman Sheriff of Madras and was the second Parsi to hold this once-honoured office, the first being Cawasji E Panday in 1893. She was also on the first international commission for Guides in India. Shortly before her death in 1975, she was awarded the Padma Vibhushan by the Government of India.

Mary Clubvala's dedication to social service began when her husband died in 1935. As a long grieving widow, she was persuaded by a friend to take up welfare work for Indian troops at the outbreak of World War II. She organised the Indian Hospitality Committee, and before the end of the war, became a 'Darling of the Army.'

The Chennai Cheshire Home was founded in December, managed by a volunteer committee. Home to 41 inmates with various disabilities and impairments, it was opened following a visit by Cheshire, who together with Mary Club, met the then Archbishop and asked for a place to start the home. Cheshire spent three weeks there at the time, and visited again with Sue Ryder, staying at the Covelong Home for another few weeks. He also stayed with M.A. Chidambaram, then Chairman of the Cheshire Chennai Home.

Cheshire, was also concerned about leprosy patients, and the Katpadi Cheshire Home was started with particular emphasis on their care. Even today, the Katpadi Home continues caring for them. His last visit to India was to Delhi in 1991, and at that time, his health was deteriorating rapidly due to a motor neuron disease.

"Discretion will protect you and understandings will Guard You." - Proverbs 2:11

Mary Clubvala Jadhav.

First Indian Jumbo Pilot

Coinciding with the report the other day that the Madras Club was being revived, there landed on my desk a little book of one of its early trainees and members 'Million Mile Pilot,' by Jaiboy Joseph. This tells the story of K.M. Mathew or Mathen, who was once named the 'First Indian Jumbo Pilot.'

Mathen learnt his flying under Tyndale-Br and M.I. Khan at the Madras Flying Club in 1939-40. The Club was founded in 1929. H. Mathen later joined the Royal IAF and was posted to Squadron one commandeered by Arjan Singh who went on to become India's Air Chief Marshal.

KM. Matthew Mathen

Pioneering Air India's Singapore-Sydney Delhi-Moscow routes, he went on to command the first non-stop delivery flight of the Boeing 707, landing in Bombay on March 7, 1960 after flying the distance in a record time. At times, he was averaging nearly 700 mph. He followed this up with being the first Indian pilot to fly a 'Jumbo' that the huge Boeing 747 was named after. By then, he had flown everything from the Puss Moth in Madras to the Jumbos in the U.S.

It was brother Mathulla, then Controller of Finance, Tata Steel, who persuaded a jobless, aimless Mathen, a couple of years out of Madras Christian College, to learn flying and join the Air Force. A decade later, in 1948, Mathulla became CEO of Air India and, before long, found across the negotiating table from him, younger brother Mathen, who had helped found the Indian Pilots Guild. When Mathen passed away in 1995 in Bombay, it was in a hospital ward that the Air India Pilots' health insurance scheme, formulated by Mathen had sponsored.

Advertised by Air India as its 'multi-million-mile pilot,' Mathen retired in 1976 as Air India's Director of Technical Planning. A born storyteller, many remember his retelling the story of the Tashkent-Moscow flight he captained with a couple of volunteers aboard. Two stewardesses helped a diplomat's wife give birth in the coat compartment, and he recall praying all the time that there wouldn't be any air pockets. The baby born at 34,000 feet was named 'Annapurna' after the aircraft. On another occasion, he commanded the flight from Rome to Delhi with Jackie Kennedy aboard, during Camelot's heyday.

No sooner the passengers were requested to get ready for landing, he received a message from his VIP passenger to the effect, "Could the Commander please delay the landing by 20 minutes as Mrs. Kennedy's hair do is not yet complete?" There was never a dull moment in Mathen's life from the time he entered the portals of the Madras Flying Club in Meenambakkam.

The Museum Story That Needs Telling

The Madras Museum is getting ready to celebrate its 150th year with a series of events. It was about a year ago, when it was proposed to release a stamp for this celebration that I wrote about the beginnings of the Museum in Madras. Surgeon Edward Balfour started it with 1100 geological specimens. There were many other additions by different officers-in-charge. Capt. Jesse Mitchell, Commandant of the Madras Mounted Police, added 70,000 main zoological specimens (1859-72), Surgeon George Birdie (1872-81) enriched it with a botanical collection, and Surgeon Edgar Thurston (1885-1908) contributed anthropological, ethnographical and prehistory wealth. Mitchell also started the library that grew into the Connemara Public Library. Bidie grew exotic trees and medicinal plants in the Museum garden — today a pale shadow of what it was, but which Director Dr. Kannan tries hard to keep clean. Thurston will always be remembered for his monumental 7-volume 'Castes and Tribes' of Southern India.

I owe this information to an unpublished monograph by N. Harinarayana, a former Director of the Museum, who has dug deep to tell the story of the first 50 years of the institution.

The English Influences

The British rule and management practices have left behind a legacy which lingers on. Whether we like it or not, every institution, from the railways to the army regiments and estate management has colonial roots. I am an admirer of European systematic management, tenacity and attention to detail in every work they do.

Also, we need to remember that Europe gave the world Socialism, the first French Revolution, Communism and also wide spread Literacy – to all classes of people when the lower class in India was in Darkness.

The Causes of French Revolution was Absolute Monarchy, Corrupt Leadership, Unfair Land Distribution, Unfair Tax code, Rigid Social Class Structure, Privileges for the first and second Estates, spread of enlightened ideas, Government Debt Deficient financing, Poor Harvest, Inflation and Failure of Louis XIV to accept reforms.

Formation of the Assembly and the storming of the Bastille was Very Similar to the socio-economic systems in the 18th century. In the course of time, we took their good points that empowered us to become a developing nation through our efficient leaders and eventually, liberated community. We take all good things from our past and reject what was wrong.

Guillotine National Assembly of French revolution.

"To become more creative, one must become more of your true self" - Bryant McGill

The Romance of the British Raj with Wood, Metal and Ivory

The chairs of the Madras Presidency

Kerosene   Fan Anglo-French Credo   Palanquin

The Beginning of Inequality among Humans

Palanquins grew out of 'litter' and 'sedan chairs' as early as inequalities set in among humans. A litter is usually carried by peoples, and, therefore, a type of human-powered transport. Another form, commonly called 'sedan chair,' consists of a chair or windowed cabin suitable for a single occupant. These porters were known in London as "chairmen." These have been very rare since the 19th century, but such enclosed, portable litters have been used as an elite form of transport for centuries, especially in cultures where women are kept secluded. In Pharaonic Egypt and many oriental realms, the ruler and divinities (in the form of an idol) were often transported thus in public.

A palanquin, also known as *palkhi*, is a covered sedan chair (or litter) carried on two poles. It derives from the Sanskrit word for a bed or couch, presumably via *pallakku*, the Tamil word for 'bed or couch.' Palanquins began to fall out of use after rickshaws were introduced in 1615.It does not seem to take its name from the city of sedan.

The tasteful, neoclassical sedan chair made for Queen Charlotte remains at Buckingham Palace. Sedan chairs could pass in streets too narrow for a carriage. By the mid-17th century, sedans for hire were a common mode of transportation. In London, 'chairs' were available for hire in 1634, each assigned a number and the chairmen licensed, because the operation was conducted in London streets, and was the earliest instance of traffic congestion. A trip within a city cost six pence, and day's rental was four shillings. A sedan was even used as an ambulance in Scotland's Royal Infirmary. Benjamin Franklin used a sedan chair until late in the 1700s.

During the 17-18th centuries, palanquins were very popular among European traders in Bengal, so much so that in 1758, an order was issued prohibiting their purchase by certain lower-ranked employees. In Europe, it took four strong chairmen to carry the corpulent Henry VIII of England in his chair towards the end of his life, but the expression 'Sedan Chair' was not used in print until in the 1930s

The original Royal Palanquin reached here from English soil and still carries the Royal Insignia. During the mid-1900's, the Queen was scheduled to visit the Brahadeeswara Temple of Tanjore during her visit to the Madras presidency. It was her childhood dream to see for her the magic of the steeple shadow not touching the ground. A sudden outbreak of plague made the authorities cancel the trip. This palanquin, a property of the British Empire in India, was already sent to carry the queen around the temple. But it was never taken back. A temple trustee had it in his custody for several years until it was sourced, restored and listed in 'The Steve Borgia' heritage Museum.

Dressing Table Ivory Brass cot.

Colonial Cot The Hide-away Bar and the Duchess Dressing Table

The Albion Printing Press

Oil extractor ...

When the British travelled to exotic lands in the nineteenth century, they adapted to new climates and cultures with sola topees, verandahs and caned furniture. This was used and left behind as their reminiscence, making the native owner proud of their possessions.

Initially, the visitors found it strange to see the native Indians sit under banyan trees and shaped rocks to conduct business. The lack of understanding of this culture forced them to go back to their own. Chairs were the first things that were imported. Very soon, the British, in India, took it wherever they went. All that came in was used in the East India Company, which was later taken by royalty into the Fort St. George as colonial furniture. The household furniture got into English settlements.

The immigration contained furniture starting from the pilgrim style of the 17th century, The William and Mary style, and Queen Anne style, Chippendale style, Windsor Chairs and the Revival and Gothic style. Needless to say, it was the Victorian, Cast Iron and the Wicker that dominated the period.

The Steve Borgia Heritage Museum has been carefully sourcing, collecting and restoring some of the rare furniture of the East India Company. The rare ones are, today, exhibited at INDeco Hotels Mahabalipuram, Swamimalai and Yercad.

Picnic hamper

From 1860-1916, the Uniform Regulations for the British Army required every soldier to have a moustache.

Indian Army Officer wearing medals. Signed portrait photo Charles Edward Hendley, 81st Pioneers,

The year 2015 November and December witnessed the worst floods after the floods of 1903, and Chennai bounced back to its normal life as major work was initiated by the Government.

Social Reformers and Politicians

"Strong people don't put others down; they lift them up."

The Great Social Reformer: E V. Periyar

Erode Venkata Ramasamy (17 September 1879 – 24 December 1973), affectionately called by his followers as Periyar, Thanthai Periyar or E. V. R., was a social activist, politician and businessman. He started the Self-Respect Movement or the Dravidian Movement, and proposed the creation of an independent state called Dravida Nadu, comprising the states of South India. He is also the founder of political party, Dravidar Kazhagam.

Periyar was born as Raghav Erode Venkata Ramasami Naicker (Naidu) on 17 September 1879, in the town of Erode, then a part of the Coimbatore District of the Madras Presidency. Periyar's father, a rich businessman, was Venkatappa Naicker (or Venkata), and his mother was Chinna Thayammal, alias Muthammal. He had one elder brother named Krishnaswamy and two sisters named Kannamma and Ponnuthoy. He later came to be known as 'Periyar' meaning 'respected one' or 'elder' in Tamil.

In 1929, Periyar announced the deletion of his caste surname Naicker (Naidu) from his name at the First Provincial Self-Respect Conference of Chengalpattu. He could speak three Dravidian languages – Tamil, Telugu and Kannada, with Kannada being his mother tongue.

Periyar was born to a wealthy family of Balijas. At a young age, he witnessed numerous incidents of racial, caste and gender discrimination. Periyar married when he was 19 and had a daughter who lived for only 5 months. His first wife, Nagammai, died in 1933. He married for a second time in July 1948 to Maniammai, who continued Periyar's social work after his death in 1973. His thoughts and ideas were, however, being spread by the Dravidar Kazhagam.

Periyar joined the Indian National Congress in 1919, but resigned in 1925 when he felt that the party was only serving the interests of the Brahmins. In 1924, Periyar led a non-violent agitation (Satyagraha) in Vaikom, Kerala. From 1929 to 1932, he toured Malaysia, Europe and Russia, which had an influence on him. In 1939, Periyar became the head of the Justice Party, and he changed its name to Dravidar Kazhagam in 1944. The party later split, and one group led by C. N. Annadurai, formed the Dravida Munnetra Kazhagam (DMK) in 1949. While continuing the Self-Respect Movement, he advocated for an independent Dravida Nadu (Dravidistan).

Periyar propagated the principles of rationalism, self-respect, women's rights and eradication of caste. He opposed the exploitation and marginalisation of the non-Brahmin, indigenous Dravidian people of South India and the imposition of what he considered, Indo-Aryan India. His work has greatly revolutionised Tamil society and has significantly removed caste-based discrimination. He is also responsible for bringing new changes to the Tamil alphabet. However, at the same time, Periyar is also held responsible for making controversial statements on the Tamil language, Dalits and Brahmins, and for endorsing violence against Brahmins.

The citation awarded by the UNESCO described Periyar as "the prophet of the new age, the Socrates of South-East Asia, father of social reform movement and arch enemy of ignorance, superstitions, meaningless customs and base manners."

In 1904, Periyar went on a pilgrimage to Kasi to worship in the revered Siva temple of Kashi Vishwanath. Although regarded as one of the holiest sites of Hinduism, he witnessed immoral activities, begging and floating dead bodies. His frustrations extended to functional Hinduism, in general, when he experienced what he called Brahmanic exploitation.

However, one particular incident in Kasi had a profound impact on Periyar's ideology and future work. At the worship site, there were free meals offered to the guests. To Periyar's shock, he was refused meals at *choultries*, which exclusively fed Brahmins. Due to extreme hunger, Periyar felt compelled to enter one of the choultries disguised as a Brahmin with a sacred thread on his bare chest, but was betrayed by his moustache. The gatekeeper at the temple concluded that Periyar was not a Brahmin, as Brahmins were not permitted by the Hindu *shastras* to have moustaches. He not only prevented Periyar's entry, but also pushed him rudely into the street.

As his hunger became intolerable, Periyar was forced to feed on leftovers from the streets. Around this time, he realised that the choultry which had refused him entry was built by a wealthy non-Brahmin from South India. This discriminatory attitude dealt a blow to Periyar's regard for Hinduism, for the events he had witnessed at Kasi were completely different from the picture of Kasi he had in mind, as a holy place which welcomed all. Ramasami was a 'theist' until his visit to Kasi, after which, his views changed and he became an atheist.

Member of Congress Party (1919–1925)

In Vaikom (then Travancore), a small town in Kerala state, there were strict laws of untouchability in and around the temple area. Dalits, also known as Harijans, were not allowed into the close streets around and leading to the temple, let alone inside it. Anti-caste feelings were growing, and in 1924, Vaikom was chosen as a suitable place for an organised Satyagraha, passive resistance campaign as practised by Gandhi. Under his guidance, a movement had already begun with the aim of giving all castes the right to enter the temples. Thus, agitations and demonstrations took place. On 14 April, Periyar and his wife, Nagamma, arrived in Vaikom.

They were arrested and imprisoned for participation. Despite Gandhi's objection to non-Keralites and non-Hindus taking part, Periyar and his followers continued to give support to the movement until it was withdrawn. He received the title Vaikom Veeran, mostly given by his Tamil followers who participated in the Satyagraha. However, a considerable section of intellectuals feels that Periyar's participation in the Indian independence movement and his contributions in the Vaikom Satyagraha have been highly exaggerated.

Self-Respect Movement

Periyar during the early years of Self-Respect Movement

Periyar and his followers campaigned constantly to influence and pressure the government to take measures to remove social inequality, even while other nationalist forerunners focused on the struggle for political independence. The Self-Respect Movement was described from the beginning as 'dedicated to the goal of giving non-Brahmins a sense of pride based on their Dravidian past.'

In 1952, the Periyar Self-Respect Movement Institution was registered with a list of objectives of the institution, and accordingly quoted as,

"…for the diffusion of useful knowledge of political education. To allow people to live a life of freedom from slavery to anything against reason and self-respect.

To do away with needless customs, meaningless ceremonies and blind superstitious beliefs in society.

To put an end to the present social system in which caste, religion, community and traditional occupations based on the accident of birth, have chained the mass of the people and created "superior" and "inferior" classes.

To give people equal rights to completely eradicate untouchability, and to establish a united society based on brother/sisterhood.

To give equal rights to women.

To prevent child marriages and marriages based on law favouring to one sect.

To conduct and encourage love marriages, widow marriages, inter-caste and inter-religious marriages, and to have the marriages registered under the Civil Law.

To establish and maintain homes for orphans and widows, and to run educational institutions."

Propagation of the philosophy of self-respect became the full-time activity of Periyar since 1925. A Tamil weekly, *Kudi Arasu*, started in 1925, while the English journal, *Revolt*, started in 1928, carrying on the propaganda among the educated people. The Self-Respect Movement began to grow fast and received the sympathy of the heads of the Justice Party from the beginning. In May 1929, a conference of Self-Respect Volunteers was held at Pattukkotai under the presidency of S. Guruswami.

K.V. Alagiriswami took charge as the head of the volunteer band. Conferences followed in succession throughout the Tamil districts of the former Madras Presidency. A training school in Self-Respect was opened at Erode, the home town of Periyar. The object was not just to introduce social reform but to bring about a social revolution to foster a new spirit and build a new society.

International travel (1929–1932)

Between 1929 and 1935, under the strain of World Depression, political thinking worldwide received a jolt from the spread of international communism. Indian political parties, movements and considerable sections of leadership were also affected by inter-continental ideologies. The Self-Respect Movement also came under the influence of the leftist philosophies and institutions. Periyar, after establishing the Self-Respect Movement as an independent institution, began to look for ways to strengthen it politically and socially. To accomplish this, he studied the history and politics of different countries, and personally, observed these systems at work.

Periyar toured Malaysia for a month, from December 1929 to January 1930, to propagate the self-respect philosophy. Embarking on his journey from Nagapattinam with his wife, Nagammal, and his followers, Periyar was received by 50,000 Tamil Malaysians in Penang.

During the same month, he inaugurated the Tamils Conference, convened by the Tamils Reformatory Sangam in Ipoh, and then, went to Singapore. In December 1931, he undertook a tour of Europe, accompanied by S. Ramanathan and Erode Ramu, to personally acquaint himself with their political systems, social movements and way of life, economic and social progress and administration of public bodies. He visited Egypt, Greece, Turkey, Russia, Germany, England, Spain, France and Portugal, staying in Russia for three months. On his return journey, he halted at Ceylon and returned to India in November 1932.

The tour shaped the political ideology of Periyar to achieve the social concept of Self-Respect. The communist system obtained in Russia appealed to him as appropriately suited to deal with the social ills of the country.

Thus, on socio-economic issues, Periyar was Marxist, but he did not advocate for abolishing private ownership. Immediately after his return, Periyar, in alliance with the enthusiastic communist, M. Singaravelu Chettiar, began to work out a socio-political scheme, incorporating socialist and self-respect ideals. This marked a crucial stage of development in the Self-Respect Movement which got politicised and found its compatibility in Tamil Nadu.

Opposition to Hindi

In 1937, when Chakravarthi Rajagopalachari became the Chief Minister of Madras state, he introduced Hindi as a compulsory language of study in schools, thereby, igniting a series of anti-Hindi agitations. Tamil nationalists and the Justice Party under Sir A. T. Panneerselvam and Periyar, organised anti-Hindi protests in 1938, which ended with numerous arrests by the Rajaji government.

During the same year, the slogan "Tamil Nadu for Tamilians" was first raised by Periyar in protest against the introduction of Hindi in schools. He explained that the introduction of Hindi was a dangerous mechanism used by the Aryans to infiltrate Dravidian culture. He reasoned that the adoption of Hindi would make Tamils subordinate to Hindi-speaking North Indians. Periyar explained that Hindi would not only halt the progress of Tamilians but would also completely destroy their culture and nullify the progressive ideas that had been successfully inculcated through Tamil in the recent decades.

Cutting across party lines, South Indian politicians rallied together in their opposition to Hindi. There were recurrent anti-Hindi agitations in 1948, 1952 and 1965.

As President of the Justice Party (1938–1944)

A political party known as the South Indian Libertarian Federation (commonly referred to as Justice Party) was founded in 1916, principally to oppose the economic and political power of the Brahmin groups. The party's goal was to render social justice to non-Brahmin groups. To gain the support of the masses, non-Brahmin politicians began propagating an ideology of equality among non-Brahmin groups. Brahmanical priesthood and Sanskritic social class-value hierarchy were blamed for the existence of inequalities among non-Brahmin groups.

In 1937, when the government required that Hindi be taught in the school system, Periyar organised opposition through the Justice Party to this policy. After 1937, the Dravidian movement derived considerable support from the student community. In later years, opposition to Hindi played a big role in the politics of Tamil Nadu. The fear of the Hindi language had its origin in the conflict between Brahmins and non-Brahmins.

To the Tamils, acceptance of Hindi in the school system was a form of bondage. When the Justice Party weakened in the absence of mass support, Periyar took over the leadership of the party after being jailed for opposing Hindi in 1939. Under his tutelage, the party prospered, but the party's conservative members, most of whom were rich and educated, withdrew from active participation.

DravidarKazhagam (1944–onwards)

Formation of the Dravidar Kazhagam

At a rally in 1944, Periyar, in his capacity as the leader of the Justice Party, declared that the party would, henceforth, be known as the Dravidar Kazhagam, or 'Dravidian Association.' However, a few who disagreed with Periyar started a splinter group, claiming to be the original Justice Party. This party was led by veteran Justice Party Leader, P. T. Rajan, and survived until 1957.

The Dravidar Kazhagam came to be well-known among the urban communities and students. Villages were influenced by its message. Hindi and ceremonies that had become associated with Brahmanical priesthood were identified as alien symbols that should be eliminated from Tamil culture. Brahmins, who were regarded as the guardians of such symbols, came under verbal attack. From 1949 onwards, the Dravidar Kazhagam intensified social reformist work and put forward the fact that superstitions were the cause for the degeneration of Dravidians. The Dravidar Kazhagam vehemently fought for the abolition of untouchability among the Dalits. It also focused its attention on the liberation of women, women's education, willing marriage, widow marriage, orphanages and mercy homes.

Split with Annadurai

In 1949, Periyar's chief lieutenant, Conjeevaram Natarajan Annadurai, established a separate association called the DMK, or Dravidian Advancement Association. This was due to differences between the two, where Periyar advocated a separate independent Dravidian or Tamil state, while Annadurai compromised with the Delhi government combined with claims of increased state independence. Periyar was convinced that individuals and movements that undertake the task of eradicating the social evils in the Indian subcontinent have to pursue the goal with devotion and dedication without deviating from the path and with uncompromising zeal. Thus, if they contest elections, aiming to assume political power, they would lose vigour and sense of purpose. But among his followers, there were those who had a different view, wanting to enter into politics and have a share in running the government. They were looking for an opportunity to part with Periyar. Thus, when Periyar married Maniammai on 9 July 1948, they quit the Dravidar Kazhagam stating that Periyar had set a bad example by marrying a young woman in his old age – he was 70 and she 30. Those who parted company with Periyar joined the DMK.

Though the DMK split from the Dravidar Kazhagam, the organisation made efforts to carry on Periyar's Self-Respect Movement to villagers and urban students. The DMK advocated the thesis that the Tamil language was much richer than Sanskrit and Hindi in content, and thus, was a key which opened the door to subjects to be learnt. The Dravidar Kazhagam continued to counter Brahminism, Indo-Aryan propaganda, and uphold the Dravidians' right of self-determination.

Later Years

In 1956, despite warnings from P. Kakkan, the President of the Tamil Nadu Congress Committee, Periyar organised a procession to the Marina to burn pictures of the Hindu God, Rama. Periyar was subsequently arrested and confined to prison.

The activities of Periyar continued when he went to Bangalore in 1958 to participate in the All India Official Language Conference. There, he stressed the need to retain English as the Union Official Language instead of Hindi. Five years later, Periyar travelled to North India to advocate the eradication of the caste system. Nearing Periyar's last years, an award was given to him by the United Nations Educational, Scientific and Cultural Organisation (UNESCO), and it was presented to him by the Union Education Minister, Triguna Sen in Madras (Chennai), on 27 June 1970. In his last meeting at Thiagaraya Nagar, Chennai on 19 December 1973, Periyar declared a call for action to gain social equality and a dignified way of life. On 24 December 1973, Periyar died at the age of 94.

Principles and Legacy

Periyar spent over 50 years giving speeches, propagating the realisation that everyone is an equal citizen and the differences on basis of caste and creeds were man-made to keep the innocent and ignorant as underdogs in the society. Although Periyar's speeches were targeted towards the illiterate and more mundane mass, scores of educated people were also swayed. Periyar viewed reasoning as a special tool. According to him, all were blessed with his tool, but very few used it. Thus, Periyar used reasoning, with respect to subjects of social interest, in his presentations to his audience. Communal differences in Tamil society were considered by many to be deep-rooted features until Periyar came to the scene.

Cho Ramaswamy Remarked in India Today:

"Periyar was accepted and acclaimed as the leader by a significant section of the Tamil population in spite of all his contempt for Tamil and disdain for Tamils, only because he was perceived to be a genuine individual, a rarity among those in public life. There was no shade of hypocrisy in him, and he never attempted sophistry while propounding his social philosophy."

Rationalism

The bedrock of Periyar's principles and the movements was rationalism. He thought that an insignificant minority in society was exploiting the majority and is trying to keep them subordinates forever. He wanted the exploited to sit up and think about their position and use their reasoning to realise that they were being exploited by a handful of people. If they started thinking, they would realise that they were human beings like the rest – that birth did not and should not endow superiority over others and that they must awaken themselves and do everything possible to improve their own lot.

Likewise, Periyar explained that wisdom lies in thinking and that the spearhead of thinking is rationalism. On caste, he stated that no other living being harms or degrades its own class. But man, said to be a rational living being, does these evils. The differences, hatred, enmity, degradation, poverty and wickedness, now prevalent in the society, are due to lack of wisdom and rationalism and not due to God or the cruelty of time. EVR Periyar had written in his books and magazines dozens of times of various occasions, which the British rule is better than self-rule.

Periyar also blamed the capitalists for their control of machineries, creating difficulties for workers. According to his philosophy, rationalism, which has to lead the way for peaceful life, had resulted in causing poverty and worries to the people because of dominating forces. He stated that there was no use in acquiring titles or amassing wealth, if one has no self-respect and scientific knowledge. An example he gave was the West sending messages to the planets, while the Tamil society in India were sending rice and cereals to their dead forefathers through the Brahmins.

In a message to the Brahmin community, Periyar stated, "…in the name of god, religion and sastras, you have duped us. We were the ruling people. Stop this life of cheating us from this year. Give room for rationalism and humanism." He added, "…any opposition not based on rationalism, science or experience will one day or another, reveal the fraud, selfishness, lies and conspiracies."

Periyar was listed among the top 100 most influential people among Tamil society of the 20th century.

Thoughts on Thirukkural

Periyar hailed the Thirukkural as a valuable scripture with many scientific and philosophical truths and praised the secular nature of the work, including

Thiruvalluvar, for his description of God as a formless entity with only positive attributes. He suggested that the reader of the Thirukkural will become a self-respecter, absorbing knowledge in politics, society and economics. Although certain items in this ancient book of ethics may not relate to today, it permitted such changes for modern society.

On caste, he believed that the Kural illustrates how Vedic laws of Manu were against the Sudras and other communities of the Dravidian race. On the other hand, Periyar opined that the ethics were comparable to the Christian Bible. The Dravidar Kazhagam adopted the Thirukkural and advocated that Thiruvalluvar's Kural alone was enough to educate the people of the country. One of Periyar's quotes on the Thirukkural from 'Veeramani's Collected Works of Periyar' was "when Dravida Nadu (Dravidistan) was a victim to Indo-Aryan deceit, Thirukkural was written by a great Dravidian, Thiruvalluvar, to free the Dravidians."

Self-determination of Dravidistan

The Dravidian-Aryan conflict was believed to be a continuous historical phenomenon that started when the Aryans first set their foot in the Dravidian lands. Even a decade before the idea of separation appeared, Periyar stated, "As long as Aryan religion, Indo-Aryan domination, propagation of Aryan Vedas and Aryan 'Varnashramas' existed, there was need for a 'Dravidian Progressive Movement' and a 'Self-Respect Movement. Periyar became very concerned about the growing North Indian domination over the South, which appeared to him no different from foreign domination."

He wanted to secure the fruits of labour of the Dravidians to the Dravidians, and lamented that fields such as political, economic, industrial, social, art and spiritual were dominated by the North for the benefit of the North Indians. Thus, with the approach of independence from Britain, this fear that North India would take the place of Britain to dominate South India became more and more intense.

Periyar was clear about the concept of a separate multi-linguistic nation, comprising Tamil, Telugu, Malayalam and Kannada areas. This roughly corresponded with the then existing Madras Presidency with adjoining areas into a federation, guaranteeing protection of minorities, including religious, linguistic and cultural freedom of the people. A separatist conference was held in June 1940 at Kanchipuram when Periyar released the map of the proposed Dravida Nadu but failed to get British approval. On the contrary, Periyar received sympathy and support from people such as Bhimrao Ramji Ambedkar and Muhammad Ali Jinnah for his views on the Congress and for his opposition to Hindi. They then decided to convene a movement to resist the Congress.

The concept of Dravida Nadu was later modified down to Tamil Nadu. This led to a proposal of a union of the Tamil people of not only South India but also Ceylon. In 1953, Periyar helped to preserve Madras as the capital of Tamil Nadu, which later was the name he substituted for the more general Dravida Nadu. In 1955, Periyar threatened to burn the national flag, but convinced by Chief Minister Kamaraj that Hindi would not be compulsory, he postponed the action. In his speech of 1957, 'Suthantara Tamil Nadu En?' (Why an independent Tamil Nadu?), he criticised the Central Government of India, inducing thousands of Tamilians to burn the constitution of India. The reason for this action was that Periyar held the Government responsible for maintaining the caste system. After stating reasons for separation and turning down opinions against it, he closed his speech with a "war cry" to join and burn the map of India on 5 June. Periyar was sentenced to six months' imprisonment for burning the Indian constitution.

Advocacy of such a nation became illegal, when separatist demands were banned by law in 1957. Regardless of these measures, a Dravida Nadu Separation Day was observed on 17 September 1960, resulting in numerous arrests. However, Periyar resumed his campaign in 1968. He wrote an editorial on 'Tamil Nadu for Tamilians,' in which he stated that by nationalism, only Brahmins had prospered and nationalism had been developed to abolish the rights of Tamils. He advocated the separate establishment of a Tamil Nadu Freedom Organisation.

Anti-Brahmanism vs. Anti-Brahmin

Periyar was a radical advocate of anti-Brahmanism. His anti-Brahmanism was evident from his comments to his followers, that if they encountered a Brahmin and a snake on the road they should kill the Brahmin first. He also used violent and vulgar language in his writings against Hindu gods.

In 1920, when the Justice Party came to power, Brahmins occupied about 70 percent of the high level posts in government. After reservation was introduced by the Justice Party, it reversed this trend, allowing non-Brahmins to rise in the government of the Madras Presidency. Periyar, through the Justice Party, advocated against the imbalance of the domination of Brahmins who constituted only 3 percent of the population in government jobs, judiciary and the Madras University. His Self-Respect Movement espoused rationalism and atheism. Periyar stated, "Our Dravidian movement does not exist against the Brahmins or the Banias (a North Indian merchant caste). If anyone thinks so, I would only pity him. But we will not tolerate the ways in which Brahminism and the Banianism is degrading Dravida Nadu. Whatever support they may have from the government, neither I nor my movement will be of cowardice."

However, at the same time, Periyar has also advocated the destruction of Brahmins.

"Only if the Brahmin is destroyed, caste will be destroyed. The Brahmin is a snake entangled in our feet. He will bite. If you take off your leg, that's all. Don't leave. Brahmin is not able to dominate because power is in the hands of the Tamilian."

Periyar also criticised Subramanya Bharathi in the journal *Ticutar* for portraying mother Tamil as a sister of Sanskrit in his poems,

"They say Bharati is an immortal poet…Even if a rat dies in an akrakāram, they would declare it to be immortal. All of Tamil Nadu praises him. Why should this be so? Supposedly because he sang fulsome praises of Tamil and Tamil Nadu. What else could he sing? His own mother tongue, Sanskrit, has been dead for years. What other language did he know? He cannot sing in Sanskrit. He says Tamil Nadu is the land of Aryas."

Comparisons with Gandhi

In the Vaikom Satyagraha of 1924, Periyar and Gandhi both cooperated and confronted each other in socio-political action. Periyar and his followers emphasised the difference in point of view between Gandhi and himself on the social issues such as fighting the Untouchability Laws and eradication of the caste system.

Peiryar, in his references to Gandhi, used opportunities to present Gandhi as a principal serving the interests of the Brahmins. In 1927, Periyar and Gandhi met at Bangalore to discuss this matter. The main difference between them came out when Periyar stood for the total eradication of Hinduism, to which Gandhi objected saying that Hinduism is not fixed in doctrines but can be changed.

In the *Kudi Arasu*, Periyar explained, "With all his good qualities, Gandhi did not bring the people forward from foolish and evil ways. His murderer was an educated man. Therefore, nobody can say this is a time of high culture. If you eat poison, you will die. If electricity hits the body, you will die. If you oppose the Brahmin, you will die. Gandhi did not advocate the eradication of Varnasrama Dharma structure, but sees in it a task for the humanisation of society and social change possible within its structure. The consequence of this would be continued high-caste leadership. Gandhi adapted Brahmins to social change without depriving them of their leadership."

On the 'Temple Entry' issue, Gandhi never advocated the opening of Garbha Griha to Harijans in consequence of his Hindu belief. These sources which can be labelled 'pro-Periyar' with the exception of M. Mahar and D.S. Sharma clearly show that his followers emphasised that Periyar was the real fighter for the removal of untouchability and the true uplifter of Hairjans, whereas Gandhi was not. This did not prevent Periyar from having faith in Gandhi on certain matters.

Religion and Atheism

Periyar was generally regarded as a pragmatic propagandist who attacked the evils of religious influence on society, mainly what he regarded as Brahmin domination. At a young age, he felt that some people used religion only as a mask to deceive innocent people and considered it as his life's mission to warn people against superstitions and priests. Anita Diehl explains that Periyar cannot be called an atheist philosopher. He repudiated the term as without real sense, "…the talk of the atheist should be considered thoughtless and erroneous. The thing I call God… that makes all people equal and free, the God that does not stop free thinking and research, the God that does not ask for money, flattery and temples can certainly be an object of worship. For saying this much, I have been called an atheist, a term that has no meaning."

Anita Diehl explains that Periyar was against incompatibility of faith with social equality and not religion itself. In a book on revolution published in 1961, Periyar stated, "Be of help to people. Do not use treachery or deceit. Speak the truth and do not cheat. That indeed is service to God."

On Hinduism, Periyar believed that it was a religion with no distinctive sacred book (Bhagawad Gita) or origins, but to be an imaginary faith preaching the 'superiority' of the Brahmins, the inferiority of the Shudras and the untouchability of the Dalits (Panchamas). In 1955, Periyar was arrested for his public agitation of burning the pictures of Rama at public places, as a symbolic protest against the Indo-Aryan domination and degradation of the Dravidian leadership according to the Ramayana epic. Periyar also showed the images of Krishna and Rama, stating that they were Aryan gods that considered the Dravidian Shudras to be "sons of prostitutes."

Maria Misra, a lecturer at Oxford University, compares him to the philosophies, by stating that "His contemptuous attitude to the baleful influence of Hinduism in Indian public life is strikingly akin to the anti-Catholic diatribes of the enlightenment philosophies."

Periyar openly suggested to those who were marginalised within the Hindu communities to consider converting to other faiths such as Islam, Christianity or Buddhism. On Islam, he stated how it was good for abolishing the disgrace in human relationship, based on one of his speeches to railway employees at Tiruchirapalli in 1947. Periyar also commended Islam for its belief in one invisible and formless God and for advocating of social unity.

At the rally in Tiruchi, Periyar said, "Muslims are following the ancient philosophies of the Dravidians. The Arabic word for Dravidian religion is Islam. When Brahmanism was imposed in this country, it was Mohammad Nabi who opposed it by instilling the Dravidian religion's policies as Islam in the minds of the people."

Periyar viewed Christianity similar to the monotheistic faith of Islam. He explained that their faith says that there can be only one God which has no name or shape. Periyar took an interest in Rev Martin Luther, where both he and his followers wanted to liken him and his role to that of the European reformer. Thus, Christian views such as that of Ram Mohan Roy's 'The Precepts of Jesus' has had, at least, an indirect influence on Periyar.

Apart from Islam and Christianity, Periyar also found in Buddhism a basis for his philosophy, although he did not accept that religion. It was again an alternative in the search for self-respect, and the object was to get liberation from the discrimination of Hinduism. Through Periyar's movement, Temple Entry Acts of 1924, 1931 and up to 1950, were created for the non-Brahmins. Another accomplishment took place during the 1970s when Tamil replaced Sanskrit as the temple language in Tamil Nadu, while Dalits were finally eligible for priesthood.

Periyar with Muhammad Ali Jinnah and Dr. B.R. Ambedkar

M. G. Ramachandran paying homage to Periyar on his funeral 1973.

Controversies on Factionism in the Justice Party

When B. Munuswamy Naidu became the Chief Minister of Madras Presidency in 1930, he endorsed the inclusion of Brahmins in the Justice Party, saying, "So long as we exclude one community, we cannot as a political speak on behalf of or claim to represent all the people of our presidency. If, as we hope, provincial autonomy is given to the provinces as a result of the reforms that may be granted, it should be essential that our Federation should be in a position to claim to be a truly representative body of all communities. What objection can be there to admit such Brahmins as are willing to subscribe to the aims and objects of our Federation? It may be that the Brahmins may not join even if the ban is removed. But surely, our Federation will not, thereafter, be open to objection on the ground that it is an exclusive organisation."

Though certain members supported the resolution, a faction in the Justice Party known as the 'Ginger Group' opposed the resolution and eventually, voted it down. Periyar, who was then an observer in the Justice Party, criticised Munuswamy Naidu, saying, "At a time when non-Brahmins in other parties were gradually coming over to the Justice Party – being fed up with the Brahmin's methods and ways of dealing with political questions – it was nothing short of folly to think of admitting him into the ranks of the Justice Party."

This factionism continued till 1932 when Muniswamy Naidu stepped down as the Chief Minister of Madras and the Raja of Bobbili became the Chief Minister.

Thanthai Periyar statue at Vaikom town near Kottayam, Kerala

Born 15[Th] July 1903 at Virudhunagar, Tamil Nadu
Died 2nd October 1975 at Chennai

Parents were Kumaraswami Nadar and Sivakami Ammal. His name was originally Kamatchi, later changed to Kamarajar. His father, Kumaraswami, was a merchant. Kamaraj had a younger sister named Nagammal.

Kamaraj was first enrolled in a traditional school in 1907, and in 1908, he was admitted to Yenadhi Narayana Vidhya Salai. In 1909, Kamaraj was admitted in Virudupatti High School. Kamaraj's father died when he was six years old, and his mother was forced to support the family. In 1914, Kamaraj dropped out of school to support his mother.

The founder and the president of the Indian National Congress (Organisation), widely acknowledged as the "Kingmaker" in Indian politics during the 1960s, he also served as the president of the Indian National Congress for two terms i.e. four years between 1964–1967 and was responsible for the elevation of Lal Bahadur Shastri to the position of Prime Minister of India after Nehru's death, and Indira Gandhi after Shastri's death. Kamaraj was the 3rd Chief Minister of Madras State (Tamil Nadu) during 1954–1963 and a Member of Parliament, Lok Sabha during 1952–1954 and 1969–1975. He was known for his simplicity and integrity. He played a major role in developing the infrastructure of the Madras State and worked to improve the quality of life of the needy and the disadvantaged.

As Chief Minister, Kamaraj removed the family vocation based Hereditary Education Policy introduced by Rajaji. The State made immense strides in education and trade. New schools were opened so that poor rural students had to walk no more than three kilometres to their nearest school. Better facilities were added to existing ones. No village remained without a primary school and no panchayat without a high school. Kamaraj strived to eradicate illiteracy by introducing free and compulsory education up to the eleventh standard. He introduced the Midday Meal Scheme to provide at least one meal per day to the lakhs of poor school children. Later, it was expanded to four more schools. This was the precursor to the free noon meal schemes introduced by K. Kamaraj in 1960's and expanded by M. G. Ramachandran in the 1980s. He introduced free school uniforms to weed out caste, creed and class distinctions among young minds.

Kamaraj Statue in Marina Beach, Chennai depicting his contribution to education in the state

Perunthalaivar Kamarajar Statue in Kamaraj Colony, Hosur

During the British regime, the education rate was only 7%. But after Kamaraj's reforms, it reached 37%. Apart from increasing the number of schools, steps were taken to improve standards of education. To improve standards, the number of working days was increased from 180 to 200, unnecessary holidays were reduced and syllabi were prepared to give opportunity to various abilities. Kamaraj and Bishnuram Medhi (Governor) took efforts to establish IIT Madras in 1959.

Major irrigation schemes were planned in Kamaraj's period. Dams and irrigation canals were built across Upper Bhavani, Mani Muthar, Aarani, Vaigai, Amaravathi, Sathanur, Krishnagiri, Pullambadi, Parambikulam and Neyyaru among others. The Lower Bhavani Dam in Erode district brought 207,000 acres (840 km^2) of land under cultivation. 45,000 acres (180 km^2) of land benefited from canals constructed from the Mettur Dam. The Vaigai and Sathanur systems facilitated cultivation across thousands of acres of lands in Madurai and North Arcot districts respectively. Rs 30 crores were planned to be spent for Parambikulam River scheme, and 150 lakhs of acres of lands were brought under cultivation; one-third of this (i.e. 56 lakhs of acres of land) received a permanent irrigation facility. In 1957–61, 1,628 tanks were de-silted under the Small Irrigation Scheme and 2,000 wells were dug with outlets. Long term loans with 25% subsidy were given to farmers. In addition, farmers who had dry lands were given oil engines and electric pump-sets on an instalment basis.

Industries with huge investments in crores of Rupees were started in his period: Neyveli Lignite Corporation, BHEL at Trichy, Manali Refinery, Hindustan raw photo film factory at Ooty, surgical instruments factory at Chennai and a railway coach factory at Chennai were established. Industries such as paper, sugar, chemicals and cement took off during the period.

He was involved in the Indian independence movement. As the president of the INC, he was instrumental in navigating the party after the death of Jawaharlal Nehru. As the chief minister of Madras, he was responsible for bringing free education to the disadvantaged and introduced the free Midday Meal Scheme while he himself did not complete schooling.

Personal Life

During his tenure as Chief Minister, when the municipality of Virudhunagar provided a direct water connection to his house in his hometown, Kamarajar ordered it to be disconnected immediately as he did not want any special privileges. He refused to use the Z-level security that was provided to him as the CM of Tamil Nadu and instead, travelled with just one police patrol vehicle. He did not marry, did not own any property and was never tempted by power. When he died, he left behind 130 rupees, two pairs of sandals, four shirts, 4 dhotis and a few books.

Death

Kamaraj died at his home, on Gandhi Jayanti day (2 October 1975), which also was the 12th anniversary of his resignation. He was aged 72 and died in his sleep due to a heart attack.

Legacy

Kamaraj was awarded India's highest civilian honour, the Bharat Ratna, posthumously in 1976. He is widely acknowledged as "Kalvi Thanthai" (Father of

Education) in Tamil Nadu. The domestic terminal of the Chennai airport is named "Kamaraj Terminal." Marina beach road in Chennai was named as "Kamarajar Salai." North Parade Road in Bengaluru and Parliament road in New Delhi were also renamed after Kamaraj. Madurai Kamaraj University is named in his honour. In 2003, the Government of India released a commemorative coin on his birthday.

Once, Tamil Nadu Chief Minister Kamaraj was traveling in a car with Indian Prime Minister Jawaharlal Nehru to attend a rally in Madurai.

Nehru asked as he got into the car on the way, "Kamaraj, is your house somewhere in this area? What if we go up there?"

"Why?"

"I want to see your mother!"

"Why would a Prime Minister of 60 crore people waste time visiting my mother without any need?"

The direction Kamaraj should turn after private conversation was showed to the driver. Nehru looked around from his car when Kamaraj asked the driver to stop the car which was speeding along an endless field. Nehru, who could not be found in the vicinity of a shop or a house, was also taken aback. Why did Kamaraj ask to park your car here? When Nehru turned his eyes to Kamaraj inside the car, he stretched his head out of the car window and looked out into the field.

Kamaraj called out to no one, "Mom are you there?"

When he saw that no one was listening, Kamaraj raised his head a little and called out loud again, "Mom, this is me, Kamaraj."

An elderly woman from a group of women working in the fields stood up, looked at the car, raised her hand and asked back, "Mone, (Son) are you all right?"

"I'm fine. I just called as I went this way."

"What's up, Mone? I was with someone in a little hurry"

"Going to Madurai."

"Can he come to his mother's place to see his mother?"

"Anyway, mother is here. When Nehru saw an old woman walking towards the car, she wiped the sweat off with a towel." Nehruji came out of the car and could not utter a word.

"This is my mother." Nehru regained consciousness.

When he shook hands with his mother, Kamaraj said to his mother, "This is the Prime Minister of India Jawaharlal Nehru."

The mother, who was completely surprised, greeted Nehru with her bare hands and said, "Hello."

(Tail piece – Today's political lords have you heard this.)

C. N. Annadurai

Conjeevaram Natarajan Annadurai, popularly called Anna or Arignar Anna, was an Indian politician who served as 1st Chief Minister of Tamil Nadu for 20 days in 1969 and fifth and last Chief Minister of Madras State from 1967 until 1969 when the name of the state of Madras was changed to Tamil Nadu.

He was the first member of a Dravidian party to hold either post.

He was well-known for his oratorical skills and was an acclaimed writer in the Tamil language. He scripted and acted in several plays. Some of his plays were later made into movies. He was the first politician from the Dravidian parties to use Tamil cinema extensively for political propaganda. Born in a middle-class family, he first worked as a school teacher. Then, he moved into the political scene of the Madras Presidency as a journalist. He edited several political journals and enrolled as a member of the Dravidar Kazhagam. As an ardent follower of Periyar E. V. Ramasamy, he rose in stature as a prominent member of the party.

With differences looming with Periyar, on issues of separate independent state of Dravida Nadu and union with India, he crossed swords with his political mentor. The friction between the two finally erupted when Periyar married Maniammai, who was much younger than him. Angered by this action of Periyar, Annadurai, with his supporters, parted from Dravidar Kazhagam and launched his own party, DMK.

The DMK initially followed ideologies the same as the mother party, Dravidar Kazhagam. But with the evolution of national politics and the constitution of India after the Sino-Indian war in 1962, Annadurai dropped the claim for an independent Dravida Nadu. Various protests against the ruling Congress government took him to prison on several occasions; the last of which was during the Madras Anti-Hindi agitation of 1965. The agitation itself helped Annadurai to gain popular support for his party. His party won a landslide victory in the 1967 state elections. His cabinet was the youngest at that time in India. He legalised Self-Respect marriages, enforced a two language policy (in preference to the three language formula in other southern states), implemented subsidies for rice and renamed Madras State to Tamil Nadu.

C. N. Annadurai and E. V. Ramasami (Periyaar)

Dravida Nadu magazine owned and edited by Annadurai

However, he died of cancer just two years into office. His funeral had the highest attendance of any to that date. Several institutions and organisations are named after him. A splinter party launched by M. G. Ramachandran in 1972 was named after him as All India Anna Dravida Munnetra Kazhagam.

M. G. Ramachandran commemorative stamp

Maruthur Gopalan Ramachandran

Born: 17 January 1917, Kandy, Sri Lanka

Died: 24 December 1987, Chennai

Popularly known as MGR, Ramachandran was an Indian politician and film actor who served as the Chief Minister of Tamil Nadu for ten years between 1977 and 1987. He was also a philanthropist and a humanitarian icon. In 1988, MGR was awarded India's highest civilian honour, the Bharat Ratna, posthumously.

In his youth, MGR and his elder brother, M. G. Chakrapani, became members of a drama troupe to support their family. Influenced by Gandhian ideals, MGR joined the Indian National Congress. After a few years of acting in plays, he made his film debut in the 1936 film *Sathi Leelavathi* in a supporting role. By the late 1940s, he graduated to the lead roles, and for the next three decades, dominated the Tamil film industry.

MGR became a member of the C. N. Annadurai-led DMK party) and rapidly rose through its ranks, using his enormous popularity as a film star to build a large political base. In 1972, three years after Annadurai's death, he left the DMK, then led by Karunanidhi, MGR's once friend and now rival, to form his own party – the All India Anna Dravida Munnetra Kazhagam (AIADMK).

Five years later, MGR steered an AIADMK-led alliance to victory in the 1977 election, routing the DMK in the process. He became Chief Minister of

Tamil Nadu, the first film actor to become a chief minister in India. Except for a six-month interregnum in 1980, when his government was overthrown by the Union government, he remained as chief minister till his death in 1987, leading the AIADMK to two more electoral triumphs in 1980 and 1984.

In October 1984, MGR was diagnosed with kidney failure as a result of diabetes. He died on 24 December 1987 in his Ramavaram Gardens residence in Manapakkam after his prolonged illness. MGR is regarded as a cultural icon in Tamil Nadu and is regarded as one of the most influential actors of Tamil cinema. He was popularly known as "Makkal Thilagam" (People's King) as he was popular with the masses. His autobiography *Naan Yaen Piranthaen* (*Why I was Born*) was published in 2003.

MGR with his wife Janaki in *Mohini* (1948)

MGR's Tomb and Memorial at Marina beach, Chennai

Muthuvel Karunanidhi (3 June 1924 – 7 August 2018) an Indian writer and politician who served as Chief Minister of Tamil Nadu for almost two decades over five terms between 1969 and 2011. He had the longest tenure as Chief Minister of Tamil Nadu with 6,863 days in office. He was also a long-standing leader of the Dravidian movement and ten-time president of the Dravida Munnetra Kazhagam political party. Before entering politics, he worked in the Tamil film industry as a screenwriter. He also made contributions to Tamil literature, having written stories, plays, novels and a multiple-volume memoir. He was popularly referred to as "Kalaignar" (Artist) and "Mutthamizharignar" (Tamil Scholar) for his contributions to Tamil literature. Karunanidhi died on 7 August 2018 at Kauvery Hospital in Chennai after a series of prolonged, age-related illnesses.

Born: 24 February 1948, Melukote Died: 5 December 2016, Chennai

Full name: Jayalalithaa Jayaraman

Indian politician and film actress who served six times as the Chief Minister of Tamil Nadu for over 14 years between 1991 and 2016. From 1989, she was the general secretary of the All India Anna Dravida Munnetra Kazhagam (AIADMK), a Dravidian party whose cadre revered her as their *"Amma"* (mother) and *Puratchi Thalaivi* (revolutionary leader). Her critics in the media and the opposition accused her of fostering a personality cult and of demanding absolute loyalty from AIADMK legislators and ministers, who often publicly prostrated themselves before her.

Jayalalithaa first came into prominence as a leading film actress in the mid-1960s. Although she had entered the profession reluctantly, upon the urging of her mother to support the family, Jayalalithaa worked prolifically. She appeared in 140 films between 1961 and 1980, primarily in the Tamil, Telugu and Kannada languages. Jayalalithaa received praise for her versatility as an actress and for her dancing skills, earning the sobriquet "Queen of Tamil Cinema."

Among her frequent co-stars was M. G. Ramachandran, a Tamil cultural icon who leveraged his immense popularity with the masses into a successful political career. In 1982, when MGR was chief minister, Jayalalithaa joined the AIADMK, the party he founded. Her political rise was rapid; within a few years, she became AIADMK propaganda secretary and was elected to the Rajya Sabha, the upper house of India's Parliament. After MGR's death in 1987, Jayalalithaa proclaimed herself his political heir, and having fought off the faction headed by Janaki Ramachandran, MGR's widow, emerged as the sole leader of the AIADMK. Following the 1989 election, she became Leader of the Opposition to the DMK-led government headed by Karunanidhi, her *bête noire*.

Early Life, Education and Family

Mysore state, now Karnataka Melukote, Pandavapura taluk, Mandya district, then in Mysore State (now Karnataka) to Jayaram and Vedavalli (Sandhya) in Tamil Brahmin Iyengar family.

The name, Jayalalithaa, was adopted at the age of one for the purpose of using the name in school and colleges. It was derived from the names of two houses where she resided in Mysore. One was "Jaya Vilas" and the other "Lalitha Vilas." Her paternal grandfather, Narasimhan Rengachary, was in the service of the Mysore kingdom as a surgeon, and served as the court physician to Maharaja Krishna Raja Wadiyar IV of Mysore. Her maternal grandfather, Rangasamy Iyengar, moved to Mysore from Srirangam to work with Hindustan Aeronautics Limited. He had one son and three daughters— Ambujavalli, Vedavalli and Padmavalli. Vedavalli was married to Jayaram, son of Narasimhan Rengachary. The couple Jayaram-Vedvalli had two children – a son, Jayakumar, and a daughter, Jayalalitha. Her mother, her relatives and later co-stars and friends referred to her as 'Ammu.'

Jayalalithaa's father, Jayaram, was a lawyer, but never worked and squandered most of the family's money. He died when Jayalalithaa was two years old. The widowed Vedavalli returned to her father's home in Bangalore in 1950. Vedavalli learnt shorthand and typewriting to take up a clerical position to help support the family in 1950. Her younger sister, Ambujavalli had moved to Madras, working as an air hostess. She also started acting in drama and films using the screen name Vidyavathy.

On the insistence of Ambujavalli, Jayalalithaa's mother, Vedavalli, also relocated to Madras and stayed with her sister from 1952. Vedavalli worked in a commercial firm in Madras and began dabbling in acting from 1953 under the screen name Sandhya. Jayalalithaa remained under the care of her mother's sister, Padmavalli and maternal grandparents from 1950 to 1958 in Mysore. While still in Bangalore, Jayalalithaa attended Bishop Cotton Girls' School, Bangalore. In later interviews, Jayalalithaa spoke emotionally about how she missed her mother while growing up in a different city. She had the opportunity to visit her mother during summer holidays. After her aunt Padmavalli's marriage in 1958, Jayalalithaa moved to Madras and began to live with her mother. She completed her education at Sacred Heart Matriculation School (popularly known as Church Park Presentation Convent or Presentation Church Park Convent).

She excelled at school and was offered a government scholarship to pursue further education. She won Gold State Award for coming first in 10th standard in the state of Tamil Nadu. She joined Stella Maris College, Chennai; however, discontinued her studies due pressure from her mother and became a film actress. She was fluent in several languages, including Tamil, Arabic, Telugu, Kannada, Hindi, Malayalam and English.

"This lovely lass has taken her place in the centre of India's political stage, and being a Hindi-speaking Tamilian, is assured of a central role for many years to come."

– Khushwant Singh, *Filmstar MPs*, *Sunday*, 27 April 1985

The then U.S. Secretary of State Hillary Clinton met Jayalalithaa in July 2011

On 22 September 2016, Jayalalithaa was admitted to Apollo Hospitals in Chennai, as she was suffering from an infection and acute dehydration. Her official duties were handed over to her aide, O. Panneerselvam on 12 October 2016, although she continued to remain as the chief minister of the state.

She was also said to be suffering from a severe pulmonary infection and septicaemia, which were cured. On 4 December 2016, she was re-admitted to the intensive care unit after suffering a cardiac arrest around 16:45. The hospital released a press statement stating that her condition was "very critical" and that she was on life support. On 5 December 2016, the hospital announced her death.

"No culture on the planet invested as much towards knowing the inner dimension as Bharat."

–Padmashree Sadguru

The Seekers of the Harmony Within

J Krishnamurti

Born on 11th May 1895: Died on 17th February 1986 Ojai, California

Mandanapalle, Madras Presidency – Now Andhra Pardesh

The Vasanta Vihar, ensconced in a quiet corner of Chennai, is a treasure that slowly reveals itself to the seeker. A white-walled bungalow with a bright cluster of bougainvillea perched atop the balcony lies in the heart of Vasanta Vihar. The scene itself is similar to a flower pinned on someone's pocket, and this is where we will be taking our first as well as the last step.

J Krishnamurti, considered one of the greatest thinkers and philosophers of the century, made this profound statement - "First step is the last step" - during his dialogue with Pupul Jayakar, his biographer, in 1970. The meaning of it is that every first step that we've taken, we've also taken the last. Every first step has altered our perception entirely, thereby, rendering every next step anew.

Born in the small town of Mandanpalle (then in Madras Presidency, now in Andhra Pradesh), Jiddu Krishnamurti went on to become a great spiritual teacher, spending most parts of his life travelling across the world and delivering speeches. The Krishnamurti Foundation established by Krishnamurti himself runs several educational institutes around the world.

"…That wherever we are, at whatever level of conditioning, of being, the perceiving of truth, of the fact, is at that moment, the last step," is a part of J Krishnamurti's quote on the topic.

A few quotes:

It is no measure of health to be well adjusted to a profoundly sick society.

I maintain that Truth is a pathless land, and you cannot approach it by any path whatsoever, by any religion, by any sect.

Freedom from the desire for an answer is essential to the understanding of a problem.

For his 125th birth anniversary, the Krishnamurti Foundation has come up with an immersive exhibit based on this very statement, featuring his life and teachings. The exhibit itself is divided into four parts: Voice, Study, Life and Teachings, of which the first two are on the outside. Inside, a different world unfolds as we take the flight of stairs leading to Krishnamurti's teachings. There's Fear - a maze inside a dark cubicle from which you emerge, Religion - a walk leading towards the sacred, Violence - a tough descent towards nowhere, and more.

The Master of 'Yoga for the Moment'

T.K.V. Desikachar

Born: 21 June 1938, Mysuru Died: 8 August 2016, Chennai

A tribute to Desikachar's approach that protected yoga from fundamentalism – Navtej Johar

An Engineer by profession, T.K.V. Desikachar decided to devote his life to yoga after he saw his father, the legendary T. Krishnamacharya, help sick people. It was the recognition of yoga being a tool of health and healing that prompted that shift, and in time, the elimination of suffering became central to his lifelong quest.

Desikachar, who died in Chennai on 8th August 2016 at the age of 78, was neither into impressing the world with fanciful ancient philosophies nor with extraordinary feats of asana. "I have discovered through yoga that there is something called heart," he once said.

He did not project the idea of yoga upon those who came to him for therapy. Instead, he observed and listened to them with childlike receptivity while attuning himself to their condition and the social and cultural context. His yoga was the yoga of the moment, not burdened by the hoary past that had to be preserved and upheld.

When I opened my yoga school at Delhi many years ago, I called Sir for his blessings to ask him how I could identify the type. "You just call it yoga," he said and "at most Patanjali yoga, no more." He clearly saw branding or even standardisation of style as antithetical to yoga, the very nature of which was fluid in his view. "Until I breathe my last breath, I am going to fight against this," he told one of his American students, Leslie Kaminoff. "We always call it yoga," he added. "It is the individual that is important, not the style, whatever technique works is fine for us."

Similarly, when he decided to study yoga from his illustrious father, his first condition was to be taught yoga without God, to which Krishnamacharya readily agreed. Desikachar's yoga approach was unique in that it remained undogmatic, non-denominational, secular, fluid, open-minded and enquiring to the core.

These unconventional choices that he made might have come easily to him, but they reveal incredible clarity and foresight, particularly when viewed from the present context when patenting, branding and religious brandishing are threatening to become the creed. We, therefore, cannot ever lose sight of the fundamental astuteness and uprightness of Desikachar's decisions which may have protected our yoga practice from fundamentalism for all times to come.

Considering that he came from the most illustrious yoga lineage, he wore his mantel very lightly. Growing up in post Independence times, which idealised and valorised tradition and the past, he went against the grain to make yoga "un-precious" and brought attention to the present moment, and in fact, on the human. He did not lay tall claims to the past nor advocated preserving the perennial knowledge of ancient doctrines. For him, if there was one perennial tradition, it was that of human suffering and the human quest for happiness. "Whether we preserve or not," he stated with profound simplicity, "this will always continue!" And it was squarely within this basic, most ordinary human condition that he located his highly nuanced and sophisticated practice of yoga.

On this sad day, when my teacher is no more and yet, his legacy and teachings shall continue, I reflect upon what I received from him. From my perspective, all that I humbly offered him was my respect and faith, and in return, I received freedom, quite literally – perennial freedom to enquire, experiment, adapt, and in fact, play with this rich knowledge to make a practice for the moment.

What I learnt from him is to exercise common sense and sensitivity, be human, and listen and most of all 'attend' to the subtle and sensitive responses of the body, breath and mind in order to gauge that nameless "something more" that Sir sometimes alluded to in his teaching. I offer my deep gratitude and salutations to the great master who made "ordinariness" so special.

(Navtej Johar is a Bharatanatyam exponent and choreographer)

Courtesy The Hindu newspaper August 8[Th] 2016

Places of Historic Importance

Mahabalipuram - A Port of Great Strategic Route and Distinct Culture Revisited

Mahabalipuram, located on the seafront of Kancheepuram district of Tamil Nadu is around 60 km south from the city of Chennai. An ancient historic town, it was a bustling seaport during the time of Periplus (1st century CE) and Ptolemy (140 CE). Ancient Indian traders who went to countries of South-East Asia sailed from the seaport of Mahabalipuram.

By the 7th century, it was a port city of South Indian dynasty of the Pallavas. It had a group of sanctuaries, which were carved out of rock along the Coromandel Coast in the 7th and 8th centuries, rathas (temples in the form of chariots), mandapas (cave sanctuaries) and giant open-air reliefs such as the famous 'Descent of the Ganges,' and the Shore Temple, with thousands of sculptures to the glory of Shiva. Megalithic burial urns, cairn circles and jars with burials dating to the very dawn of the Christian era have been discovered near Mamallapuram.

The Sangam age poem, Perumpāṇāṟṟuppaṭai, relates the rule of King Thondaiman Ilam Thiraiyar at Kanchipuram of the Tondai Nadu port, 'Nirppeyyaṟu' which scholars identify with the present day Mamallapuram. Chinese coins and Roman coins of Theodosius I in the 4th century CE have been found at Mamallapuram, revealing the port as an active hub of global trade in the late classical period. Two Pallava coins bearing legends read as Srihari and Srinidhi have been found at Mamallapuram. The Pallava kings ruled Mamallapuram from Kancheepuram, the capital of the Pallava dynasty from the 3rd century to 9th century CE. The port was used to launch trade and diplomatic missions to Sri Lanka and Southeast Asia.

Mahabalipuram has an average elevation of 12 metres (39 feet). The modern city of Mahabalipuram was established by the British Raj in 1827 with the group of monuments being classified as a UNESCO World Heritage Site.

Kanchipuram

Kanchipuram, otherwise known as Kanchi, (previously romanised as Kānci-pura, Conjevaram) is 72 kilometres or 45 miles from Chennai, the capital of Tamil Nadu. Chennai International Airport is the nearest domestic and international airport to the city, which is located at Tirusulam in Kanchipuram district.

Located on the banks of the Vegavathy River, Kanchipuram has been ruled by the Pallavas, the Medieval Cholas, the Later Cholas, the Later Pandyas, the Vijayanagar Empire, the Carnatic kingdom, and the British. The city's historical monuments include the Kailasanathar Temple and the Vaikunta Perumal Temple. Historically, Kanchipuram was a centre for education and was known as the ghatikasthanam, or 'place of learning.' The city was also a religious centre of advanced education for Jainism and Buddhism between the 1st and 5th centuries. Kanchipuram based Buddhist institutions were instrumental in spreading Theravada Buddhism to South-East Asia.

In Hindu theology, Kanchipuram is one of the seven Indian cities to reach final attainment. The city houses Varadharaja Perumal Temple, Ekambareswarar Temple, Kamakshi Amman Temple and Kumarakottam Temple, which are some of major Hindu temples in the state. The city is a holy pilgrimage site for both Saivites and Vaishnavites. Of the 108 holy temples of the Hindu god Vishnu, 14 are located in Kanchipuram. Known for its hand woven silk saris, most of the city's workforce is involved in the weaving industry.

Bodhidharman

Kanchipuram is administered by a special grade municipality that was constituted in 1947. It is the headquarters of the Kanchi Matha, a Hindu monastic institution believed to have been founded by the Hindu saint and commentator Adi Sankaracharya, and Pallava Kingdom's capital city between the 4th and 9th centuries.

Fabric Tour of India

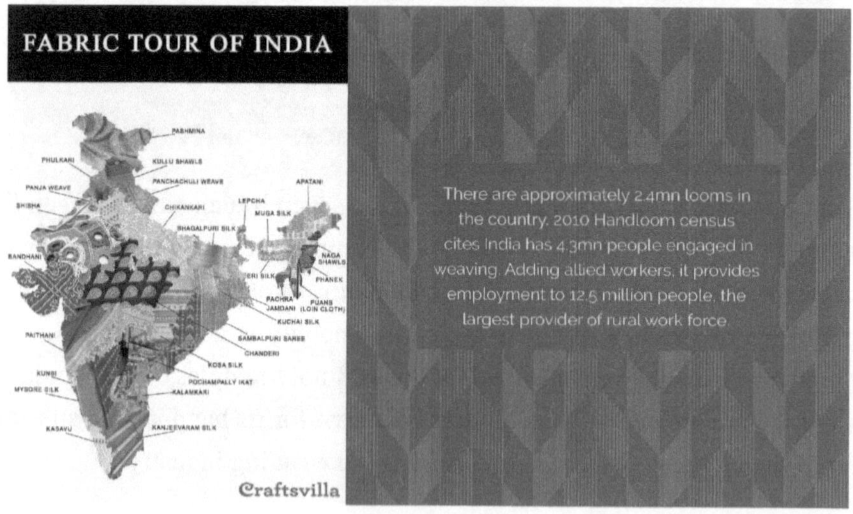

Kanjivaram: The Romance of Silk

The vivid colours and opulence of the heavy Kanjivaram silk are iconic, as are its designs inspired by the grand temples of the land it comes from. But few who drape this or admire its richness realise how old this silk is or even how it represents a coming together of traditions which thrived under the royal patronage of the Pallava rulers who lorded over the town of Kancheepuram, where it comes from. The Kancheepuram silk saris are popularly known as Kanjivaram saris after the old British name for the town '*Congeevaram.*'

Kancheepuram silk saris are popularly known as Kanjivaram saris after the old British name for the town 'Congeevaram.'

The city of Kancheepuram had well-laid out roads, high fortifications and prominent buildings, which attracted visitors from around the world. It was also a great seat of Hindu and Buddhist learning. The renowned Chinese pilgrim and traveller, Xuanzang, who visited Kancheepuram in 640 CE, described it as a large city, 6 miles in circumference and its people were known for their bravery and love for learning. After the Pallavas, the town was ruled by the Cholas, Pandyas, the Vijayanagara Empire, Nawabs of Arcot and finally, the British. While the kingdoms rose and fell, the Kanjivaram silk industry continued to thrive.

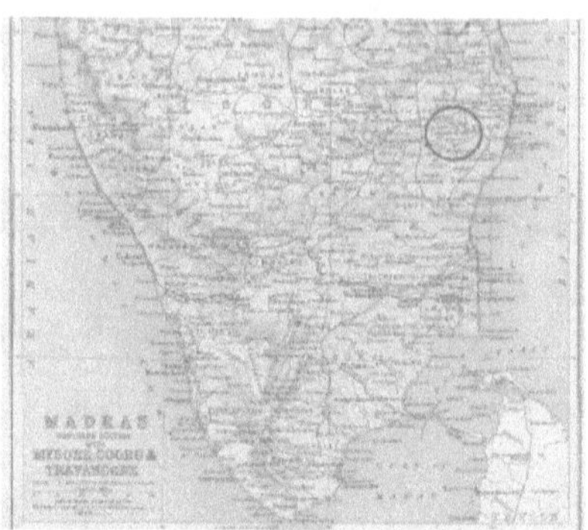

The map showing city of Kancheepuram (Congeevaram) in Madras Presidency|Wikimedia Commons

Like everything else from antiquity, the Kanjivaram silk too has a legend woven around it. It claims that the traditional weavers who have been weaving the Kanjivaram Silk for hundreds of years are descendants of Sage Markanda, the master weaver of the Gods who is supposed to have woven tissue from the lotus fibre. However, the historical facts tell a different story.

Scholars trace the origins of the Kanjivaram silk industry to the patronage of the Chola dynasty, which succeeded the Pallavas. It is believed that Raja Raja Chola I, between 985 CE – 1014 CE, invited a large number of weavers from Saurashtra in Gujarat to settle down in the area and establish looms. However, during this time, it was just a local specialised craft, produced on a small scale.

First Carnatic War |Wikimedia Commons

The transition of Kanjivaram silk from a local craft to a massive thriving industry happened only 500 years later, in the reign of Krishna Deva Raya (1509-1529 CE), the ruler of Vijayanagara Empire. During his reign, the weaving communities of Andhra Pradesh, the Devangas and Saligars, migrated south and settled in different parts of the empire. This second wave of migration of weavers meant that the old silk tradition of Kanchi was infused with new skills, new designs and techniques, taking the industry to new heightsThe transition of Kanjivaram silk from a local craft to a massive thriving industry happened in the reign of Krishna Deva Raya.

The Kanjivaram silk industry thrived for a few hundred years, but a war between two foreign powers almost brought the industry to the brink of extinction. In the 18th century CE, the English and the French fought a series of wars known as the Carnatic wars, for supremacy and control of the Coromandel Coast. In 1757 CE, the city was burnt by the French during the war. This was a big blow to the industry. However, with the British victory, and a period of relative peace, the Kanjivaram silk industry rose again like the proverbial phoenix. It thrives to this day!

Weaving of Kanjivaram silk |WIkimedia Commons

The Kanjivaram silk saris are prepared from pure raw silk known as mulberry silk and are characterised by the heavy use of *zari* in gold and silver. Although the actual weaving takes places at Kancheepuram in Tamil Nadu, the silk for the same comes from Karnataka and the *zari* is brought from Surat in Gujarat.

Kanjivaram Silk as a weaving art has been passed down for generations within the weaving community. The handloom industry suffered a major setback a couple of decades ago when the Indian government tried to encourage power looms instead of the traditional handloom. This led to mass unemployment among the weavers and availability of cheaper copies of Kanjivaram silk in the market.

It was only in 2005 that Kanjivaram silk or Kancheepuram Silk has been recognised under the Geographical Indicator by the government of India. This indicator acknowledges the unique design and traditional weaving method using the traditional technique, weight and other details and means that this silk can only be produced from the town of its origin. Today, more than 30,000 weavers are a part of this thriving industry.

Textile weavers and fabrics of india Bottom of Form

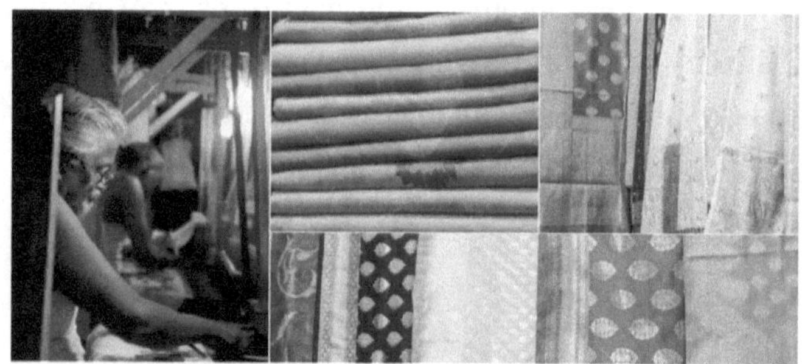

Varanasi - The Sacred Land of Silks

Despite the chaos there is always an air of serenity on the *ghats* of Varanasi (Benaras), there's a sense of being part of a continuum. Of being one of the billions of people who have stood exactly where you have over millennia and wondered about life and death. So, it is ironical that this city of death or salvation, whichever way you look at it, is also home to one of the most opulent extravagances of the world - the spectacular silks that have been woven here for centuries. Over the centuries pilgrim routes and trade routes converged at Varanasi. Bizarre as it may sound the ghats and the silks of Varanasi have a strong connection - they both represent a confluence of roads and travellers who have passed through this city. Over the centuries pilgrim routes and trade routes converged to interweave through the looms of Benaras. Not surprisingly then, that pick any classic Banarasi sari, and you will find influences from all over - Persia, China, South-East Asia and different parts of the Indian subcontinent, as well.

An 1890 CE sketch of the Ghats of Varanasi |Wikimedia Commons

Banarasi cotton finds mention in Buddhist texts dating back to 500-800 CE

Varanasi was a well-known cotton weaving hub during the early Buddhist period. The fineness of the cottons of Varanasi has been mentioned in early texts like the *Mahaparinibbana Sutta*, a Buddhist text, dating back to 500-800 CE. In this work there is mention of how *vihita kappasa* or calendared cloth (calendaring is a process used to make paper or cloth smooth and glossy), from Varanasi was used to cover the mortal remains of an important ruler as it does not absorb oil. *Majjhima Nikaya*, another Buddhist scripture dating back to the 3rd-2nd century BCE, also talks about the fineness of the cotton produced in Varanasi, the skills of the women spinners and weavers and the softness of the water which was considered to be good for bleaching. During this period silk, too, was produced in Varanasi and it is said that Buddha sanctioned the use of *kauseya-pravara* (silken shawls) or *chadar* to the *bhikkhus* or Buddhist monks.

An 1825 CE painting that depicts Kabir weaving|Wikimedia Commons

Even though the usage of silk fabric has been mentioned in Buddhist Texts, it was mainly the cotton industry that flourished during the ancient times. It gained more prominence during the time of Mughal Emperor Akbar (1556-1605 CE) and it is during his time that the influx of Persian motifs, because of the influence of Persian masters in his courts, took place.

Persian motifs gained prominence in the designs during the reign of Mughal Emperor Akbar However, brocade weaving gained prominence with the influx of skilled brocade weavers who migrated from Gujarat in the 17th century CE and enriched the craft with their skills, techniques and designs which, later, got incorporated into the Banarasi silk sari. The influx from Persia and Central Asia led to the evolution of the workmanship that involved the use of *zari* made of gold and silver and the procuring of certain silk material from China and Central Asia to create the weaves we see today.

Persian motifs that were incorporated into Banarasi Silk|Wikimedia Commons

The *Banarasi* silk gained prominence only in the 19th century CE

For a long time, Banarasi silk was used mainly for furnishing fabrics, light turban cloths, yardages and loom-engineered garments and it reached its peak during Shah Jahan's time (1628-1657 CE). However, it was only in the 19th century CE that the quintessential Banarasi silk sari gained prominence. The combination of these influences can further be seen in the motifs of a Banarasi silk sari.

Look at the motifs and you will see how complex and varied the influences have been. In fact, over the centuries weavers here have even developed a hierarchy and system that makes this specialisation possible. Different weaver *gharanas* or houses specialise in different kinds of weaves and they have their own pocket boroughs across the old city.

For instance, the weavers of Mauval Gharana, residing in the northern part of Varanasi, were of Gujarati origin and followed the standard norm of design. The designs mainly comprised corner-paisley (*konia*), diagonally-flowing shrubs (*ari-jhari*) and figure-centric embellishments which are loosely termed as *shikargarh*.

The weavers of Banaraswal Gharana, residing in the central-southern parts of the town were more open to design experimentation thanks mainly to the patronage the gharana received and their Pan-India trade. However, two Mauval nakshabands, or designers belonging to the Mauval Gharana during the 'Empire of India' exhibition in London in 1895 CE, added a new range of designs inspired by European wall-papers which remained in vogue until the 1940s.

Different weaver gharanas or houses specialise in different kinds of weaves

Butidar Sari|Harsunit

The Different Banarasis

The Butidar sari is a quintessential example of the many influences that have worked their way into the Banarasi loom. These saris are marked by gold and silver thread work, showcasing the confluence of the rivers Ganga and Jamuna whose waters are believed to be black and white respectively. The commonly used motifs here include flowers, betel leaves, the moon, and tiny flowers.

Jamdani Sari|Harsunit

The Jamdani, considered to be the finest among the Banarasi silk saris, is a blend of cotton and silk. While the fabric used is silk, cotton threads are woven onto it. The motifs include embroidered Jasmine, emeralds, flowers like the marigold, betel leaves, diagonal stripes and floral mango brocades.

Tanchoi Sari|Harsunit

Tanchoi, another popular variety of Banarasi Silk has an interesting story behind it. It's believed that around 1856 CE three weavers from a Joshi family of Surat were commissioned by Jamsetji Jeejeebhoy, a Parsi Merchant, to travel to China and learn the skill of weaving this particular silk. On returning, they adopted the name of their Chinese Teacher, *Chhoi,* who had taught them the skill of silk weaving. *Tan,* close to the Gujarati word *tran* meaning 'three', referred to the three brothers. Hence, the silk came to be known as Tanchoi. The fabric made its way to India through Gujarat. It got incorporated into the Banarasi silk industry only in the 1950s. In Varanasi, the Tanchoi fabric has paisley motifs all over the sari and is highly inspired by the Jamawar shawls of Kashmir.

Harsunit|Jangla Sari

The Jangla has motifs made of the *muga* silk, an indigenous silk from Assam. The sari has motifs of spread vegetation wherein the flowers and creepers are made of silver and gold threads respectively. The borders have brocades made of *muga* silk and silver *zari*.

Tissue Sari|Harsunit

The Banarasi Tissue sari, often part of wedding trousseau has densely patterned lotuses on it, done with gold *zari*, seen floating in a glimmering pond. The effect of 'drops of water' is created by using the cut-work technique. The borders have a diamond pattern which is enclosed by a running paisley. These motifs were, perhaps, inspired by Buddhism since clouds, lotus flowers and flames as motifs are said to have been made by the weavers of Benaras for Buddhist monasteries earlier.

DID YOU KNOW

The Banarasi brocades have been the most showcased of the Banarasi saris internationally and were, in fact, on display at the Great Exhibition at London in 1851 CE.

At the end of the exhibition, Prince Albert felt the need to keep the momentum going and suggested the creation of a 'District of Museums and Colleges' for the study of arts and sciences in order to promote British manufacturing. This gave birth to the South Kensington School of Art, as well as the Victoria and Albert Museum in London. Meanwhile, it was a visit to the exhibition that inspired Lockwood Kipling, the father of Rudyard Kipling, to pursue a career in the arts and design. Even Sir Jamsetjee Jeejeebhoy decided to establish the Sir JJ School of Arts in the city of Mumbai after seeing the exhibition.

The Great Exhibition may be a distant memory, but it did leave quite a legacy. It inspired Britain to be even more aggressive in its ambitions, it shaped the way India came to be seen and it left behind some lasting institutions.

L H 1: 4

The Mapping of Indian Textiles

More than 150 years ago, a former East India Company surgeon decided to try something new – to create a portable museum on the famed Indian textiles that British mill owners inManchester and Lancashire were desperately trying to copy.

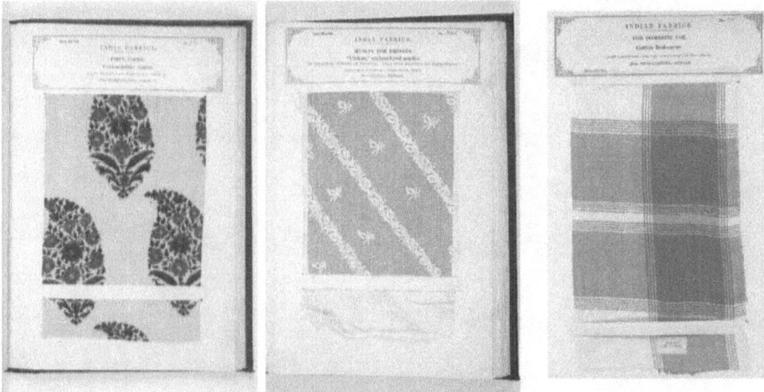

While this documentation was to help the British factories, we do have to thank Sir John Forbes Watson for creating an extraordinary 18-volume catalogue, *Collections of the Textile Manufactures of India* (1866). This work remains a window to many Indian textile traditions that have since died. But then, did this book also sound the death knell of these very weaves?

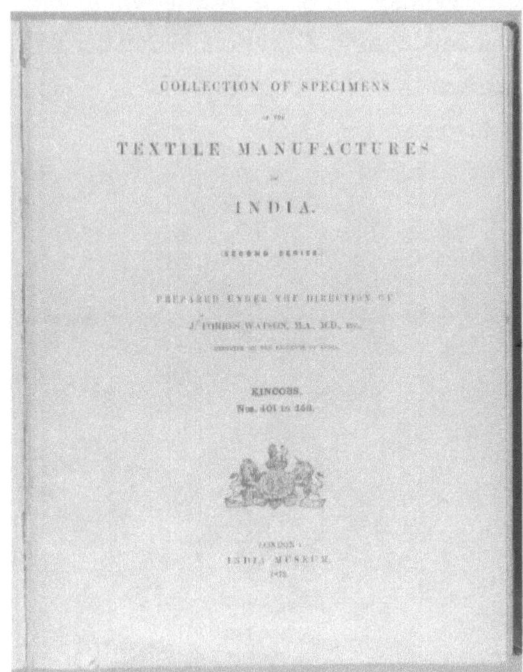

Title page of the book| MET

John Forbes Watson| VandA Museum

As the name suggests, *Collections of the Textile Manufactures of India* was a hard-nosed attempt at cataloguing. It was created under Watson, who was, by then, Director of the then India Museum in London, which later evolved into the famous VandA Museum.

People of India, Kanyang Hill Tribe, Assam | V and A Museum

A major project he undertook was to document the people of India through a photographic series. *The People of India* was published in eight volumes from 1868-75. But Watson was a curious man, and his research interests were varied. He was most interested in botany and the plant life of India. He went on to study various types of cotton in India, which led to further interest in the study of Indian textiles.

The portable museum as envisaged by Watson |V and A Museum

This set the stage for his monumental work – the 18-volume *Collections of the Textile Manufactures of India*, which contained 700 samples of fabrics, published in 1866. This series was accompanied by a companion volume titled *The Textile Manufactures and the Costumes of the People of India,* also published in the same year.

The catalogue contained thorough documentation of Indian fabrics. It contained many technical and practical bits of information, like the use of the fabric, cost of production, material requirements, etc. The volumes were divided on the basis of use, type of fabric and the style of print or embroidery on it. For example, there were volumes on turbans, fabrics for men, fabrics for women, cotton, silks and woollens, and these went into great detail about different fabrics used in different places, locations and people. Having been trained as a doctor and deeply interested in botany, Watson approached the exercise more like a natural historian than a museum curator. As Watson wrote in the companion volume:

The 700 specimens…show what the people of India affect and deem suitable in the way of textile fabrics, and if the supply of these is to come from Britain, they must be imitated there. What is wanted, and what it is to be copied to meet that want, is thus accessible for study in these museums.

Watson didn't include all the fabrics manufactured in India in the catalogue, only those he thought British manufacturers could produce. His work wasn't intended for the scientist or scholar but was for practical use by manufacturers or administrators.

The Paris exhibition of 1855|Wikimedia Commons

The way the catalogue was compiled is a fascinating tale, and almost sacrilegious for a museum expert. Watson wasn't a textile or crafts expert, and his knowledge of textiles itself was rather limited. The India Museum had a large volume of samples of Indian textiles in its collection. Most of these samples had reached the museum through the Paris exhibition of 1855 and some had been acquired through trade. Watson and his assistants cut up the collection to create these books. The information too came from the labels which had already been attached to the fabrics. His role was that of a compiler.

Twenty copies of this great catalogue were created, of which 13 were distributed in England and seven were sent to India. They were sent to the public libraries in the textile manufacturing towns in the United Kingdom like Bradford, Liverpool, Manchester, Edinburgh, and in India like Allahabad, Nagpur, Bombay and Calcutta.Today, one can find some volumes of the book at the Vand A Museum in London, the Metropolitan Museum of Art in New York, the Cooper Hewitt Library of the Smithsonian Museum and the Bhau Daji Lad Museum in Mumbai.

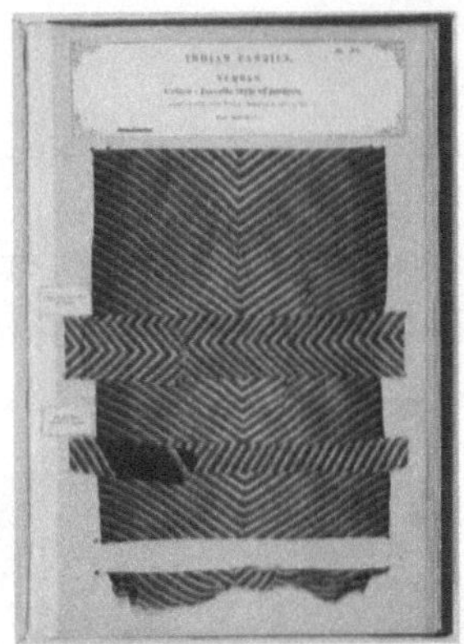

Page from the book|V&A Museum

LHI 5

Costumes of India

Pondicherry

A lovely French bastion lovingly called the 'French quarter.'

Stroll around its seafront promenade caressed by the waves of Bay of Bengal. Here lived Sri Aurobindo who brought to life his ideas of universal harmony.

The Booty from Pondicherry

General Eyre Coote, who ransacked Pondicherry in 1761, brought back to Madras a whole lot of booty. One small part of that loot was to contribute significantly in the years that followed. It was 'a hand-press, types of cases and other equipment.' This was the first printing equipment to reach Madras.

Printing in India started in Goa and the Malabar Coast, faded out and was revived in Danish Tranquebar (Tarangambadi) by the German Priests from Halle in the early 1700s. One of the later Tranquebar missionaries walked all the way to Madras and found himself being made the representative for the Society for Promoting Christian Knowledge, London. The society was unable to send out its own missionaries due to the East India Company not permitting British missionaries to come to India.

The missionary from Tranquebar who settled in Vepery was Johann P. Fabricius, a scholar who soon became fluent in Tamil and Telugu. He requested the

Government of Madras for the equipment that had been found in Governor-General de Lally's' mansion, where it had been lying unused from 1758. Fabricius offered to run the press in Vepery, giving priority to Government work and only then taking up the Mission's. The Government agreed, and so was born the East India Company's Press, aka the Vepery Press.

In time, the two names were to develop as separate units, the former becoming today's Government Press, the latter the SPCK Press, then the Diocesan Press and now, the CLS Press Fabricius. Running schools, translating Christian literature and doing a modicum of missionary work, Fabricius also found time to be a successful manager of the press. In 1766, he expanded the press by acquiring another printing machine from Tranquebar, imported Tamil type castings from Halle and got a Tamil printer named Thomas from Tranquebar.

It was this wing of the Vepery Press that enabled its growth over the years, making it one of the biggest printing presses in South India until the 1960s. The first publication in Tamil from the Vepery Press was a catechism that Fabricius had translated. It was printed in 1766. The first major work of the Press was released six years later, which was Fabricius's revised version of the Malabar (Tamil) New Testament.

In 1799, the Vepery Press issued its greatest publication, the Malabar-English Dictionary. Fabricius and his colleague, Breithaupt, then brought out the second part of this monumental work of theirs in 1786. Today, what survives of the press is its reputation as the oldest surviving printing press in India. Obviously, some good came out of the Carnatic Wars.

"Let the beauty of what you love, be what you do"

– **Rumi -The 13th century author (1207-1273).**

Ajit Koujalgi

The Icon of Indian Heritage Conservation

Nothing perhaps captured Ajit Koujalgi's (Born 1948- Died 2014) commitment to heritage preservation than the story of how this Chief Architect and Co-Convener of the Puducherry chapter of the Indian National Trust for Art and Cultural Heritage (INTACH), saved the Indian Coffee House. When he heard of the plan of the management to demolish the building, he swiftly met Chief Minister N. Rangasamy and convinced him of its iconic stature. Today, the Indian Coffee House on Nehru Street, beautifully restored by Ajit and his team at INTACH, stands for all that is possible in heritage conservation, whether it is streetscapes or landmark buildings. It was thus with much grief and shock that Pondicherry and Auroville heard the news of Koujalgi's passing away at Apollo Hospitals in 2014 in Chennai. Arul, an INTACH architect, said his untimely death amounted to a 'huge loss' to Puducherry. "We will all miss him more than words can express," was the message left by the INTACH staff on a banner at their office on Aurobindo Road.

INTACH has restored several colonial and heritage buildings which have been converted to boutique hotels. Recalling his immense contribution to the restoration of Maison Perumal and Palais De Mahé, Sam John, manager at Maison Perumal, said that Koujalgi's death was a loss for heritage conservationists, and added that Koujalgi was a source of inspiration to all who worked with him.

"In today's trend of building concrete blocks in the name of development, it was not an easy job, but Ajit never gave up." Koujalgi is survived by his wife, Ratna, also an architect.

He graduated from the School of Planning and Architecture, New Delhi in 1970, and had been working at Auroville and Puducherry since 1971. His stint in Europe in the early 1980s exposed him to heritage conservation and was instrumental in his work here. He had been involved with INTACH since 1987. His work gained recognition with the UNESCO Asia Pacific Heritage Award for Culture Heritage Conservation conferred on him and his wife in 2000 for their restoration of Hotel de l'Orient. In 2008, his team won the UNESCO Asia Pacific Heritage Award for Culture Heritage Conservation for the restoration of Vysial Street.

"Ajith championed the cause of heritage conservation. His contribution to conservation of Pondicherry is extraordinary, including Tranquebar (Tharanganbadi). The Maison Perumal and Palais de Mahé, two hotels in Pondicherry are his creations. Also, the Kalari Kovilakom, which is an 18th century palace of the Vengunad Rajas in Kollengode, Kerala, is restored and adapted for use as an Ayurveda Treatment facility. The success of these ventures owes much to the architect Mr. AjitKoujalgi."

– Jose Dominic Chairman CGH Earth Group.

Trade between Western Asia and the West Coast of India took place at least 1000 years before Christ. Hebrew texts refer to the port of Ophir located along this same patch of coast line. Babylonian builders, as far back as the 7th century BC, used Indian teak and cedar.

An anonymous Greek document, written sometime in the 1st century, describes various ports along the coast of India with details about the active Roman trade in South India. British archaeologist Sir Mortimer Wheeler, during an excavation at Arikkamedu near Pondicherry, uncovered a Roman settlement as well as pieces of pottery that had been manufactured near Rome. Pottery made in Tunisia, when it was under Roman control has been uncovered at Ranuswaram. In central Kerala, in 1983, more than 200 gold coins minted in Rome in the 2nd century were discovered by workers digging for clay to make bricks.

Tranquebar

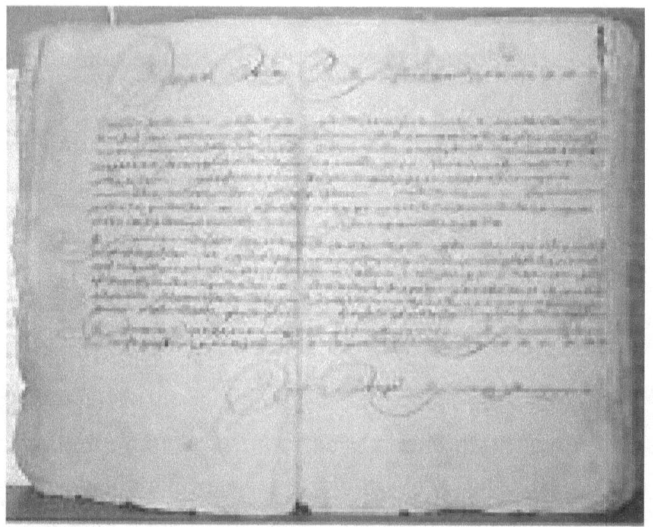

Example of VOC document in Tamil language, 1747

Once a forgotten Dutch seaside trading port, this is now lovingly dusted down to life. Tharangambadi, formerly Tranquebar, is a panchayat town in Nagapattinam district in the Indian state of Tamil Nadu, 15 km north of Karaikal. It is located near the mouth of a tributary of the Kaveri River. Tharangambadi is the headquarters of Tharangambadi taluk. Its name means 'place of the singing waves.' It was a Danish colony from 1620 to 1845, and in Danish, it is still known as Trankebar.

History

The place dates back to the 14th century, where Masilamani Nathar (Shiva) temple was built in 1306, in a land given by Maravarman Kulasekara

Pandyan I. As of now, this temple is the oldest monument. Until 1620, when Danish people came, the place was under Thanjavur Nayak kingdom. Danish admiral Ove Gjedde felt the place would be a potential trading centre, made a deal with Raghunatha Nayak and built a fort, which is known as Fort Dansborg. Nevertheless, a Jesuit Catholic church was already in place before that, catering to the Indo-Portuguese community. The Catholic Church was probably demolished to build the fort. This fort was the residence and headquarters of the governor and other officials for about 150 years, but is now a museum, hosting a collection of artefacts from the colonial era.

Among the first Protestant missionaries to set foot in India were two Lutherans from Germany, Bartholomäus Ziegenbalg and Heinrich Pluetschau, who began work in 1705 in the Danish settlement of Tranquebar. Ziegenbalg translated the Old and New Testaments into Tamil, imported a printing press, and printed the New Testament in Tamil in 1714.

They were forced to teach broken Portuguese, which was the lingua franca between Indians and Europeans at the time, and later on, translated the Bible into the local Tamil language. They also established a printing press, which within a hundred years of its establishment in 1712, had printed 300 books in Tamil. At first, they only made little progress in their religious efforts, but gradually, the mission spread to Madras, Cuddalore and Tanjore. Today, bishop of Tranquebar is the official title of a bishop in the Tamil Evangelical Lutheran Church (TELC) in South India, which was founded in 1919 as a result of the German Lutheran Leipzig Mission and Church of Sweden Mission. The seat of the Bishop, the Cathedral and its Church House (Tranquebar House) is in Tiruchirappalli.

The Zion church was sanctified in 1701, one of the oldest Protestant church in India. In 1718, The New Jerusalem Church was constructed. Moravian Brethren missionaries from Herrnhut, Saxony established the Brethren's Garden at Porayar near Tranquebar and operated it as a missionary centre for a number of years.

An Italian Catholic Father, Constanzo Beschi, who worked in the colony from 1711 to 1740, found himself in conflict with the Lutheran pioneers at Tranquebar, against whom he wrote several polemical works.

Tranquebar came under the control of the British in February 1808 during the Napoleonic Wars in Europe, but was restored to Denmark following the Treaty of Kiel in 1814. Along with the other Danish settlements in India (Serampore and the Nicobars), it was sold to the British in 1845. Tranquebar was then, still a busy port, but later, it lost its importance after a railway was opened to Nagapattinam.

Danish Museum

The antiquities connected with the colonial period, and the Danish settlement at Tharangampadi have been exhibited at the museum which contains porcelain ware, Danish manuscripts, glass objects, Chinese tea jars, steatitle lamps, decorated terracotta objects, figurines, lamps, stones, sculptures, swords, daggers, spears, sudai (stucco) figurines and wooden objects. There is also a part of a whale skeleton and small cannonballs.

Danish Fort

Construction of Fort Dansborg started in 1620. Most parts of the fort have been reconstructed several times. The rampart wall is a fairly large four-sided structure, with bastions at each cardinal point. A single storied building was constructed along three inner sides of the rampart, with barracks, warehouse, kitchen and jail. The rooms on the southern side remain in good condition, but the rooms on the western and northern sides have been substantially damaged. On the eastern side of the fort, there was a two storied building facing the sea. It was the main building of the fort. The vaulted lower storey served as a magazine and a warehouse, while the vaulted upper storey contained the church and the lodging of the governor, the senior merchants and the chaplain. The sea on the eastern and western side protected the fort. The fort was surrounded by a moat, with the access to the fort being over a drawbridge. The moat has completely disappeared.

Fort Dansborg at Tharangambadi built by Danish Admiral, Ove Gjedde in 1620 and partially renovated during 2002 by the Tranquebar Association. View from the governor's bungalow.

Remembering Ziegenbalg

The week ahead will recall the arrival in India, 300 years ago, of Bartholomaeus Ziegenbalg and the significant contribution he and his fellow 'Pietists' made to India and, particularly, to South India. Ziegenbalg, of the Danish Halle Mission to Tranquebar (Tarangambadi), was the first Protestant missionary to arrive in Asia with a mandate for missionary activity. But being a Pietist – one of those 17th century Lutherans who pioneered a search for enlightenment at home and abroad – Ziegenbalg and his successors made a greater success of becoming Tamil scholars. They spread and acquired knowledge, introducing the achievements of the New World to the Old, rather than in the pursuit of strictly focused missionary activities. They were an honoured roll call of German missionaries; Ziegenbalg and Plutschau and Grundler in Tranquebar, Schultze and Gericke, Fabricius and Breithaupt in Madras, Schwartz in Tanjore, Kiernander in Serampore and many others. It was Ziegenbalg who showed them the way.

Quickly becoming a Tamil scholar, he spent as much time translating Tamil wisdom as he did the Old and New Testaments. After printing had died out in India by the end of the 17th century, he reintroduced it in Tranquebar, where he set up a printing press and ink and paper manufacturing units in 1712-14. He offered Europe, insights into such Indian knowledge as Ayurveda, Astronomy and Hindu Philosophy. Looking back on his contribution, printing was, perhaps, the most significant part of it, for it was after those beginnings that Serampore helped Carey, Marshman and Ward to spread the word throughout India and the rest of Asia.

The commemoration of Ziegenbalg's arrival in India will begin on July 2nd with the inauguration at the Raja Muthiah Library, 'Taramani' (near the M.S. Swaminathan Foundation), of a week long pictorial exhibition. This is organised by the Francke Foundation, Halle on Ziegenbalg's life and times. The Foundation, founded in 1698 by a Lutheran theologian and educationist, August Hermann Francke, a contemporary of Ziegenbalg, has today, one of the largest collections of South Indian artefacts in Europe as well as the largest collection of papers on the Mission in Danish Tranquebar, which curiously, was from the Germans.

The formal tercentenary celebrations of Ziegenbalg's arrival will get underway on July 3rd at the Gurukulam Lutheran Theological College, Kelly's. The highlight of the inauguration will be the release of a stamp commemorating Ziegenbalg and the handing over to the Gurukulam of the microfilms of all the Indian written material now held by the Francke Foundation. This material will be of immense value to researchers and those studying such subjects as Tamil, early mission activities in India and South Indian history. The next day, there will be a day-long seminar at the Gurukulam on the Tranquebar Mission's contribution to civil society. Several outstanding scholars are expected to participate in this discussion on the secular contribution by Ziegenbalg and others. On July 5th and 6th the Gurukulam will host a two-day international consultation on the role of Christian missions in the world today. A special jubilee convocation at the Gurukulam on the 7th will be followed by the celebrations moving to Tranquebar. On July 9 2006, the 300th anniversary of Ziegenbalg's arrival in India will be commemorated by a grand Ecumenical Jubilee Thanks giving Service with religious leaders of the major Christian denominations participating.

It has been a curious fact that while Pope, Caldwell, Beschi – whose work was printed at Tranquebar in a nice touch of ecumenism – have all been honoured with status by the Government of Tamil Nadu, Bartholomaeus Ziegenbalg, who first trod the track of Tamil scholarship that was followed by the other Christian scholars from abroad, has been forgotten. I hope the tercentenary of his arrival will see him not only honoured but also lead to greater study of the contributions of the Pietists to India.

"The soul becomes dyed with the colour of its thoughts."

– Marcus Aurelius

Bartholomäus Ziegenbalg monument in Tranquebar

Danish church Tarangampadi Goldsmith Street now restored by INTACH in Tranquebar

100

VEPERY MISSION STATISTICS.—TABLE I.

The following Comparative Table shows the progress of the Vepery, Tanjore, Trichinopoly, Tinnevelly and Telugu Missions.

	Missionaries.			East Indian Catechists.	Native Catechists.	Schoolmasters, &c.	No. of Souls belonging to the Congregation.	No. of Children in Schools.	Catechumens.
	European.	East Indian.	Native.						
1826.									
Vepery M.	2	...	...	...	6	11	389	116	...
Tanjore M.	2	...	...	...	38	46	3,502	863	...
Trichinopoly M.	2	...	...	...	2	1	300	43	...
Tinnevelly M.	...	...	...	...	22	15	4,161	210	...
Total...	6	...	...	...	68	73	8,352	1,232	...
1836.									
Vepery M.	4	...	...	6	8	33	2,293	1,523	...
Tanjore M.	3	1	2	2	33	52	4,263	1,011	...
Trichinopoly M.	1	...	...	...	9	13	835	455	...
Tinnevelly M.	2	...	...	...	26	13	4,352	269	...
Total...	10	1	2	8	76	111	11,743	3,258	...
1846.									
Vepery M.	2	2	2	4	18	52	4,112	1,495	100
Tanjore M.	3	4	...	3	57	73	5,396	1,737	192
Trichinopoly M.	...	1	...	...	3	7	585	396	13
Tinnevelly M.	5	1	...	3	83	53	6,524	2,156	6,839
Total...	10	8	2	10	161	185	16,617	5,784	7,144
1856.									
Vepery M.	2	3	2	1	3	27	1,714	771	38
Tanjore M.	3	3	1	2	1	60	3,044	827	57
Trichinopoly M.	...	2	...	...	1	32	1,252	426	7
Tinnevelly M.	8	3	3	*3	2	138	9,824	2,489	3,674
Telugu M.	...	1	...	2	...	12	361	199	437
Total...	13	12	6	8	7	269	16,195	4,712	4,213

*2 Europeans,

101

VEPERY MISSION STATISTICS.—*Continued.*

	Missionaries.			East Indian Catechists.	Native Catechists.	Schoolmasters, &c.	No. of Souls belonging to the Congregation.	No. of Children in Schools.	Catechumens.
	European.	East Indian.	Native.						
1866.									
Vepery M.	1	2	5	1	4	39	2,724	1,359	44
Tanjore M.	3	2	2	...	4	53	2,920	1,404	62
Trichinopoly M.	1	1	3	...	2	24	1,359	581	11
Tinnevelly M.	3	1	7	...	3	108	11,633	3,574	6,832
Telugu M.	...	2	...	2	...	4	1,498	577	1,353
Total...	8	8	17	3	13	228	20,134	7,495	8,302
1876.									
Vepery M.	2	3	3	1	14	47	3,431	1,099	45
Tanjore M.	3	...	6	...	27	89	3,658	2,710	444
Trichinopoly M.	1	2	2	...	14	28	1,603	1,180	10
Tinnevelly M.	3	2	21	...	67	107	16,977	5,908	5,589
Telugu M.	...	2	...	...	5	1	2,465	810	1,781
Total...	9	9	32	1	127	272	28,134	11,707	7,899
1886.									
Vepery M.	3	1	7	...	5	78	4,079	1,752	80
Tanjore M.	1	...	5	...	4	66	2,723	1,895	125
Trichinopoly M.	2	...	7	...	6	130	2,337	2,634	31
Tinnevelly M.	4	1	21	...	15	169	30,656	8,517	9,922
Telugu M.	3	...	...	...	2	20	4,222	1,128	2,343
Total...	13	2	40	...	32	463	44,017	15,926	12,506
1896.									
Vepery M.	†2	...	16	...	5	113	5,152	2,342	54
Tanjore M.	1	...	5	...	7	110	2,709	2,417	112
Trichinopoly M.	4	...	9	...	8	129	2,691	2,706	20
Tinnevelly M.	4	...	38	...	15	365	30,687	8,528	5,316
Telugu M.	4	...	6	*1	2	132	8,065	2,161	3,548
Total...	15	...	74	1	32	849	49,304	18,154	9,050

* European Layman. † Viz: the Principal, Theological College, and the missionary at Negapatam, which is not now included in this division.

102

VEPERY MISSION STATISTICS.—TABLE II.

The following Comparative Table shows the progress of the various branches of the Vepery Mission.

	Missionaries.			East Indian Catechists.	Native Catechists.	Schoolmasters, &c.	No. of Souls belonging to the Congregation.	No. of Children in Schools.	Catechumens.
	European.	East Indian.	Native.						
1826.									
Vepery	2	...	...	...	5	9	231	94	...
Cuddalore	...	...	...	...	1	2	158	22	...
Total...	2	...	...	...	6	11	389	116	...
1836.									
Vepery	2	...	...	5	5	20	1,605	923	...
Cuddalore	1	...	...	1	1	10	311	473	...
Negapatam	1	...	...	...	1	2	273	97	...
Bangalore	...	...	...	...	1	1	104	30	...
Total...	4	...	...	6	8	33	2,293	1,523	...
1846.									
Vepery	1	...	...	1	2	10	1,599	328	7
Cuddalore	...	...	...	1	2	7	275	166	33
Negapatam	1	...	...	...	3	2	315	91	...
Bangalore	...	...	...	1	...	2	268	52	4
S. Thomé	...	1	...	...	2	5	678	163	36
Chintadripett	...	...	1	...	2	3	143	120	4
Poonamallee	...	1	...	...	3	3	365	77	7
Secunderabad	...	...	1	...	1	5	157	184	2
Chittoor	...	...	...	1	3	7	289	180	6
Sheemoga	...	...	...	...	...	8	23	134	1
Total...	2	2	2	4	18	52	4,112	1,495	100
1856.									
Vepery	...	1	...	1	2	8	459	175	10
Cuddalore	...	1	...	...	...	4	223	72	...
Negapatam	...	1	...	...	...	1	140	63	8
Bangalore	...	...	1	...	...	3	275	64	...
S. Thomé	2	...	...	...	...	2	349	110	20
Secunderabad	...	...	1	...	1	9	268	287	...
Total...	2	3	2	1	3	27	1,714	771	38

103

VEPERY MISSION STATISTICS.—*Continued.*

—	European.	East Indian.	Native.	East Indian Catechists.	Native Catechists.	Schoolmasters, &c.	No. of Souls belonging to the Congregation.	No. of Children in Schools.	Catechumens.
1866.									
Vepery	...	...	...	1	1	1	2	722	444	7
Cuddalore	...	...	...	1	...	1	4	216	97	9
Negapatam	...	...	1	...	...	..	8	185	177	3
Bangalore	...	...	...	1	...	..	2	318	56	2
S. Thomé	...	...	...	1	...	..	7	456	206	5
S. John's	...	...	...	1	...	...	3	236	85	7
Poonamallee	...	...	...	...	...	2	...	363	56	1
Secunderabad	...	...	1	...	...	...	11	228	226	10
Sullivan's Gardens Seminary	1	...	...	...	...	2	...	18	...
Total...	1	2	5	1	4	39	2,724	1,359	44
1876.									
Vepery	...	...	1	...	1	...	2	813	85	5
Cuddalore	...	1	...	...	...	3	7	228	94	6
Negapatam	...	...	1	...	...	1	1	385	23	...
Bangalore	...	...	...	1	...	3	1	617	120	17
S. Thomé	...	...	...	1	...	2	6	417	186	...
S. John's	...	...	1	...	...	1	2	354	53	...
Secunderabad	...	...	...	1	...	3	7	574	162	12
Hosur	...	...	...	...	...	1	...	43	...	5
Sullivan's Gardens Seminary	1	...	...	...	...	4	...	17	...
Vepery A.-V. Schl.	...	...	...	...	...	17	...	359	...
Total...	2	3	3	1	14	47	3,431	1,099	45
1886.									
Vepery	1	...	1	...	1	13	882	295	5
Cuddalore	...	...	1	...	...	13	328	203	34
Negapatam	1	...	1	...	1	4	307	57	...
Bangalore & Hosur	...	...	1	...	1	9	556	240	19
Carried over...	2	...	4	...	3	39	2,073	795	58

104

VEPERY MISSION STATISTICS.—*Continued.*

—	European.	East Indian.	Native.	East Indian Catechists.	Native Catechists.	Schoolmasters, &c.	No. of Souls belonging to the Congregation.	No. of Children in Schools.	Catechumens.
Brought over.	2	...	4	...	3	39	2,073	795	58
S. Thomé	...	1	1	...	2	9	513	167	11
S. John's	...	...	1	...	...	3	577	70	...
Secunderabad	...	...	1	...	...	8	916	190	11
Theological College	1	...	...	...	...	1	...	25	...
Vepery High Schl.	...	...	...	...	...	18	...	445	...
Cuddalore A.-V. School	...	...	...	...	...	...	...	60	...
Total...	3	1	7	...	5	78	4,079	1,752	80
1896.									
Vepery	...	...	1	...	1	12	939	326	5
Cuddalore	...	...	3	...	1	12	416	304	19
Negapatam	1	...	1	...	...	6	474	108	1
Bangalore	...	...	1	...	1	5	917	83	13
S. Thomé	...	...	2	...	...	8	442	162	...
S. John's	...	...	7	...	...	8	467	159	...
Secunderabad	...	...	1	...	1	11	496	193	...
Hosur	...	...	...	...	...	5	34	109	1
Chudderghaut	...	...	1	...	...	5	221	50	3
Bolarum	...	...	1	...	...	8	144	156	...
Coimbatore	...	...	1	...	1	5	288	82	6
Bellary	...	...	1	...	...	2	314	40	6
Theological College	1	...	1	...	...	...	...	13	...
Sullivan's Gardens School	...	...	...	...	...	4	...	105	...
Vepery High Schl.	...	...	1	...	...	16	...	356	...
Cuddalore L. S. School	...	...	...	...	...	6	...	96	...
Total...	2	...	16	...	5	113	5,152	2,842	54

Tranquebar, About 1600

The German View of Olde Madras

During the Aaron Endowment Lecture delivered by Dr. C.S. Mohanavelu of Presidency College at Ziegenbalg Auditorium of the Gurukul Lutheran

Theological College and Research Institute in Kelly's, a birds' eye view of 'Madras in Olden Times' was presented.

Aaron, born in a Saivite family in Cuddalore in 1698, was named Arumugam by his father, Chokkanatha Pillai, a well-to-do merchant. When the Tranquebar Lutheran Mission, the first Protestant mission in India, established in front of his house, Arumugam was on his way to becoming Aaron. He was one of the first students of the school and learnt from Tamil books printed in Tranquebar – the educational texts printed in the country. In 1718, he went to Tranquebar to be baptised by Bartholomaeus Ziegenbalg, who had pioneered Protestant missionary activity in India. On December 28th 1733, he was ordained a minister at the New Jerusalem Church there. A German newspaper report describes the Rev. Aaron as 'the first coloured Protestant pastor in whole world.'

The Erudite Rev Sundar Clarke, C.S.I.'s Bishop Madras in the 1980s, is descended from one of the daughters of Rev. Aaron. Her son, John Devasahayam, was the first South Indian to be ordained into the Anglican Church. Since that ordination in November 2, 1830, there has been six successive generations of the Devasahayam family who have served as Anglican Church pastors. Yet, when their ancestor, the Rev. Aaron was trying to persuade the Tranquebar Mission to ordain more Indian members of the church as priests in the early 18th century, it was a suggestion discouraged by a writer whose writings were recalled that afternoon.

Whether it was the Rev. Benjamin Schultze's differences of opinion with the other missionaries at Tranquebar or whether it was at their request, Schultze, who, in 1719, had arrived in Tranquebar, came to Madras in 1728 and served as the first Protestant missionary there. He established the first Protestant missionary church in the town about where the Reserve Bank of India building now is, and preached and taught there until he left the Coromandel in 1743. Fluent in Tamil, Telugu, Sanskrit and Hindustani, he kept a diary in Telugu. Based on the diary, he wrote a book, Madras — or Fort St George in German, which was published by the Mission's headquarters in Halle around 1752. It was later translated into English, and is the source of the first part of Dr. Mohanavelu's lecture.

The second part features the contribution of the scholarly Dr. Johann Peter Rottler, who arrived in Madras in 1803 after 27 years in Tranquebar. He was to head the Madras Mission in Vepery for the next 33 years and die in Harness, aged 87. A crusader for the poor of Vepery, he was also a dedicated teacher. His Tamil translation of the English Liturgy was bought by the College of Fort St. George and published in three parts between 1834 and 1841.

The third of the Germans to be quoted in the lecture will be Karl Graul. I'd never heard of him before, but what I've been able to learn of him is that during a three-year stay in Tranquebar, he collected several Tamil manuscripts and books, took a great deal of interest in the different kinds of thalis of South India and wrote books on Tamil grammar, culture and language. How he and his predecessors saw Olde Madras is something I'm looking forward to understand and research.

Courtesy Madras Miscellany S. Muthiah

East India Company

The British imperial history is a story of contradiction. Discovery and progress, prejudice and the oppression, we have to build upon strong foundations which lay scatted in many parts of India. Once we are free, today, we are globally connected worlds and emerged as a sizeble contributer to the new world.

The last day of the sixteenth century, the British East India Company was awarded the coveted royal charter from Queen Elizabeth to trade in the East Indies, especially India, which was then dominated by the Dutch and the Portuguese. The Company wanted the patronage of the British sovereign to facilitate their business plans of importing spices, cotton and other raw materials from the Indian subcontinent, in exchange for textiles, steel and industrial products churned out by their factories in London, Manchester and Leeds.

The East India Company, originally chartered as the Governor and Company of Merchants of London trading into the East Indies, and more properly called the Honourable East India Company.

Founder: John Watts

Founded: December 31, 1600

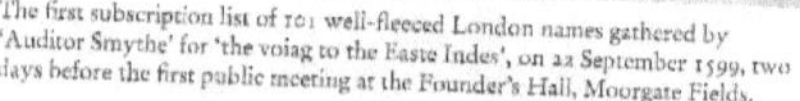

Sir Thomas 'Auditor' Smythe, the founder of the East India Company, in 1616.

Sir James Lancaster, who commanded the Company's first voyage in 1601, shown five years earlier, on his return from his first disastrous journey east.

Sir Thomas Roe, the ambassador of James I who led Britain's first official diplomatic mission to India in 1615.

The first subscription list of 101 well-fleeced London names gathered by 'Auditor Smythe' for 'the voiag to the Easte Indes', on 22 September 1599, two days before the first public meeting at the Founder's Hall, Moorgate Fields.

"We shape our buildings; thereafter, they shape us."

– Winston Churchill

In August 1765, the East India Company defeated the young Mugal Emperor and forced to establish in his richest provinces a new administartion run by English Merchants who collected taxed through means of a ruthless private army what we would now call an act of involunatary privatisation.

William Dalrymple tells the remarkable storty of how one of the the world's magnificient empires disintergrated and came to be replaced by a dangerously unregulated private company based thousands of miles overseas in one small, five window wide building and answerable only to its distant shareholders in his book *The Anarchy*.

The most importang people associated with the Rise and fall as the tides of changes took its foundations in the new age.

British

Robert Clive 1725 -1774

Warren Hastings 1732-1818

Philip Francis 1740- 1818

Charles Cornwallis.1st Marquess Cornwallis 1738-1805

Richard Colley Wellesley, 1st Marquess Wellesley 1760 – 1842

Colonel Arthur Wellesley 1769 -1852

Gerald 1st Viscount Lake 1744-1808

Edward Clive, Ist Earl of Powis 1754- 1839

French

Joseph – Franciscois Dupleix 1697-1764

Micheal Joachim Maria Raymond 1755-1798

General Pierre Culler – Perron 1755- 1834

Mughals

Alamgir Aurangazeb 1618-1707

Muhammed shah Rangila 1702-1748

Ghazi ud-Din Khan Imad ul-Mulk 1736-1800

Alangir II 1699-1759

Shah Alam 1728-1806

Nawabs

Aliverdi Khan, Nawab of Bengal 1671-1756

Siraj ud-Daula.Nawab of Bengal 1733-1757

Mir Jafar.Nawab of Bebgal 1691- 1765

Mir Quasim,Nawab of Bengal - died 1763

Shuja ud Daula,Nawab of Avadh 1732- 1774

The Rohillas

Najib Khan Yusufazai.Najib ul Daula Died 1770

Zabaita Khan Rohilla Died 1785

Ghulam Quadir Khan Rohilla 1765- 1787

The Sulthans of Mysore

Haider Ali –Died 1782

Tipu Sulthan – 1750 -1799

The Marathas

Chhatrapathi Shivaji Bhonsale Died 1680

Nanan Phadnavis 1742 -1800

Tukoji Holkar 1723- 1771

Mahadji Scindia 1730- 1794

Peshwa Baji Rao 1775- 1851

Daulat Rao Scindia 1779- 1827

Jaswant Rao Holkar 1776-1821

EAST INDIA COMPANY ™

New East India House, the East India Company headquarters in London's Leadenhall Street, after its early eighteenth-century Palladian facelift. A Portuguese traveller noted in 1731 that it was 'lately magnificently built, with a stone front to the street; but the front being very narrow, does not make an appearance in any way answerable to the grandeur of the house within'. Like so much about the power of the East India Company, the modest appearance of East India House was deeply deceptive.

Headquarters of the Dutch East India Company at Hughli by Hendrik van Schuylenburgh, 1665.

Fort William, Calcutta, by George Lambert and Samuel Scott, 1731.

Jahangir as the Millennial Sultan Preferring the Company of Sufis, by Bichitr. Jahangir is sitting enthroned with the halo of majesty glowing so brightly behind him that one of the putti has to shield his eyes from its radiance; another pair of putti are writing a banner reading 'Allah o Akbar! Oh king, may your age endure a thousand years!' The Emperor turns to hand a Quran to a sufi, spurning the outstretched hands of the Ottoman Sultan, James I, meanwhile, is relegated to the bottom corner of the frame, below Jahangir's feet, and only just above Bichitr's own self-portrait. The King shown in a three-quarter profile – an angle reserved in Mughal miniatures for the minor characters – with a look of slingary sullenment on his face at his lowly place in the Mughal hierarchy.

East India Company ships at Deptford, 1660.

East India Co is back, with Indian owner

The East India Company, now owned by Indian Origin Entrepreneur Sanjeev Mehta, has created a limited edition 24-carat Gold and silver Coin to Mark the Diamond Jubilee of queen Elizabeth's reign in 2012.

The company, which was granted the royal charter in 1600 and went on to rule India until the second half of the nineteenth century, is producing 60 pure gold and 60 pure silver coins to mark the queen's 60 years in office.

The gold coin weights a kilo and costs 1, 25,000 pounds. It is encrusted with over 100 diamonds.

It features a portrait of the current queen, with her tiara, necklace and brooch highlighted with two carat diamonds.

Mumbai-origin Mehta, 50 acquired the company in 2005, and has since opened a store off Régent Street, which reminds many of the Company Bahadur's heritages. Its coat of arms hangs on the wall while ancient Indian coins are placed across sales counters.

Launching gold and silver coins he said, "The Company has been known in the precious metal trade since 1800. It was and still is the only corporate in history to mint its own trading currency. It made sense to commission our own silver and gold coins in this day and age."

The 10cm coin fits into the palm of the hand and is made from pure gold, containing no trace of any other metal. Each one represents over 1,000 hours of craftsmanship.

Over 400 years after it was first established, the East India Company has relaunched in a new avatar – a luxury goods brand. At its peak, the company was responsible for 50% of global trade, employed a third of the British workforce and ruled much of India. Now, the brand will sell luxury gift sets, teas, coffees, jams and other goods inspired by the East India Company's history through its new e-commerce website. The site, and the company's flagship store in London, was launched on Independence Day. Mumbai-born owner Sanjiv Mehta, 48 says he is just a trustee of a brand that he is taking through the next stage of its history. "The winds are blowing eastwards, and I see the East India Company as a brand tomorrow's India can build upon," he says.

EMKE Group Chaired by M. A Yosufali from Kerala Acquires Major Stake in EIC.

A South Indian's Hand on East India Company

In 2014 October EMKE Group managing director M. A. Yusuffali has acquired a significant stake in London-based East India Company (EIC), the biggest multinational trading company operated in the world at one time.

The formalities of the acquisition are expected to be finalised in London this week. Yusuffali is expected to acquire around 10 per cent stake in the parent company, and around 40 per cent stake in East India Fine Foods Company.

"The East India Company will start operations in many more countries. Currently, the company's products include very fine quality and up market tea, coffee, chocolates, biscuits and such products, which are retailed both online and at up market locations in London. The stake in the company was acquired from its English owners, and the current chairman Sanjiv Mehta," the statement further said.

The Abu Dhabi-headquartered EMKE Group owns the Lulu Hypermarket chain in the Middle East. With an annual turnover of $6.5 billion globally, the Group employs the largest number of Indians outside India.

A journey into the founding of British Empire in India

Fort William, Calcutta

"After the Nawab of Bengal took Calcutta in 1755 and was then defeated by Clive, a new Fort William was begun by the Company's chief engineer, Captain John Bohier, in Bengal. On an island site by the river, unencumbered by buildings, Fort William's field survives as the maiden, emulated at Bombay."

COLONIAL LEGACY

The East India Company (EIC), originally chartered as the 'Governor and Company of Merchants of London trading into the East Indies', and more properly called the Honourable East India Company, was an English, and later (from 1707) British joint-stock company. It was formed to pursue trade with the East Indies but it ended up trading mainly with the Indian subcontinent, Qing Dynasty China, North-West Frontier Province and Baluchistan. The company rose to account for half of the world's trade, particularly trade in basic commodities that included cotton, silk, indigo dye, salt, salt, pepper, tea and opium. The company also ruled the beginnings of the British Empire in India.

The company received a Royal Charter from Queen Elizabeth in 1600, making it the oldest among several similarly formed European East India Companies. Wealthy merchants and aristocrats owned the company's shares. The government owned no shares and had only indirect control. The company eventually came to rule large areas of India with its own private armies, exercising military power and assuming administrative functions. Company rule in India effectively began in 1757 after the Battle of Plassey and lasted until 1858 when, following the Indian Rebellion of 1857, the 'Government of India Act (GOI) 1858' led the British Crown to assume direct control of India in the new British Raj.

The company was dissolved in 1874 as a result of the East India Stock Dividend Redemption Act passed one year earlier since the GOI Act had by then rendered it vestigial, powerless and obsolete. The official government machinery of British India had assumed its governmental functions and absorbed its presidency armies.

Soon after the defeat of the Spanish Armada in 1588, London merchants presented a petition to Queen Elizabeth I for permission to sail to the Indian Ocean. The permission was granted, and on 10 April 1591, three ships sailed from Torbay England, around the Cape of Good Hope to the Arabian Sea on one of the earliest English overseas Indian expeditions. One of them, the Edward Bonventure, then sailed around Cape Comorin and on to the Malay Peninsula, and subsequently, returned to England in 1594.

In 1596, three more ships sailed east, which were all lost at sea. On 24 September 1598, another group of merchants, having raised £30,133 in capital, met in London to form a corporation. Although their first attempt was not completely successful, they, nonetheless, sought the Queen's unofficial approval, bought ships for their venture, increased their capital to £68,373 and convened again a year later.

This time, they succeeded, and on 31 December 1600, the Queen granted a Royal Charter to "George, Earl of Cumberland, and 215 Knights, Aldermen and Burgesses" under the name – Governor and Company of Merchants of London trading with the East Indies. For a period of 15 years, the charter awarded the newly-formed company a monopoly on trade, with all countries east of the Cape of Good Hope and west of the Straits of Magellan.

"Chance can be beautiful when we are brave enough to evolve with it, and change can be Brutal when we fearfully resist it."

– Bryant McGill

The Voyages of James Lancaster

The seed from which grew the most extensive empire the world has ever seen was sown on Pulo Run in the Banda Islands at the eastern end of the Indonesian archipelago. As the island of Runnymcde is to British constitutional history, so the island of Run is to British imperial history.

How in 1603 Run's first English visitors ever lit upon such an absurdly remote destination is cause for wonder. To locate the island a map of no ordinary dimensions is needed. For to show Pulo Run at anything like scale and also include, say, Darwin and Jakarta means together a sheet of room size - and still Run is just an elongated speck. On the ground, it measures two miles by half a mile, takes an hour to walk round and a day for a really exhaustive exploration. This reveals a modest population, no buildings of note and no source of fresh water. There are, although, a lot of trees among which the botanist will recognise *Myristica fragans* Dark of foliage, willow-sized and carefully tended. It is more commonly known as the nutmeg tree.

For the nutmegs (i.e. the kernels inside the stones of the tree's peach-like fruit) and for the mace (the membrane which surrounds the stone) those first visitors, in 1603, would willingly have sailed round the world several times. Nowhere else on the globe did the trees flourish, and so, nowhere else was their fruit so cheap. In the minuscule Banda Islands of Run, Ai, Lonthor and Neira, ten pounds of nutmeg cost less than half a penny, and ten pounds of mace less than five pence. Yet, in Europe, the same quantities could be sold for respectively £1.60 and - £16, a tidy appreciation of approximately 32,000 per cent.

Not without pride would James I come to be styled 'King of England, Scotland, Ireland, France, Puloway [Pulo Ai] and Puloroon [Pulo Run].' The last named, thought one of its visitors, and could be as valuable to His Majesty as Scotland.

True, the island never quite lived up to expectations. Indeed, it would become a fraught and expensive liability. But as it happened, the importance of Run for the East India Company and so for the British Empire lay not in its scented groves of nutmeg but in one particular nutmeg seedling.

A peculiarity of the Banda islands at the beginning of the seventeenth century was that thanks to their isolation, they owed allegiance to no one. Moreover, the Bandanese recognised no supreme sultan of their own authority. Instead, authority rested with village councils presided over by *orang kaya* or headmen. In the best tradition of south-east Asian *adat* (consensus), each village or island was, in fact, a self-governing and fairly democratic republic. They could withhold or dispose of their sovereignty as they saw fit; and whereas, the inhabitants of neighbouring Neira and Lonthor had already been bullied into accepting a large measure of Dutch control, those of outlying Ai and Run had managed to preserve their independence intact.

By 1616, Run and Ai valued their contacts with the English, and when menaced by the Dutch, voted to pledge their allegiance to the men who flew the cross of St George. They did this by swearing an oath and by presenting their new suzerains with a nutmeg seedling rooted in a ball of Run's yellowish soil. As well as the symbolism, it was an act of profound trust. Seedlings were closely guarded and destroyed rather than surrendered. Who knew what effect the naturalisation elsewhere of a misappropriated seedling might have on the Bandanese monopoly?

The recipients of this gratifying presentation were, like all the other doubleted Englishmen who had so far reached Run, employees of the East India Company. But therein lay a problem. For in this, its infancy, the Company was not empowered to hold overseas territories. Its royal charter made no mention of them, only of trading rights and maritime conduct. It was, therefore, on behalf of the Crown that Run's allegiance had to be accepted. And when, after an epic blockade of the island lasting four years, the Company would eventually decide that it had had enough of Run, it was in fact the British sovereign who stood out in favour of his exotic windfall and of his Bandanese subjects.

Even Oliver Cromwell was to have a soft spot for Run, and at his instigation arrangements, would be made for reestablishing a permanent colony there. Solid Presbyterian settlers were recruited; goats, hens, hoes and psalters were piled aboard the good ship, *London;* and it was only at the very last minute that renewed hostilities with the Dutch led to the ship being redirected to St Helena in the South Atlantic. More important, although, it was with Run in mind that the Protector issued the Company with a new charter which included the authority to hold, fortify and settle overseas territories. Thanks to the *orang kaya* of Run, first St Helena, soon after Bombay, then Calcutta, Bengal, India and the East would come under British sway.

But there, Run's celebrity would end. Ironically, it was in the same year that the East India Company took over Bombay that Charles II relinquished his rights to Run. Sixty years of Dutch pressure had finally paid off. By the treaty of Breda, the British Crown would cede all rights in the Bandas, receiving by way of compensation a place on the North American seaboard called New Amsterdam together with its own spice-less island of Manhattan. It may have seemed like a good swap, but the little nutmeg of Run had arguably more relevance to future empire than did the Big Apple.

Of those first Elizabethan Englishmen, who in 1603, trooped, sea weary and surf soaked, on to Run's scorching sands we know only from the protest registered by a Dutch admiral who happened to be on the Banda island of Neira at the time. The Dutch had reached the Bandas two years earlier and, but for their sensational success there and elsewhere in the East Indies, it must be doubtful whether London's merchants would ever have entered the 'spice race' or subscribed to an East India Company. But then, the Dutch were only emulating the Portuguese who had been trading with the Indies for nearly a century; and although it was the Portuguese who had discovered the sea route round the Cape of Good Hope, even they had not invented the spice trade. Since, at least Roman times, the traffic in exotic condiments from east to west had sustained the most extensive and profitable trading network the world had yet seen. The buds of the dainty clove tree, the berries of the ivy-like pepper vine, and of course, the kernel and membrane of the nutmeg had been ideal cargoes. Dried, husked and bagged, they were light in weight, high in value and easily broken into loads. Shipped to the Asian mainland in junks, *prahus* and dhows, they were repacked as camel and donkey loads for the long overland journey to the Levant, and then, reshipped across the Mediterranean to the European markets.

In the process, their value appreciated phenomenally. What were basic culinary ingredients in south Asia had become exotic luxuries by the time they reached the Mediterranean and the Atlantic. They were the precious metals of the vegetable kingdom, and their pungency seemed to enhance their rarity by conferring a whiff of distinction on every household that could afford them. In brines and marinades, nutmeg proved a vital preservative; in stews and ragouts, pepper masked the smell of ill-cured meat and improved its flavour; and the clove, as well as its culinary uses, was credited with amazing medicinal properties. Like later, tea, coffee and even tobacco, it was as expensive health foods that spices gradually entered everyday diet. As the supply increased, the merchants' profit margins would fall, but in the sixteenth century, it was still calculated that if only one-sixth of a cargo reached its destination, its owner would still be in profit.

Control of this lucrative trade rested traditionally with the Chinese and Malays in the East, with the Indians and Arabs in its middle reaches, and with the Levantines and Venetians in the West. But around the year 1500, other interested parties had appeared on the scene. It was to reroute the spice trade to the greater advantage of Christendom and their own considerable profit that European seafarers from Spain and Portugal first ventured on to the world's oceans. Improvements in marine design, in navigational instruments, cartography and gunnery soon gave the newcomers an edge over their Asian rivals. They could sail further, faster and for longer. They had less need to hug the coastline and, since the spice-producing islands lay on the opposite side of the world, they had a choice of sailing east or west.

But what their charts failed to show was that there were other lands lay in the way. Hence, the search for the Spice Islands threw up the discovery of America, of the Pacific archipelagos, of sub-Saharan Africa, and of the Indian and south-east Asian coastlines. Knowledge of, and eventually, dominion over these "new worlds" would follow. Yet, such incidental discoveries could not immediately deflect the European parvenus from their main objective. Trade, not conquest or colonisation, was the priority. In 1511, only 23 years after first rounding the Cape of Good Hope, the Portuguese had readied Java; and in 1543, 23 years after discovering the Magellan strait near Cape Horn, a Spanish fleet from Mexico had laid claim to the islands soon christened the Philippines. Somewhere in the gap remaining between these two global pincer movements lay the Spice Islands.

The perversity of nature in lavishing her most valued products on islands so small and impossibly remote prompted wonder and fable. To what Milton called the 'islands of spicerie' an air of mystery clung. When Christopher Columbus had cast about for a sponsor for his projected voyage over the western horizon, he made much of the idea that if he did not find the spice-rich Indies he had a good chance of finding the lost continent of Atlantis. Neither was a geographical certainty; both owed much to the imagination.

Even today, with better and more comprehensive maps, it is hard to put a finger on the exact spot. 'Spice Islands' was as much a description as a proper name, and mostly, it was reserved for islands which had no other claim on the map-maker's attention. Thus, somewhere as important as Sri Lanka, although always the main producer of cinnamon bark did not qualify and neither did the main pepper-producing areas of Sumatra and of India's Malabar Coast.

The real Spice Islands were less obvious and more mysterious, and lay much further to the east between Sulawesi (Celebes), New Guinea and the Philippines. This, the Moluccan triangle, is also the epicentre of Indonesia's volcanic 'Ring of Fire.' On average, there is an eruption every five years, and deposits of volcanic soil are as crucial to the location of spice groves as the humid sea-breezes. In seventeenth century drawings, Tidore and Ternate, the main clove-producing islands, figure as smoking volcanoes rising sheer from the ocean, the only vocation being a fringe of coconut palms at their base. Horticulrurally, they look most unpromising. Yet this *is,* in fact, a fairly accurate depiction. The cones rise a mile into the sky, and only the narrowest of margins between the encircling ocean and the funnel of fire is available for clove gardens. Likewise, the Banda Islands are dominated by the great central volcano of Gunung Api which periodically showers the nutmeg groves with rich volcanic dust. If the production of spices required such an elemental setting, it was no wonder they were a rarity.

The first spice race, won by the Portuguese, was confirmed by the terms of a Papal bull which drew a sort of international date-line between the advancing fleets of Spain and Portugal. With a chain of heavily fortified bases stretching from Hormuz in the Persian Gulf to Goa in India, then Malacca near the modern Singapore, and finally, Ambon in the central Moluccas, the Portuguese made good their claim to control of the entire spice route. Barring occasional interference from the Spanish in the Philippines, they enjoyed as near a monopoly of the oceanic spice trade as they cared to enforce for most of the sixteenth century.

Other European rivals simply failed to materialise. As yet, the Dutch were still enduring the birth pangs of nationhood; and the English, who with the loss of Calais and the break with Rome, were, at last, looking away from Europe, were nevertheless looking in the wrong direction. Observing how, although the Portuguese sailed into the sunrise and the Spanish into the sunset, both had successfully found two paths to the Spice Islands, Englishmen had concluded that they too could expect to discover their own corridor to the East. The fact that that same Papal bull gave the Iberian powers a monopoly over their respective routes which might be enforced by any available means, was also good reason for Tudor seafarers to find their own route. Like their Spanish and Portuguese rivals, the English were familiar with the latest advances in marine technology and were dimly aware that being located on the European periphery should no longer be a disadvantage. In what was to be the age of the Atlantic powers, the English were not behindhand; only five years after Columbus, John Cabot, in an English vessel, had been the first to reach the American mainland. But they were unlucky. Portuguese endeavour had been handsomely rewarded by the discovery of a 'south-east passage' round the Cape of Good Hope; thereafter, the Indies had been plain sailing. Similarly, a 'south-west passage' round the Horn had awaited the Spanish. But where were their northern equivalents?

Throughout the second half of the sixteenth century English ships determinedly pushed up into the Arctic Circle. In the north-west, Frobishcr and Davis probed the sounds and channels of Canada's frozen north; none turned out to be a Magellan strait. Earlier Willoughby and Chancellor, in search of a north-east passage, had rounded Norway's North Cape and entered the Barents Sea. Novaya Zemlya was no place of balmy refreshment like Madagascar, but in an age when men still welcomed some medieval symmetry in their maps, the Norwegian cape showed a happy longitudinal correspondence to that of southern Africa.

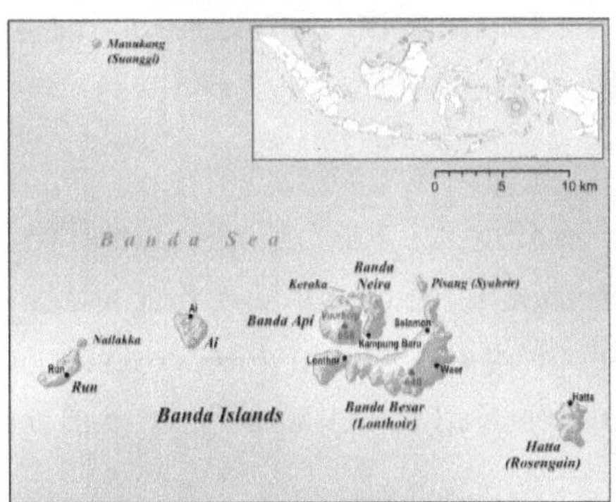

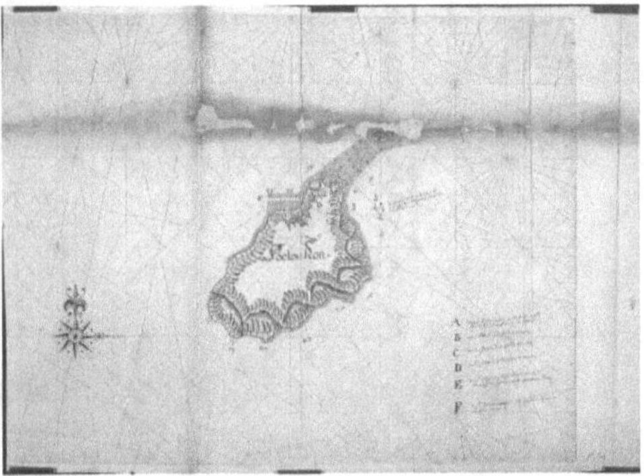

Map of Run Island Dated 1623

Run (island)

Run (also known as Pulau Run, Pulo Run, Puloroon, or Rhun) is one of the smallest islands of the Banda Islands, which are a part of Moluccas, Indonesia. It is about three kilometres (1.9 mi) long and less than one kilometre (0.62 mi) wide. According to historian John Keay, Run is comparable in its significance in the history of the English overseas possessions as Runnymede is to British constitutional history.

In the 17th century, Run was of great economic importance because of the value of the spices nutmeg and mace, which are obtained from the nutmeg tree

(Myristica fragrans), once found exclusively in the Banda Islands of which Run is one.https://en.wikipedia.org/wiki/Run_(island) - cite_note-nafta-3

During the history of the spice trade, sailors of the English East India Company of the second expedition of James Lancaster, John Davis, Sir Henry Middleton and his brother, John who stayed in Bantam on Java, first reached the island in 1603 and developed good contacts with the inhabitants.

On December 25 1616, Captain Nathaniel Courthope and 1st mate Zachary Barnett Duncan reached Run to defend it against the claims of the Dutch East India Company. A contract with the inhabitants was signed, accepting James I of England as sovereign of the island. After four years of siege by the Dutch and the death of Nathaniel Courthope in an attack in 1620, the English and their local allies departed the island with the exception of 1st mate Zachary Barnett Duncan as he fell in love with a local and was to be wed.

According to the Treaty of Westminster ending the First Anglo-Dutch War of 1652–1654, Run should have been returned to England. The first attempt in 1660 failed because of formal constraints by the Dutch. After the second attempt in 1665, the English traders were expelled in the same year, and the Dutch destroyed the nutmeg trees.

After the Second Anglo-Dutch War of 1665–1667, England and the United Provinces of the Netherlands agreed in the Treaty of Breda to the status quo. The English kept the island of Manhattan, which the Duke of York (the future James II, brother of Charles II), had occupied in 1664, renaming the city on that island from New Amsterdam to New York. In return, Run was formally abandoned to the Dutch. The Dutch monopoly on nutmeg and mace was destroyed by the transfer of nutmeg trees to Ceylon, Grenada, Singapore and other British colonies in 1817, after the capture of the main island, Bandalontor, in 1810 by Captain Cole, leading to the decline of the Dutch supremacy in the spice trade. There are, however, nutmeg still trees growing on Run today.

The First Britisher to Sail to India

Sir James Lancaster commanded the first East India Company voyage; and Sir Henry Middleton commandeered the second voyage in March 1604.

Initially, the company struggled in the spice trade due to the competition from the already well-established Dutch East India Company. The company opened a factory in Bantamonon its first voyage. Pepper imports from Java were an important part of the company's trade for 20 years. The factory in Bantam was closed in 1683. During this time, ships belonging to the company arriving in India, docked at Surat, which was established as a trade transit point in 1608.

In the next two years, the company built its first factory in South India in the town of Machilipatnam on the Coromandel Coast of the Bay of Bengal. The high profits reported by the company after landing in India initially prompted King James I to grant subsidiary licences to other trading companies in England. But in 1609, he renewed the charter given to the company for an indefinite period, including a clause which specified that the charter would cease to be in force if the trade turned unprofitable for three consecutive years.

The Company was led by one Governor and 24 directors, who made up the Court of Directors. They, in turn, reported to the Court of Proprietors which appointed them. Ten committees reported to the Court of Directors.

Foothold in India

The Red Dragon fought the Portuguese at the Battle of Swally in 1612, and made several voyages to the East Indies.

English traders frequently engaged in hostilities with their Dutch and Portuguese counterparts in the Indian Ocean. The company achieved a major victory over the Portuguese in the Battle of Swally in 1612. It decided to explore the feasibility of gaining a territorial foothold in mainland India, with official sanction of both countries and requested that the Crown launch a diplomatic mission.

Jahangir investing a courtier with a robe of honour watched by Sir Thomas Roe, English ambassador to the court of Jahangir at Agra from 1615–18, and others.

In 1612, James I instructed Sir Thomas Roe to visit the Mughal Emperor Nuruddin Salim Jahangir (r. 1605 – 1627) to arrange for a commercial treaty that would give the company exclusive rights to reside and build factories in Surat and other areas. In return, the company offered to provide the Emperor with goods and rarities from the European market. This mission was highly successful as Jahangir sent a letter to James through Sir Thomas Roe:

"Upon which assurance of your royal love I have given my general command to all the kingdoms and ports of my dominions to receive all the merchants of the English nation as the subjects of my friend; that in what place so ever they choose to live, they may have free liberty without any restraint; and at what port so ever they shall arrive, that neither Portugal nor any other shall dare to molest their quiet; and in what city so ever they shall have residence, I have commanded all my governors and captains to give them freedom answerable to their own desires; to sell, buy, and to loot."

—Nuruddin Salim Jahangir, *Letter to James I.*

The company, benefitting from the imperial patronage, soon expanded its commercial trading operations, eclipsing the Portuguese Estado da India, which had established bases in Goa, Chittagong and Bombay (which was later ceded to England as part of the dowry of Catherine de Braganza). The East India Company also launched a joint effort attack with the Dutch United East India Company on Portuguese and Spanish ships off the coast of China, which helped secure their ports in China. The company created trading posts in Surat (where a factory was built in 1612), Madras (1639), Bombay (1668), and Calcutta (1690). By 1647, the company had 23 factories, each under the command of a factor or master merchant and governor if so chosen, and had 90 employees in India. The major factories became the walled forts of Fort William in Bengal, Fort St George in Madras and the Bombay Castle.

In 1634, the Mughal emperor extended his hospitality to the English traders to the region of Bengal, and in 1717, completely waived customs duties for the trade. The company's mainstay businesses were by then in cotton, silk, indigo dye, saltpetre and tea. The company's future, however, was braked by the signing of the Treaty of Münster in 1648, which freed the Netherlands from Spanish control, allowing it to turn its full attention to expanding its trade both at home and distant waters and enter a period recognised as Holland's 'Golden Age.' The Dutch were aggressive competitors, and had meanwhile, expanded their monopoly of the spice trade in the Malaccan straits by ousting the Portuguese in 1640–41. With reduced Portuguese and Spanish influence in the region, the EIC and Dutch East India Company (VOC) entered a period of intense competition, resulting in the Anglo-Dutch Wars of the 17th and 18th centuries.

Meanwhile, in 1657, Oliver Cromwell renewed the charter of 1609 and brought about minor changes in the holding of the company. The status of the company was further enhanced by the restoration of monarchy in England.

In an act aimed at strengthening the power of the EIC, King Charles II provisioned the EIC (in a series of five acts around 1670) with the rights to autonomous territorial acquisitions, to mint money, to command fortresses and troops and form alliances, to make war and peace and to exercise both civil and criminal jurisdiction over the acquired areas.

William Hedges was sent in 1682 to Shaista Khan, the Mughal governor of Bengal, in order to obtain a firman, an imperial directive that would grant England regular trading privileges throughout the Mughal Empire. However, the company's governor in London, Sir Josiah Child, interfered with Hedges' mission, causing Mughal Emperor Aurangzeb to break off the negotiations.

In 1689, a Mughal fleet commanded by Sidi Yaqub attacked Bombay. After a year of resistance, the EIC surrendered in 1690, and the company sent envoys to Aurangzeb's camp to plead for a pardon. The company's envoys had to prostrate themselves before the emperor, pay a large indemnity and promise better behaviour in the future. The emperor withdrew his troops, and the company subsequently reestablished itself in Bombay and set up a new base in Calcutta.

Mughal Convoy Piracy Incident of 1695

In September 1695, Captain Henry Every, an English pirate on board the *Fancy*, reached the Straits of Bab-el-Mandeb, where he teamed up with five other pirate captains to make an attack on the Indian fleet making the annual voyage to Mecca. The Mughal convoy included the treasure-laden *Ganj-i-Sawai*, reported to be the greatest in the Mughal fleet and the largest ship operational in the Indian Ocean, and its escort, the Fateh Muhammed. They were spotted passing the straits en route to Surat. The pirates gave chase and caught up with the Fateh Muhammed some days later, and meeting little resistance, took some £50,000 to £60,000 worth of treasure.

Every continued in pursuit and managed to overhaul the Ganj-i-Sawai, who put up a fearsome fight but it too was eventually taken. The ship carried enormous wealth and, according to contemporary East India Company sources, was carrying a relative of the Grand Mughal, although there is no evidence to suggest that it was his daughter and her retinue. The loot from the Ganj-i-Sawai totalled between £325,000 and £600,000, including 500,000 gold and silver pieces, and has become known as the richest ship ever taken by pirates.

In a letter sent to the Privy Council by Sir John Gayer, then governor of Bombay and head of the East India Company, Gayer claims, "it is certain the Pirates...did do very barbarously by the People of the Ganj-i-Sawai and Abdul Ghaffar's ship, to make them confess where their money was." The pirates set free the survivors who were left aboard their emptied ships, to continue their voyage back to India.

When the news arrived in England it caused an outcry. In response, a combined bounty of £1,000 (considered massive by the standards of the time) was offered for Every's capture by the Privy Council and East India Company, leading to the first worldwide manhunt in recorded history. The plunder of

Aurangzeb's treasure ship had serious consequences for the English East India Company. The furious Mughal Emperor Aurangzeb ordered Sidi Yaqub and Nawab Daud Khan to attack and close four of the company's factories in India and imprison their officers, who were almost lynched by a mob of angry Mughals, blaming them for their countryman's depredations, and threatened to put an end to all English trading in India. To appease Emperor Aurangzeb and particularly his Grand Vizier, Asad Khan, Parliament exempted Every from all of the Acts of Grace (pardons) and amnesties it would subsequently issue to other pirates.

The prosperity that the officers of the company enjoyed allowed them to return to Britain and establish sprawling estates and businesses, and to obtain political power. The company developed a lobby in the English parliament. Under pressure from ambitious tradesmen and former associates of the company (pejoratively termed Interlopers by the company) who wanted to establish private trading firms in India, a deregulating act was passed in 1694.

This allowed any English firm to trade with India, unless specifically prohibited by act of parliament, thereby annulling the charter that had been in force for almost 100 years. By an act that was passed in 1698, a new "parallel" East India Company (officially titled the English Company Trading to the East Indies) was floated under a state-backed indemnity of £2 million. The powerful stockholders of the old company quickly subscribed a sum of £315,000 in the new concern, and dominated the new body. The two companies wrestled with each other for some time, both in England and in India, for a dominant share of the trade.

It quickly became evident that, in practice, the original company faced scarcely any measurable competition. The companies merged in 1708, by a tripartite indenture involving both companies and the state. Under this arrangement, the merged company lent to the Treasury a sum of £3,200,000, in return for exclusive privileges for the next three years, after which the situation was to be reviewed. The amalgamated company became the United Company of Merchants of England Trading to the East Indies.

Fort St. George, Bombay

Bombay's Fort St. George was finished in 1715. To place this in context, the Mughal Empire was beginning to rapidly come apart with Aurangzeb's death in 1707.

In the following decades, there was a constant see-saw battle between the company lobby and the Parliament. The company sought a permanent establishment, while the Parliament would not willingly allow it greater autonomy and so relinquish the opportunity to exploit the company's profits. In 1712, another act renewed the status of the company, although the debts were repaid. By 1720, 15% of British imports were from India, almost all passing through the company, which reasserted the influence of the company lobby. The licence was prolonged until 1766 by yet another act in 1730.

At this time, Britain and France became bitter rivals. Frequent skirmishes between them took place for control of colonial possessions. In 1742, fearing the monetary consequences of a war, the British government agreed to extend the deadline for the licensed exclusive trade by the company in India until 1783 in return for a further loan of £1 million. Between 1756 and 1763, the Seven Years' War diverted the state's attention towards consolidation and defence of its territorial possessions in Europe and its colonies in North America

The war took place on Indian soil, between the company troops and the French forces. In 1757, the Law Officers of the Crown delivered the Pratt-Yorke opinion distinguishing overseas territories acquired by right of conquest from those acquired by private treaty. The opinion asserted that, while the Crown of Great Britain enjoyed sovereignty over both, only the property of the former was vested in the Crown.

With the advent of the Industrial Revolution, Britain surged ahead of its European rivals. The demand for Indian commodities was boosted by the need to sustain troops and economy during the war and by the increased availability of raw materials and efficient methods of production. As home to the revolution, Britain experienced higher standards of living. Its spiralling cycle of prosperity, demand and production had a profound influence on overseas trade. The company became the single largest player in the British global market. William Henry Pyne notes in his book The Microcosm of London (1808):

"On the 1 March 1801, the debts of the East India Company to £5,393,989 their effects to £15,404,736 and their sales increased since February 1793, from £4,988,300 to £7,602,041."

Saltpetre Trade

Saltpetre used for gunpowder was one of the major trade goods of the company.

Sir John Banks, a businessman from Kent who negotiated an agreement between the king and the company, began his career in a syndicate arranging contracts for victualling the navy, an interest he kept up for most of his life. He knew that Samuel Pepys and John Evelyn had amassed a substantial fortune from the Levant and Indian trades.

He became a Director, and later, as Governor of the East India Company in 1672, he arranged a contract which included a loan of £20,000 and £30,000 worth of saltpetre — also known as potassium nitrate, a primary ingredient in gunpowder – for the King at the price it shall sell by the candle that is by auction — where an inch of candle burnt and as long as it was alight bidding could continue. The agreement included with the price 'an allowance of interest which is to be expressed in tallies.' This was something of a breakthrough in royal prerogative because previous requests for the king to buy at the company's auctions had been turned down as 'not honourable or decent.'

Outstanding debts were also agreed and the company permitted to export 250 tonnes of saltpetre. Again in 1673, Banks successfully negotiated another contract for 700 tonnes of saltpetre at £37,000 between the king and the company. So urgent was the need to supply the armed forces in the United Kingdom, America and elsewhere that the authorities sometimes turned a blind eye on the untaxed sales. One governor of the company was even reported as saying in 1864 that he would rather have the saltpetre made than the tax on salt.

Robert Clive became the first British Governor after he had instated the schismatic Mir Jafar as the Nawab of Bengal.

The Seven Years' War (1756–1763) resulted in the defeat of the French forces, limited French imperial ambitions and stunted the influence of the Industrial Revolution in French territories. Robert Clive, the Governor-General, led the company to a victory against Joseph François Dupleix, the commander of the French forces in India, and recaptured Fort St George from the French. The company took this respite to seize Manila in 1762.

By the Treaty of Paris (1763), France regained the five establishments captured by the British during the war (Pondicherry, Mahé, Karikal, Yanam and Chandernagar) but was prevented from erecting fortifications and keeping troops in Bengal (art. XI). Elsewhere in India, the French were to remain a military threat, particularly during the War of American Independence and up to the capture of Pondicherry in 1793 at the outset of the French Revolutionary Wars without any military presence. Although these small outposts remained French possessions for the next two hundred years, French ambitions on Indian territories were effectively laid to rest, thus eliminating a major source of economic competition for the company.

In contrast, the company, fresh from a colossal victory and with the backing of a disciplined and experienced army, was able to assert its interests in the region from its base at Madras and in Bengal from Calcutta, without facing any further obstacles from other colonial powers.

Military expansion

The Mughal Emperor Shah Alam II, who, with his allies, fought against the East India Company during his early years (1760–1764), only, accepts the protection of the British in the year 1803, after he had been blinded by his enemies and deserted by his subjects.

The company continued to experience resistance from local rulers during its expansion. Robert Clive led company forces against Siraj Ud Daulah, the last independent Nawab of Bengal, Bihar and Midnapore district in Odisha to victory at the Battle of Plassey in 1757, resulting in the conquest of Bengal.

This victory estranged the British and the Mughals, since Siraj Ud Daulah was a Mughal feudatory ally. With the gradual weakening of the Marathas in the aftermath of the three Anglo-Maratha wars, the British also secured the Ganges-Jumna Doab, the Delhi-Agra region, parts of Bundelkhand, Broach, some districts of Gujarat, the fort of Ahmmadnagar, province of Cuttack (which included Mughalbandi/the coastal part of Odisha, Garjat/ the princely states of Odisha, Balasore Port, parts of Midnapore district of West Bengal), Bombay (Mumbai) and the surrounding areas, leading to a formal end of the Maratha empire and firm establishment of the British East India Company in India. Hyder Ali and Tipu Sultan, the rulers of the Kingdom of Mysore, offered much resistance to the British forces. Having sided with the French during the Revolutionary War, the rulers of Mysore continued their struggle against the company with the four Anglo-Mysore Wars. Mysore finally fell to the company forces in 1799, with the death of Tipu Sultan.

The fall of Tipu Sultan and the Sultanate, during the Battle of Seringapatam in the year 1799.

The last vestiges of local administration were restricted to the northern regions of Delhi, Oudh, Rajputana and Punjab, where the company's presence was ever-increasing amidst infighting and offers of protection among the remaining princes. The hundred years from the Battle of Plassey in 1757 to the Indian Rebellion of 1857 were a period of consolidation for the company, which began to function more as an administrator and less as a trading concern.

A cholera pandemic began in Bengal, and then, spread across India by 1820. 10,000 British troops and countless Indians died during this pandemic. Between 1736 and 1834, only some 10% of the East India Company's officers survived to take the final voyage home.

In the early 19th century, the Indian question of geopolitical dominance and empire-holding remained with the East India Company. The three independent armies of the company's Presidencies, with some locally raised irregular forces, expanded to a total of 280,000 men by 1857. First recruited from mercenaries and low-caste volunteers, the Bengal Army, especially, eventually became composed largely of high-caste Hindus and land-owning Muslims.

Within the Army, British officers who initially trained at the company's own academy at the Addiscombe Military Seminary, always outranked Indians, no matter how long their service. The highest rank to which an Indian soldier could aspire for was Subadar-Major (or Rissaldar-Major in cavalry units), effectively a senior subaltern equivalent. Promotion for both British and Indian soldiers was strictly by seniority, so Indian soldiers rarely reached the commissioned ranks of Jamadar or Subadar before they were middle aged at best. They received no training in administration or leadership to make them independent of their British officers.

During the wars against the French and their allies in the late eighteenth and early nineteenth centuries, the East India Company's armies were used to seize the colonial possessions of other European nations, including the islands of Reunion and Mauritius.

There was a systemic disrespect in the company for the spreading of Protestantism, although it fostered respect for Hindu and Muslim castes and ethnic groups. The growth of tensions between the EIC and the local religious and cultural groups grew in the 19th century as the Protestant revival grew in Great Britain. These tensions erupted at the Indian Rebellion of 1857, and the company ceased to exist when the company dissolved through the East India Stock Dividend Redemption Act 1873.

Victoria Memorial Kolkata

The idea and the plan for Victoria memorial hall was conceived by Lord Curzon, to build a stupendous memorial for Queen Victoria. Kolkata was then the capital of British India and an ideal choice. Edward the Prince of Wales laid the foundation on 4th January, 1906 and the Memorial was opened to Public by the Duke of Windsor on 21st December, 1921.

Victoria Memorial & Some Astounding Facts

It's called the 'Taj of the Raj', and with good reason. It's jaw-dropping, it's built of the same white Makrana marble as is the Taj Mahal, and just like the monument it tries to emulate, it too honours the memory of a woman.

The Victoria Memorial was built as a tribute to England's Queen Victoria, Empress of India during the Raj, when India was ruled by the British Crown. It was constructed between 1906 and 1921, after Victoria's death in 1901.

Victoria Memorial in Kolkata | Author

A grand museum in Kolkata today, the monument still casts a regal air and is possibly the most awesome reminder of the Raj in India. But even a monument as well-known as this has a few secrets.

Here are five facts about the Victoria Memorial that you may not know.

1. ONCE A PRISON!

Presidency Jail

Long before the Victoria Memorial was built here, this was the site of Kolkata's Presidency Jail. Established in 1778, one of the jail's famous inmates was

James Hickey, who launched India's first newspaper, *Hickey's Bengal Gazette*. Hickey was imprisoned here, on trumped-up charges, for exposing the corruption of Warren Hastings. Older texts refer to this area as 'Harinbari' or 'deer house', suggesting that there may have once been a hunting lodge here. Some say it was a 'zoo' because the jail inmates were treated like 'animals inside a cage'! In 1906, the jail was shifted to Alipore and the site was used to build the Victoria Memorial.

THE BONG CONNECTION

The contract to build the Victoria Memorial was awarded to Messrs Martin & Co, which was part-owned by a Bengali, Sir Rajen Mookerjee. Initially hired to build only the foundation, the firm's work impressed the British and it ended up building the entire monument. Mookerjee was later knighted. Martin & Co continues to exist, although Mookerjee's family is no longer at the helm.

BUILT OF THE SAME MARBLE AS THE TAJ

Victoria Memorial | LHI

Known as the 'Taj of the Raj', the British wanted the Victoria Memorial to boast the finest quality as did the Taj Mahal in Agra. So they used the same marble from Makrana in Rajasthan. Martin & Co set up a quarry in Makrana and the East India Railways transported the marble to Calcutta for free.

VICTORIA MEMORIAL WAS ONCE COVERED IN DUNG

An old picture of Victoria Memorial

During World War II (1939-1945), as the Japanese inched closer to Calcutta, the former capital of the Empire (it had long since shifted to Delhi) became a target. At midnight on 20th December 1942, the Japanese bombed Calcutta, endangering the beloved memorial of the British. A unique attempt was made to 'hide' the Victoria Memorial, so it was covered in cow dung!

OTHER VICTORIA 'MEMORIALS' IN INDIA

Victoria Memorial, Lucknow

When Queen Victoria died in 1901, the British wanted to build many small memorials in her honour all over India. But Viceroy Lord Curzon wanted one grand monument in the imperial capital that would captivate every visitor to

Calcutta. Ironically, the British capital was shifted to Delhi even as the memorial was being built, in 1911. But did you know that there are smaller versions or mini 'Victoria Memorials' in cities such as Lucknow and Allahabad, where a statue of the Empress is housed under modest canopies?

The Victoria Memorial houses hundreds of fascinating exhibits from the days of the Raj, including weapons and armour from the Revolt of 1857. But who knows what secrets lurk within its walls?

Credit Author Deepanjan Ghosh

Live History India

Victoria House built in 1798.

A Great Romance

August 8th is the 230th anniversary of the culmination of the great romances in world history. It grew unnoticed on the high seas, blossomed in Madras and culminated in the wedding in Calcutta on August 8, 1777 of Warren Hastings, Governor-General of INDIA and his Maid Marian, Anna Maria Appolonia Chapusettin Imhafl, a French Huguenot.

Hastings, who was aboard the *Duke of Grafton*, sailing from Lend to Madras to take his seat in the Council as Third Member, fell quite seriously ill during the voyage. The Count Baron von Imhoff, an impecunious German, was also on board, sailing to India to try and make his fortune as a painter — he did have a modicum of talent. With him was his petite and rather striking and vivacious wife, Marian. When Marian Imhoff saw the sad state Hastings was in, she decided to become his nurse — and charm him to health she did during the rest of the voyage. A grateful Hastings, also smitten by her attention to him, offered the Imhoffs hospitality of his house in Madras. Before long, Hastings became Second in Council — and packed the Baron off to Calcutta, stating that the portrait pickings would be greater there.

When Hastings was transferred to Calcutta and appointed, in due course, the first Governor-General of what was becoming Birtish India, he bought off Imhoff (Say that in whispers!) and married Maid Marian, the divorcee. Calcutta may have been scandalised, but their 'love was cut short only by Hastings' death in 1818. Together, they had survived all the blows of fortune they had to endure. But what was remarkable about their romance was the impassioned love letters they wrote to each other whenever they were parted, even by a few miles. Typical of the dry-as-dust Governor-General's alter ego were letters with passages like this – "Yes, my lovely Marian, you are before me; your delightful looks, your enchanting voice and your divine touch! Oh God! Once more make them substantially mine!" Who said Nehru and Edwina?

Thomas Babington Macaulay, 1st Baron Macaulay (25 October 1800 – 28 December 1859) was a British historian and Whig politician. He wrote extensively as an essayist and reviewer; his books on British history were hailed as literary masterpieces.

Macaulay held political office as the Secretary at War between 1839 and 1841 and as Paymaster-General between 1846 and 1848. He played a major role in introducing English and western concepts to education in India. He supported the replacement of Persian by English as the official language, the use of English as the medium of instruction in all schools and the training of English-speaking Indians as teachers.

In his view, Macaulay divided the world into civilised nations and barbarism, with Britain representing the high point of civilisation. In his Minute on Indian Education of February 1835, he asserted, "It is, I believe, no exaggeration to say that all the historical information which has been collected from all the books written in the Sanskrit language is less valuable than what may be found in the paltriest abridgement used at preparatory schools in England." He was wedded to the Idea of Progress, especially in terms of the liberal freedoms. He opposed radicalism while idealising historic British culture and traditions.

Macaulay was the eldest child of Zachary Macaulay, a Scottish Highlander, who became a colonial governor and abolitionist and Selena Mills, who was a former pupil of Hannah More. Thomas Macaulay was born in Leicestershire, England, where he was noted as a child prodigy. As a toddler, gazing out of the window from his cot at the chimneys of a local factory, he is reputed to have asked his father whether the smoke came from the fires of hell.

He was educated at a private school in Hertfordshire and at Trinity College, Cambridge. While at Cambridge, he wrote much poetry and won several prizes, including the Chancellor's Gold Medal in June 1821. In 1825, he published a prominent essay on Milton in the Edinburgh Review. He studied law, and in 1826, he was called to the bar but showed more interest in a political than a legal career.

India (1834–1838)

Macaulay was Secretary to the Board of Control under Lord Grey from 1832 until 1833. After the passing of the Government of India Act 1833, he was appointed as the first Law Member of the Governor-General's Council. He went to India in 1834 and served on the Supreme Council of India between 1834 and 1838.

Later on, he introduced English-medium education in India through his famous Minute on Indian Education of February 1835. Macaulay called for an educational system to create a class of anglicised Indians who would serve as cultural intermediaries between the British and the Indians, and brought to an end a lively debate on the appropriate language for education and administration.

Macaulay, thereby, succeeded in implementing ideas previously put forward by Lord William Bentinck, the governor-general from 1829, who, inspired by utilitarian ideas and calling for "useful learning," had favoured the replacement of Persian with English as the official language, the use of English as the medium of instruction and the training of English-speaking Indians as teachers.

Macaulay convinced the Governor-General to adopt English as the medium of instruction in secondary education, from the sixth year of schooling onwards, rather than the Sanskrit or Persian then used in the institutions supported by the East India Company. Macaulay's argued that Sanskrit and Arabic were wholly inadequate for students studying history, science and technology. Referring to the orientalist, he observed, "I have never found one among them who could deny that a single shelf of a good European library was worth the whole native literature of India and Arabia."

He argued, "We have to educate a people who cannot, at present, be educated by means of their mother tongue. We must teach them some foreign language." The solution was to teach English. His final years in India were devoted to the creation of a Penal Code as the leading member of the Law Commission.

In the aftermath of the Indian Mutiny of 1857, Macaulay's criminal law proposal was enacted. The Indian Penal Code in 1860 was followed by the Criminal Procedure Code in 1872 and the Civil Procedure Code in 1909. The Indian Penal Code inspired counterparts in most other British colonies, and to date, many of these laws are still in effect in places as far apart as Pakistan, Singapore, Bangladesh, Sri Lanka, Nigeria and Zimbabwe, as well as in India itself.

In Indian culture, the term "Macaulay's Children" is sometimes used to refer to people born of Indian ancestry who adopt Western culture as a lifestyle, or display attitudes influenced by colonisers (Macaulayism) – expressions used disparagingly, and with the implication of disloyalty to one's country and one's heritage.

Macaulay's Minute formed the basis for the reforms introduced in the English Education Act of 1835. In 1836, a school named La Martinière, founded by Major-General Claude Martin, had one of its houses named after him.

In independent India, Macaulay's idea of the civilising mission has been used by Dalitists, in particular by neo liberalist Chandra Bhan Prasad, as a "creative appropriation for self-empowerment," based on the view that Dalit folk are empowered by Macaulay's deprecation of Hindu civilisation and an English education.

Later life (1857–1859)

Macaulay sat on the committee to decide on the historical subjects to be painted in the new Palace of Westminster. The need to collect reliable portraits of notable figures from history for this project led to the foundation of the National Portrait Gallery, which was formally established on 2 December 1856. Macaulay was among its founding trustees and is honoured with one of only three busts above the main entrance.

During his later years, his health made work increasingly difficult for him. He died of a heart attack on 28 December 1859, aged 59, leaving his major work, The History of England from the Accession of James the Second incomplete. On 9th January 1860, he was buried in Westminster Abbey in Poets' Corner, near a statue of Addison. As he had no children, his peerage became extinct on his death.

Macaulay's nephew, Sir George Trevelyan, BT, wrote a best-selling "Life and Letters" of his famous uncle, which is still the best complete life of Macaulay. His great-nephew was the Cambridge historian G. M. Trevelyan. Macaulay likely had an eidetic memory.

The Funeral of Thomas Babington Macaulay

"I have travelled the length and breadth of India, and I have not seen one person as a beggar, who is a thief. Such wealth I have seen in the Country." That was according to Lord Macaulay - in 1835. He was addressing the British Parliament. He then proposed to replace India's ancient education system for, "if Indians think all that is foreign and English is good and greater, they will lose their self esteem and truly become a dominated nation."

Lord Macaulay's speech in the British Parliament on 2nd February 1835.

Lord Robert Clive - portrait after Gainsborough.

That one moves two centuries ago still have repercussions, and we come across some lasting bond India shares with the colonial history within the pages.

In a counter to this, I have an observation that misinterpreted teaching of the Vedas. Vedas are teaching invaluable for the harmony of the world when taught in its truth and real purpose. For vested interest, it was kept away from the underprivileged to live a life safeguarding their self-esteem. They considered it as their fate in the blindness of the outer world or not to look into the light of freedom or prosperity. The right for asking for alms to a higher caste was denied for the caste on the lowest tier of the social system. The right for asking for alms to a higher caste was denied for the caste on the lowest tier of the social system.

Once education and enterprise was introduced by the Three European power that colonised India in a more systematic manner for the interests of the British Empire, there was a major turnaround in our Socio-Economic strata. That is the main reason why the following lines by N Ram is so relevant.

"India needs to recognise the inescapability of history without romancing the Raj. It is possible to understand the centrality of the British rule to the evolution of the modern day India." N.RAM -2009 -Chairman The Hindu News Paper of Kasturi and Sons.

I believe that our great leaders took good things from all the leaders of the world as they all thought we believed the World as a family and took lessons from all civilisations and added it our heritage. So, the present state of our country needs to be read as metaphor along the lines of a vibrant mix of thoughts and actions of chain reactions of Colonial rule and India's underlying ideologies. This helps us today to hang on as a democracy. So, we hold guilty if we rob our countrymen and deny their rights.

Design and the Construction of Victoria Memorial Hall in Kolkata

Victoria Memorial, which is about 184 feet tall, has been built in an area of 64 acres in the heart of the city of Kolkata. This Memorial was designed by Sir William Emerson, who was the President of the British Institute of Architects. The architecture of the Victoria memorial hall is similar to the Belfast City Hall. Sir William Emerson had used Indo Sarcenic style of Architecture, incorporating some Mughal elements also to make the hall look attractive. You can see miniature paintings and images of Queen Mary King George V and Queen Victoria. You can also see about 3500 articles associated with the everlasting memory of Queen Victoria in the inside rooms of the Victoria Memorial.

While going through them you will get an idea of how Queen Victoria lived, the way the Queen dressed as well as the numerous artillery weapons used in the Battle of Plassey and the famous Rosewood piano the Whispering Gallery in the dome of the Memorial. Not only the Royal gallery, you are also asked to visit Kolkata Gallery for more insight into the historical legacy of Kolkata right from Job Charlock's discovery of Kolkata until the year 1911, when the capital of India was relocated to Delhi. Other than these, you can also see the Ivory chair of Warren Hastings, medals awarded to Prince Dwarkanath Tagore by Queen Victoria, the Nawab's throne and the pistols used by Warren Hastings in actual warfare and many more interesting bits and pieces of news.

STATUES ADORNING VICTORIA MEMORIAL

Howrah Bridge

The Men Who Delved into Ancient India

James Prinsep: Decoding Ancient India

It was on an early morning sometime in 1837 that one of the biggest 'Eureka' moments in Indian history took place. The Brahmi script, an ancient Indian script that had for long flummoxed historians and researchers studying India's past, had finally been deciphered. Finally, Indians could understand their distant past as never before. And the man who achieved this was an extraordinary Indologist and polymath, an Englishman named James Prinsep (1799-1840).

In the 18th and early 19th century, very little was known of India's past before Islamic rule. Noted author and historian John Keay, in his book *India Discovered* (1981), quotes 18th century English scholar Thomas Twining, who while studying Indian history wrote in 1790,

> "It is at this epoch [1000 CE] that we come to a line of shade beyond which no object is distinctly discernible. What treasures might not be discovered if the light of science should ever penetrate this darkness."

As the British empire began expanding across India following the Battle of Plassey in 1757, a number of British writers, travellers, scholars, merchants and officials attempted to cross this 'line of shade' to rediscover India's ancient past. They were traversing newly conquered British territories to marvel at and study the ruins at Khajuraho, Ellora and Madurai.

Among these was a young Englishman who started life in India as a junior employee at the Calcutta Mint and went on to leave an indelible mark on Indian history. His name was James Prinsep.

This remarkable man was born on 20th August 1799 CE into a wealthy English family. His father had made a huge fortune as an indigo planter in India. After completing his studies in England, Prinsep decided to follow in his father's footsteps. He arrived in India in 1819 at the age of 20 to work as an 'Assay Master' at the Calcutta Mint. His job was to ensure quality control at the mint but his life was to take another direction.

Horace Hayman Wilson| Wikimedia Commons

Prinsep's superior at the Calcutta mint was Horace Hayman Wilson (1786-1860), the most eminent Orientalist of his time. Wilson was a Sanskrit scholar, who had an interest in Ayurveda, and was the first person to translate the *Rigveda,* the *Vishnu Purana* and Kalidasa's *Meghaduta* in English.

In Benares, Prinsep studied Indian temple architecture, making a series of watercolours that were published between 1830 and 1834 in London, titled *Benares Illustrated, In a Series of Drawings*. He also designed the new mint building and a church in Benares, and a series of canals in Bengal. But, while working in the mint, he developed a great interest in the study of coins.

Lithograph of *Kupuldhara Tulao, Benares* by Prinsep (1834) |Wikimedia Commons

In 1830, Prinsep was transferred back to the Calcutta Mint, where his boss, Wilson, had been puzzling over different coins found in Rajasthan and Punjab. Prinsep offered to catalogue these coins, which in turn, aroused his interest in the indecipherable inscriptions found on them. The same year, Prinsep also became the founding editor of *The Journal of the Asiatic Society* published by the Asiatic Society of Bengal.

Around 1833 CE, the remains of a pillar very similar to one found at Feroze Shah Kotla in Delhi, were found in the Allahabad Fort. Prinsep later noted in his diary, *'I could not see the highly curious column lying at Allahabad, falling to rapid decay, without wishing to preserve a complete copy of its several inscriptions...'*

MODIFICATIONS OF THE SANSKRIT ALPHABET. VOWELS.

INITIALS — MEDIALS

1. FIFTH CENT. B.C.
2. CENT. B.C.?
3. THIRD CENT. B.C.
4. SECOND CENT. A.D. (also)
5. FIFTH CENT. A.D.
6. SEVENTH CENT. A.D.
7. NINTH CENT. A.D.
8. TENTH CENT. A.D.
9. MODERN
SQUARE PALI

Brahmi notes of Prinsep| Wikimedia Commons

With the help of a Sanskrit expert, Prinsep managed to decipher a part of the inscription, which spoke of conquests of a king named 'Samudragupta.' But he could not connect with another ruler, 'Chandragupta' [Maurya], who had appeared in Buddhist texts and as Sandracottus in Greek texts.

> What a disappointed Prinsep did not realise is that he had accidently stumbled upon the 'Imperial Gupta' dynasty, which until then, had been completely forgotten.

Finally, he hit upon his first success. He wrote:

'Upon carefully comparing them [the three inscriptions] with a view to finding any other words that might be common to them, I was led to a most important discovery; namely that all three inscriptions were identically the same.'

But he still had no idea what it meant! For the next four years, Prinsep worked assiduously on his project. He spent his days in the mint and his nights in the company of coins and inscriptions. He developed a huge network of 'correspondents' all across India, who would keep sending him anything interesting that they came across. These were merchants, military officers, doctors and anyone else who was interested in history. Then, in 1837, some vital clues emerged.

On Prinsep's suggestion, Captain Edward Smith, a military engineer from Allahabad, had made a long journey through the jungles of Central India, to archaeological remains in a village called 'Sanchi' in the Kingdom of Bhopal. Along with the main inscriptions here, Captain Smith had also sent to Prinsep [in his words] *'trivial fragments of rude writing'* found on the stone railings around the main stupa. He noticed that most of the inscriptions ended with the same two characters, which he deciphered as *'Danam.'* And, slowly, the rest revealed itself. The entire Brahmi script had finally been decoded.

Danam on Sanchi Inscription|Wikimedia Commons

In 1838, Prinsep presented his findings to the Asiatic Society. It came to be known that the edicts had been inscribed on the orders of a king named 'Devanampiya Piyadasi,' who had changed his religion. And the dots began to connect. From Ceylon (now Sri Lanka), George Turnour, a historian studying Buddhist history, wrote back saying that from Sri Lankan Buddhist texts he had come to know that 'Piyadasi' was an epithet for an Indian king known as 'Ashoka.' It was further stated that Ashoka was the grandson of Chandragupta.

Kharosthi coins|Wikimedia Commons

In addition to deciphering Brahmi, Prinsep also deciphered the 'Kharosthi' script, an ancient script used in the North-Western regions of India to write Sanskrit and Prakrit. For this, he used the coins of the Indo-Greek kings that had ruled Punjab. The coins had the names of the rulers written in Greek on one side and in Kharosthi on the other.

Sadly, the heavy workload took a toll on Prinsep's health. He kept working despite poor health but was forced to return to London for treatment. He died on 23rd April, 1840 of a brain aliment at the age of 41. In 1843, the citizens of

Calcutta built a memorial in his honour on the banks of the Hooghly River, which is still called 'Prinsep Ghat.'

Prinsep Ghat|Wikimedia Commons

While much of James Prinsep's work remained incomplete, what he discovered would prove invaluable for future historians and archaeologists – he opened up entire chapters of India's history.

LH1 6

Viceroy of India

Lord and Lady Curzon on the elephant Lakshman Prasad, 29 December 1902

The Victorian Cupboard is indeed unique because it is structured Victorian and contains Gothic Features as well terms of details.

The Victorian age 1837-1901 was a time the past was plundered for design ideas, a great electric mix of styles came together with influences including the Rococo, the baroque, the neo classical and the gothic.

This royal piece of colonial furnite was once housed in the Victoria House in Calcutta. It is hard to believe that all the Gothic pillars are hand-carved, yet so very identical. Lord Wellesley in 1798 decided to build a magnificent house in Calcutta in Bengal to represent British Authority in India.

The design he chose was based upon one of Robert Adam's greatest neo classical residences. Lord Viscount Valentia who witnessed its inaugural ceremony said, "A noble structure although not without faults in the architecture; and upon the whole, not unworthy of its destination, and the sums expended upon it. India is a country of splendour, of extravagance and outward appearances; that the head of a mighty empire (Wellesley) out to conform the to the prejudices of the country he rules over. In short, I wish India to be ruled from a palace not from a counting house with the ideas of a Prince not with those of a retail dealer in muslin and Indigo." Lord Valentia's remark only mirrors the queen's concern for the locals and their culture.

This Victorian Cupboard was sourced from Orissa in 1998 and restored by Madras Craftsmen and listed in Steve Borgia's Indian Heritage Museum in Tamil Nadu.

"You must do things you think you cannot do"

– Elenor Roosevelt

Gentleman Indologist -William Jones

On September 25 1783, a frigate named the Crocodile sailed up the Hooghly River in Bengal and docked at Calcutta's Chandpal Ghat. On board were a 36-year-old Welsh scholar and barrister, bearing essentials for what he expected to be a six-year stint in India.

These included two large sheep and an intrepid young wife whom he had married just four days before embarking from England. Awaiting him in Calcutta was an East India Company judgeship with a salary far greater than he had ever known. His hope was to incorporate Hindu and Muslim laws into his own rulings so that the British could govern Indians according to Indians' own "manners and sentiments." During the leisurely journey from England, he put to paper an exhaustive list of topics he needed to study.

"The Laws of the Hindus and Mohammedans; The History of the Ancient World; Modern Politics and Geography of Hindustan; Best Mode of Governing Bengal; Arithmetic and Geometry and the mixed Sciences of the Asiatics; Medicine, Chemistry, Surgery, and Anatomy of the Indians; The Poetry, Rhetoric, and the Morality of Asia; Music of the Eastern Nations."

The list went on. Ambitious as it was, this plan would eventually be dwarfed by what he achieved in his 11 years in India. Sir William Jones was to become the greatest Orientalist of his time. Two hundred years later, Edward Said and his epigones would turn that word – 'Orientalist' – into a slur, but Jones produced a revolution in knowledge about language and history. "A far-seeing man," the German Romanticist Goethe would say of Jones, "he seeks to connect the unknown to the known."

Jones brought to Calcutta something more useful than sheep – an uncanny mastery of languages. Eventually, he would learn 28 languages, or as friends ribbed him, every language but his native Welsh. When he turned this prodigious skill to ancient Sanskrit texts, the effects were profound. He would go on to change not just the way the world sees India, but how Indians see their history and culture.

Charles Stuart: More 'Hindoo' than British

Charles Stuart (c. 1758 – 31 March 1828) was an officer in the East India Company Army and is well known for being one of the few **British** officers to embrace Hindu culture while stationed there, earning the nickname **Hindoo Stuart**.

Visit the British Museum in London and you will come across a spectacular image of 'Harihara,' representing the amalgamation of Vishnu and Shiva. But did you know that this thousand-year-old image from Khajuraho and a substantial portion of Indian idols (some say as many as 70% to 80%) displayed in the British Museum from the collection of a 19th century British East India company official, Major-General Charles Stuart? Known for his eccentricities, Major-General Stuart became a Hindu, regularly performed Pujas, greeted Indians with '*Jay Sittaramjee*,' and even raised his voice against conversion activities of missionaries in India. This earned him the epithet of 'Hindoo Stuart.'

Little is known about this eccentric Irishman's early life. Stuart is believed to have been born in Galway in Ireland in 1757 or 58. He came to India in his late teens and developed a deep fascination with Hinduism and the people of India. Stuart authored two pamphlets in his early days. The first of these was in response to the arguments forwarded by the prominent missionary, Claudius Buchanan, about the conversion of Indians to Christianity.

Stuart warned about the dangers of attempting mass-scale conversion. He wrote, "*Is it wise, is it politic, is it even safe to institute a war of sentiment against the only friends of any importance we seem to have left in India, our faithful subjects of the Ganges, by suffering missionaries, or our own Clergy, to preach among them, the errors of idolatry and superstition; and thus, disseminating throughout the public mind the seeds of distrust and disaffection?*" "*Hinduism*", Stuart notes, "*little needs the meliorating hand of Christianity to render its votaries a sufficiently correct and moral people for all the useful purposes of a civilised society.*"

Chelsea McGill and Tathagata Neogi

But Stuart is more remembered for his series of letters published in Calcutta newspapers, advising British women in India on how to dress. These were later collected and published under the title, *Ladies' Monitor*. Historian William Dalrymple refers to the *Ladies' Monitor* in his book *White Mughals* (2002). Stuart, in his articles, urged British women to take up the *sari*, insisting that it was much more attractive than contemporary European fashions.

While Stuart was commanding one of the largest cavalry regiments in North India, his deputy was William Linnaeus Gardener, who referred to him in a number of his letters. The first reference to Stuart comes on the eve of his joining the regiment as a commanding officer. Gardener writes that in contrast to his predecessor, Stuart isn't much for parties and does not pride himself on his capacity to overeat – a leitmotif of colonial life in India. Stuart instead, regularly performed his "*pooja*" and avoided "the sight of beef."

"From this point on," writes Dalrymple, "Stuart features regularly in Gardener's correspondence, usually referred to as 'Pundit Stuart' or 'General Pundit.'" On one occasion, Gardener wrote, *"The General is an odd fish. He wrote to me to come to him at Chukla Ghat where the Hindoos bathe... On this point, he is going to build a pagoda! Every Hindoo he salutes with 'Jey Sittaramjee.'"*

LHI 7

The Scotsman Who Befriended Vivekananda and Tagore

The Scottish ecologist and the Bengali poet were brought together by many things: by their common interests in an integrated and experiential approach to learning, by their internationalism, by their love of nature and their deep respect for the limits of human knowledge

Arguably the two greatest modern Bengalis were Swami Vivekananda and Rabindranath Tagore. Both have had a colossal and still enduring influence on their state, their country and the world. Tagore and Vivekananda were close contemporaries, and both lived in and around Calcutta. And yet, while they undoubtedly knew of each other's work, they seem to have met only once, at a tea party hosted by the wife of the American consul-general in January 1899.

This column is about a remarkable Scotsman who befriended both Vivekananda and Tagore. His name was Patrick Geddes. While admired in ecological and town-planning circles around the world, Geddes is not someone even the most educated Bengali is likely to have heard of. Yet, this was a man of whom Tagore once remarked that he had "the precision of the scientist and the vision of a prophet; and at the same time, the power of an artist to make his ideas visible."

These words are quoted in the fine new book, Patrick Geddes's Intellectual Origins (Edinburgh University Press), by the historian Murdo Macdonald. Macdonald stresses Geddes's interdisciplinary approach to knowledge. He was at once a botanist, an ecologist, a geographer, a sociologist and, not least, a town-planner, in which profession all these disciplines were synthesised. Unlike most scientists (as well as most social scientists), Geddes also had a strong visual imagination.

Patrick Geddes first met Swami Vivekananda in America early in 1900, when both were lecturing in that country. They then met again in Paris in the summer of the same year, when the French capital was hosting a World Fair in which Geddes had a stall. Accompanying the Swami in his travels was his disciple, Sister Nivedita. Although Vivekananda died shortly afterwards, Geddes kept in close touch with Nivedita. The Scotsman and the Irishwoman got along famously. Nivedita introduced him to Indian spirituality via the teachings of Ramakrishna; Geddes introduced her to human geography through the works of the French scholar, Frédéric le Play. Nivedita's book, The Web of Indian Life, was dedicated to Geddes, for "teaching me to understand a little of Europe."

In 1903, Sister Nivedita wrote to Patrick Geddes about a planned university in India. The funds for this venture would come from the industrialist, Jamsetji Tata, who had been advised by Swami Vivekananda to invest in the scientific future of India. The Swami was now dead; so Nivedita asked Geddes, as a long time professor himself, to send some suggestions about how this new Indian university should be structured. He wrote her a stream of letters, which provided a panoramic survey of medieval and modern universities in Europe and America, of their systems of teaching and learning and of what lessons and warnings they held for those wishing to start a university in India.

When the Indian Institute of Science was started with Tata funds in 1909, it had no department of geography or of what Geddes had called "nature-study." It was only in the 1980s that the institute established a Centre for

Ecological Sciences, which has since done excellent research on human-nature interactions.

Sister Nivedita died in 1911. Three years later, inspired by her memory, Patrick Geddes came to India. He spent much of the next decade in the subcontinent, studying the processes of urbanisation. I have written about his precocious and still relevant work on Indian town-planning elsewhere. Here, I wish to focus rather on his connections with Rabindranath Tagore.

Tagore and Geddes first met in Calcutta in 1915. They met again in Darjeeling in the summer of 1917, in the home of the scientist, Jagadish Chandra Bose (whose biography the Scotsman was later to write.) For many years thereafter, they carried on a sporadic but always interesting correspondence (reproduced in The Tagore-Geddes Correspondence (Kolkata: Visva-Bharati, 2004) edited by Bashabi Fraser.) Thus, in April 1919, Geddes wrote to Tagore, "Congratulations on your lectures on 'Education' and on 'Forest,' each so fine in its own way."

Three years later, Geddes sent Tagore a scheme for the integrated teaching of disciplines, a scheme that he somewhat presumptuously suggested could be used in the university Tagore was building in Santiniketan.

In reply, Tagore told Geddes, "I have often wished for my mission the help of men like yourself who not only have a most comprehensive sympathy and imagination but a wide range of knowledge and critical acumen. It was with a bewilderment of admiration that I have so often followed the architectural immensity of your vision. But at the same moment, I have had to acknowledge that it was beyond my power to make a practical use of the background of perspective which your vision provides us with. The temperamental characteristics of my own nature require the greatest part of my work to remain in the sub-soil obscurity of mind. All my activities have the character of 'play' in them – they are more or less like writing poems, only in different media of expression. Your own schemes also, in a great measure, have the same element which strongly attracts me, but they have a different idiom, which I have not the power to use."

In 1924, Geddes returned to Europe where he set up an institute in the French town of Montpellier. Two years later, he wrote to Tagore, "At a recent discussion here, we were all lamenting that though the various revolutionary parties have plenty of songs, the more truly progressive ones are still mostly without them. We especially bewailed the lack of any song which could express the movement of international sympathy and good-will, of which the League of Nations, with all its limitations, is the expression… So, as the conversation went on, all with one voice agreed that we must ask that needed song from — Tagore! Will you write it? An admirable musician, a true idealist who is head of our Conservatoire of Music in Montpellier and an invaluable influence accordingly, will be able not only to get us a good translation into French, by one of our young poets, but will himself do his utmost to set it to European music, if yours proves difficult for us in the west."

Replying to this request, Tagore said: "I shall try to write the song you asked from me but you must know that your language does not surrender itself to my muse as easily as my own mother tongue. The initial barrier of diffidence frightens me off from the task." (It seems the internationalist song asked for was, in the end, not written.)

In August 1929, Geddes wrote to Tagore, "Last night, I was reading again your 'Creative Unity,' and with fresh interest and renewed pleasure. How I wish I could put ideas as you do! We have ideas that need also to be expressed, but (for lack of the Love-Unity, I fear) expression is lacking!"

In 1930, Geddes invited Tagore to Montpellier. That summer, Tagore was giving the Hibbert Lectures at Oxford. He was all set to see his friend in France, but then, he had a pain in his chest and his doctor advised him that to be fit for his Oxford assignment, he should cancel his Montpellier trip. So he did, to both men's sorrow and regret. They never saw each other again.

Geddes's intellectual legacy was admirably carried forward by his American disciple, Lewis Mumford, whose great books, Technics and Civilisation and The Culture of Cities, bear the impress of his master's teachings. Mumford once remarked of his mentor, "Geddes's Scotland embraced Europe, and his

Europe embraced the world." We can likewise say of Geddes's friend that "Tagore's Bengal embraced India, and his India embraced the world." When the love of nation and the love of science thrived together.

"The policy of being too cautious is the greatest risk of life."

– Jawaharlal Nehru Bottom of Form

Pandemics Through Indian Literary Lens

As the world tries desperately to contain the coronavirus pandemic that has already claimed more than half a million lives, there is a sinking feeling that we never seem to learn from past experiences. During every pandemic, there comes a time when the reality is so grim that we begin to count the cost in cold statistics – the number of lives lost, jobs snatched, economic fallout and in 2020, a haunting phrase that has emerged, the 'number of positive cases.'

The outbreaks of deadly diseases like typhoid, smallpox, cholera, malaria and the plague are not recent phenomena. They are as old as civilisation itself. As explorers 'discovered' new lands and emperors dispatched armies to conquer new territories, they either took with them or brought back diseases that eventually wiped out large sections of the population.

Pieter Bruegel's *The Triumph of Death* reflects the social upheaval and terror that followed plague, which devastated medieval Europe. |Wikimedia Commons

The great Roman and Byzantine Empires, for instance, battled frequent epidemics as they kept pushing their geographical boundaries. And then, there was Black Death in the mid-14th century, which wiped out more than one-third of Europe's population and altered the course of history.

A French allegory of a cholera pandemic, c. 1832|https://www.pbslearningmedia. org/

One of the earliest references to this is in *The Indian Cholera* (1835), a play written by Norwegian poet, Henrik Wergeland. The play captures the role of British colonialism in transforming cholera, which was endemic to the eastern part of the Indian subcontinent, into a worldwide pandemic in the first half of the 19th century.

We know that the 19th century witnessed three major waves of a cholera pandemic in quick succession: 1817-24, the 1830s and 1846-60. On each occasion, it started in the Ganges delta in India and spread to other parts of the world, such as West Asia, Europe, the Americas, China and Japan through colonial trading networks.

But the best piece of epidemic-oriented literature is undoubtedly noted French writer, Albert Camus's *The Plague* (1947). Although Camus's novel is set in the French Algerian city of Oran in the 1940s. He used sources pertaining to the cholera outbreak that killed a large proportion of the population in Oran in 1849. Considered mainly an existentialist classic, *The Plague* has been written in allegorical fashion, which depicts the powerlessness of the individual and high-handedness of the state during an epidemic-like situation. In fact, history tells us that epidemics have always been used by the state to tighten their grip on the population.

Another novel, written by Colombian novelist, Gabriel Garcia Marquez titled *Love In The Time of Cholera* (1985), explores death and decay as well as love against the backdrop of recurring civil wars and cholera epidemics in the South American continent. In this novel, Marquez presents the conflict between tradition and modernity as embodied by two of his central characters. While one of them represents the traditionalist attitude towards cholera and advocates accepting it as a part of life, the other echoes the modernist approach, which emphasises its eradication.

Ironically, when the wrestler was alive, he was the only ray of hope for his fellow villagers as he beat his drum from evening till morning amidst the horror of the cholera epidemic. Renu says the unbroken rhythm of Luttan Singh's drum used to fill the despairing village with *sanjeevani shakti* (cosmic, healing energy).

Epidemics find references in works of noted Hindi writer Mushi Premchand's works as well. Premchand's short stories *Idgah* (1933) and *Doodh Ka Daam* (1934) also make tangential references to cholera and the plague, respectively.

LHI 8

"You need power only when you want to do some thing harmful, otherwise Love is enough to get everything done."

– Charlie Chaplin

The Heartbreaking Truth Behind Malaysian Tamils and the Death Railway

Malaysia is a beautiful country known for its multiracial citizens living together in harmony. But how did Tamils from South India end up in Malaya and become an important part in forming Malaysia?

The ill-fated story of 'the railway of death' may have been forgotten by many – or not even known by some younger Malaysians. But as Malaysians, we need to learn what happened and how our ancestors contributed to the nation we live in today! The peaceful life we enjoy today would not be possible without the immense sacrifice of our forefathers – our ancestors who lost their lives during the British-Japanese governance.

The British Era

In 1907, the British government formed the 'Tamil Immigration Fund,' which was later replaced by 'South Indian Labour Fund,' to overcome the labour shortages in Malaya, especially in plantations. The formation of this fund marked the beginning of 31 years of assisted migration from India to Malaya, and was managed by a statutory body known as the 'Immigration Committee.'

The objective of the body was to recruit labourers from India in stages and manage their welfare in Malaya. The committee was also in charge of managing the train trips of labourers and their dependents from their villages to camps in Madras and Nagapatinam, provide food and medical treatment while awaiting ships, quarantine charges upon arrival in Malaya, transport charges within Malaya and so on. In 1938, the United Planting Association of Malaya (UPAM) wanted to reduce rubber tappers' wages from 50 cents a day to 40 cents, which caused the Government of India to ban the emigration of unskilled labourers to Malaya.

Despite having the funds in place to manage their welfare, the labourers who migrated to Malaya were struggling. But their suffering got even worse when the British abandoned Malaya during World War II (WW11).

The labourers lost even that meagre pay. They were left with no money, proper clothing or medical supplies, and even struggled to get a decent meal. They were dressed in rags and suffered ill health.

The Japanese Era

When the Japanese conquered Malaya during WWII, Tamils had three options:

1. Join the Indian National Army to fight alongside the Japanese
2. Work on the death railway in Siam (Thailand)
3. Join the Malayan Peoples Anti-Japanese Army (MPAJA) to fight against the Japanese

Over 300,000 labourers were forced to work on the construction of the Siam-Burma Railway, known to many as the Death Railway, under Japanese soldiers who were known to be very cruel and inhuman.

The Death Railway

The construction of the 415-km Thai-Burma Death Railway started in June 1942 and lasted up to October 1943.

The Japanese brought Malayan Indians, war prisoners, romusha (Javanese labourers) and other Malayans to work on the railway construction - some were deceived into taking up the job on empty promises of high pay while others were forced into it. In a 2016, interview with R.AGE, Death Railway survivor Arumugam Kandasamy said he wanted to flee to Singapore, but took up the construction job at Siam when the Japanese soldiers threatened to kill his family. He continued the journey to Siam to look for his brother, despite being warned by others about the tragic fate of the railway's workers.

"We walked for 12 days, and dead bodies were lying on the walking path throughout the way."

The workers were required to cut through cliffs and mountains, and many died due to the brutal treatment, starvation, overwork and diseases. Some even committed suicide due to their unbearable situation. Thousands of workers were also massacred to prevent their deseases from spreading, while many women lost their lives due to rape.

An estimated 45,000 Tamilians died during the construction, leaving their families bereft. Some report that the number exceeds 60,000. But the actual number of Tamilians who died during the construction is unknown.

Kalingarayar Canal: Carrying a Royal Grudge

Western Tamil Nadu would have been very different if it didn't have the Kalingarayar Canal to nourish it. Velvet paddy fields and waving coconut palms kiss the canal's banks for the better part of its 90-km run, but its calm waters run deep. The story goes that the canal, over 730-year-old hydrological wonder, was built on the back of a royal snub and a vow to never give anyone a chance to cast such aspersions on the ruling dynasty again.

There may or may not be truth to the tale, but the fact is that the canal, which connects three tributaries of the Cauvery River in Tamil Nadu – Bhavani, Noyyal and Amaravathi – was built by the Kalingarayar family, which played a very important role in Coimbatore's history until as recently as the 1950s.

Over the centuries, the canal has brought great wealth and prestige to the family, which also lent its name to a strain of paddy – 'Kalingan' paddy – grown on their lands. Today, the canal irrigates 30,000 acres and benefits more than 50,000 farmers and remains a lifeline for the region.

Kalingarayar Canal|Wikimedia Commons

The Kalingarayars are now based in Uttukuli, 65 km from Coimbatore, but they originally ruled from their capital Vellode in Kongunadu, when the dynasty was founded in the 13th century CE. Kongunadu was one of five divisions of Tamil Nadu, the other four being Cheranadu, Cholanadu, Pandyanadu and Thondainadu.

Most of the old records connected to the Kalingarayar family's early history were destroyed during the wars with Tipu Sultan in the late 18th century, but there are some traces of their past recorded on Cadjan leaves. Apparently, the Pundurai division of the Coimbatore region, consisting of 32 villages, was bestowed on Sathandhai Kalingan by a Chola king, and he was anointed as a local chieftain. Sathandhai Kalingan, thus established the Kalingarayar dynasty which ruled the region till the abolition of the *Zamindari* system after India's independence in 1947.

The story of the Kalingarayars is enriched by the construction of the eponymous canal by the family during the reign of its founder. According to one story, Sathandhai Kalingan, the ruler of Pundurai, had approached his brother-in-law Pannai Kulathan in Karur, to ask for his daughter's hand in marriage for his son. The alliance was accepted, and wedding plans were soon underway.

Golden Grove, Uthukuli Palace|Author

The wedding would have proceeded without a hitch – and Tamil Nadu would not have had its canal – if not for a careless remark made by the father of the bride-to-be. It appears that Kalingarayar overheard the cook asking the bride's father whether he should use fine rice or coarse rice to serve the guests at the wedding reception. The cook was told, "What does it matter whether you cook coarse or fine rice for people living in dry lands?"

Kalingarayar was deeply offended and vowed that the wedding would take place only after wetland crops grew in his lands. He returned to his capital and decided not to shave until he achieved his goal. Legend has it that Lord Subramanya appeared to him in a dream and advised him to construct an anicut, or a small dam, at Bhavani, while he dug a larger canal to irrigate the entire territory. He was also advised to choose a place where a peacock had chased a snake.

Kalingarayar realised that if Kongunadu was to be blessed with crops like rice, he would have to build a long and meandering canal. Work on the canal began in 1270 CE and it took 12 years to complete. It wasn't easy, and it came at a great cost. As the ruler of the region, Kalingarayar could have had almost anything he wanted, but he was a fair man and acquired the land needed for the canal by paying over 1,000 units of gold as compensation. The land thus acquired was used to create a road between the construction site and the Urachi Hills. Another 1,000 units were paid for the boulders used in the canal's construction.

Chandira Saalaai, Uthukuli Palace|Author

There are many other anecdotes that embellish the story of the canal. It is said that to choose the site of the anicut, Kalingarayar went on a coracle ride with a fisherman, whom he granted special privileges at a temple festival. These privileges continue to this day. He also gave some people privileges at the Elamalai Sellandiamman temple celebrations as they had provided implements for the construction of the anicut.

When the canal was completed in 1282 CE, Kalingarayar shaved for the first time in 12 years and to honour his barber, named a village after his community, Navithan Palayam.

As a ruler, he knew he had to take everyone along. In that same spirit, Kalingarayar was quick to introduce social reforms by permitting some backward classes to paint and plaster their houses and to also wear footwear. He even allowed them to play musical instruments on special occasions.

Besides the canal, Kalingarayar constructed several check dams, tanks and water bodies in Kongunadu. After he was satisfied that his beloved Kongunadu was properly irrigated, he went to Karur to keep his promise and celebrate his son's wedding. Since then, the peacock has been the emblem of the Kalingarayar family.

The winds of change in the 14th century altered the political landscape in South India, and the territory ruled by the Kalingarayar family came under the mighty Vijayanagara Empire. From then on, the Kalingarayars became one of the 72 'Polygars' or 'Palayakkarars' in the empire and reported to the Nayaka (Viceroy) of Madurai. Each Palayakkarar governed a *palayam,* which was an administrative division.

Under the Madurai Nayakas, the Kalingarayars functioned as a semi-independent principality and their power and might grew exponentially.

They had a standing army, owned palaces and forts, collected taxes, owned private estates, dispensed justice, maintained law and order, held *durbars,* maintained water bodies while expanding the land under cultivation, built and managed temples and indulged in philanthropy in a big way. The paraphernalia of royalty was funded by retaining a quarter of the revenue they collected, while depositing the rest at Madurai.

Until the 15th century, the Kalingarayar family had been based in Pundurai, and it was the Vijayanagara emperor, Devaraya, who asked Kalingan's descendant, Nanjiya Kalingarayar, to clear the forests of Uttukuli and establish his base there. On the king's orders, he built a new capital, which included wells and channels for irrigation and even a temple to his deity – Agathuramman.

Agathuramman temple|Author

When the Vijayanagara Empire went into decline after its defeat by the Deccani Sultanates in the Battle of Talikota in 1565 CE, the Kongunadu region came under the suzerainty of the Wodeyars of Mysore. Again, luck was on their side and the Kalingarayars enjoyed the patronage of the Wodeyars in exchange for the family's support.

The Polygars of Uttukuli had under them 5,000 footmen, 5,000 horsemen and a kadagam of elephants.

They were stationed at Anaimalai (63 km from Coimbatore) and placed at the disposal of the palace. In return, the Polygars were allowed to levy tolls on goods passing through their territory en route to Kerala, a very lucrative source of income for the Uttukuli Polygars.

By the 1750s, Hyder Ali became the de facto ruler of Mysore and was succeeded in 1728 by his son Tipu Sultan. The Polygars of the Coimbatore region were harassed by Tipu Sultan, and the Polygar of Uttukuli was forced to send his family to Bombay under British protection. The defeat and death of Tipu Sultan in 1799 brought Uttukuli under the British East India Company, which asked the Polygar to pay seven-tenths of the revenue he collected to the Company.

If that was a huge price to pay, there was an upside too. British rule brought peace to the region and the Polygars were able to pay attention to the affairs of their estate and improve their accounting system. This, in turn, increased revenues a great deal, which enabled the Uttukuli family to make huge donations to charitable causes in and around Coimbatore.

The 33rd Polygar of Uttukuli, Agathur Muthuramaswami Kalingarayar, also played an important role in the politics of the Madras Presidency. He was the Vice-President of Madras Zamindars' and Landowners' Association and a Member of the South Indian Liberal Federation. He gave money to start a school in Uttukuli and resources for the Pasteur Institute and Lawley Hospital, both in Coonoor. He was also one of the driving forces behind the establishment of the Coimbatore Spinning and Weaving Mills (1888), a first-of-its-kind in the region, and one that would transform Coimbatore into South India's textile hub.

Lastly, Uttukuli was also famous for its Dusshera celebrations, which were considered the grandest in the Coimbatore region. This can be gauged from an interesting account in *The Madras Mail* dated 23rd October 1912,

"The Dasra festivities at Uttukuli Zamindari commenced on the morning of 11th October 1912 with the installation of the Goddess amidst the chanting of Vedic hymns and mantras on one side of the Chandrasala, a tastefully decorated and beautifully illuminated Mandapam and the other portion being reserved for the holding of the Durbar by the Zamindar."

"The Zamindar with his family and children attended the customary worship, and a Durbar was held every night. As soon as the Zamindar took his seat in the Durbar Hall, he was presented with prasadams from all temples and a number of retainers presented arms in semi-military fashion. Then, all the tenants of the Zamindari paid their respects to the Zamindar."

"Afterwards, a regular programme of music and nautch was gone through. Every evening, there were Kalakshepams by Bhagavathars and others, and numerous people were daily fed. This continued for nine days, and the tenth-day ceremony was an imposing one. After the worship of the Goddess in the morning, the Zamindar held a Durbar and was given a dagger and sword in commemoration of the fact that his ancestors were military chieftains ruling over that part of the country."

The centuries-old rule of the Uttukuli Kalingarayars ended post independence, when the *Zamindari* system was abolished in Madras, in keeping with the

Madras Big Estates Abolition Act, 1948. But the good deed by the first Kalingarayar, in transforming the dry and arid region of Kongunadu into a fertile one, lives on in the hearts of the locals even today.

A statue of Sathandhai Kalingan was recently on 13th May 2018 unveiled at Bhavani in Erode district of Tamil Nadu, while the government of Tamil Nadu has declared the fifth day of the Tamil month of Thai (January) as 'Kalingarayar Day,' which the local agrarian community celebrates as 'Kalingarayan Pongal,' as a mark of gratitude.

The Uthukuli Palace of Kalingarayar Dynasty!

The sprawling palace of the Zamindars of Uthukuli is spread over four acres and is vested with Siddharth and his cousin, Vishnu. The palace has several bedrooms, a library, sheds for bullock carts and cars, a large granary, a kutchery were the Zamindars held court during the yesteryears in addition to a large garden which provides produce for the palace and flowers for the 12 temples managed by the royal family. Large parts of the palace were restored by Siddharth (grandson) and his parents Arunkumar and Seetha, who happens to be the grand daughter of the doyen of the Murugappa Group – A.M.M. Murugappa Chettiar. The ancestors ruled the Vellode part of the Kongu country and around the year 1282, they dedicated the Kalingarayar canal to the people of Western Tamil Nadu by creating a union between the rivers Bhavani, Amaravathi and Noyyal – the three tributaries of river Cauvery. The canal measures 56.5 miles and has been irrigating over 30,000 acres of land for the past seven centuries. "We created our own strain of paddy which came to be known as the Kalingan paddy. Even today, water flows through the Kalingarayar canal for ten and a half months a year. The ruler of Vijayanagar bestowed the title 'Rayar' on us for perpetuity in recognition of our services, and our family moved over to Uthukuli near Pollachi in order to ensure that the benefits of the Kalingarayar canal were completely given to the farmers of the region. The grateful agrarian community continues to celebrate the 5th of the Tamil month of Thai each year as the Kalingarayar day," states the dynamic Siddharth.

The Kalingarayars fought wars on behalf of both the Nayaks of Madurai and the Wodeyars of Mysore in Tirunelveli and Coorg respectively. The Uthukuli Palayam came under the East India Company after the death of Tipu Sultan and the rulers were granted a Zamindari Sanad by the British Monarch during the 19th century.

LHI 9

Epilouge

This book has come out of my realization and a truism that we live in a time when human identities -civilizations, cultures, tribes and individuals -are being erased everywhere across the globe; identities built up often over hundreds of years are lost in a generation in a time where the past and the present jostle for space. The truth may be lost in the ancient dust … But let the memories forever persist. This is a humble compilation written for posterity. The book is also a journey through my understanding that God had to send his messengers as potters to pick up the broken pieces on our ever-changing world, their thoughts, words and deeds have remoulded our destiny – This a Tribute to them all.

This compilation can work as a little catalyst to start on their journey to learn more of the heritage of Tamilnadu and their tall people, its magnificent past and how they made its mark of this ancient land of our pride.

Neither will exploration, the world makes sure that we have a sturdy supply of exciting, new information passionately collected at all times. We have discovered this truth over by looking back. This book gives us an opportunity to delve deeper, and we are only too happy to share our new found knowledge with you.

No tall claims are made from my part, as I claim only to be a compiler rather than an author. I have heavily depended upon information available on the internet; upon excerpts from books published from as early as 1900 to the present day; upon websites of various companies. I have journeyed through Google for endless hours to pack this information in a readable form in print. There is always a narrative tension between these differing tasks of the historian, me being a compiler have just tried to put pieces together, so a deeper study to every subject will always lead to greater insights.

Compilers Note and Acknowledgments

The compiler takes pleasure in acknowledging the kindness of authors and publishers who, very generously, have granted permission to use extracts and excerpts from their copyrighted publications, Blogs and research materials. Among those is whom acknowledgements are due being the following:

A Madras Miscellany S. Muthiah Copyright Late S Muthiah, The Hindu and Westland 2011

2014 Outlook Traveller February edition

Outlook February 29th 2016 edition.

The Hindu Newspaper 2014.2015 and 2016 various editions.

William Dalrymple. The Anarchy Bloomsbury Publishing Plc

Indrani Ramachandra

The images in this book, unless specifically mentioned, are either from open sources or from Private collection given to me by various relatives of person associated with the contents of the book.

Very Special Credits are due to the Following Authors who built up the Live History of India with daily historical treasure, which I have heavily depended.

The Authors list

LHI 1 Karthik Venkatesh…

LHI 2 Mini Menon

LHI3 Leora Pezarkar

LHI4 Kritika Sarda

LH15 Anshika Jain…

LHI6 Akshay Chavan…

LHI 7 Deepanjan Ghosh… Deepanjan Ghosh is a broadcast professional from Kolkata, India. A history buff, a landscape and architecture photographer and blogger, writing since 2013.

LHI 8 Saurav Kumar Rai…

LHI 9 Rajesh Govindarajulu…

Special to Mini Menon Editor Live History India, Adithi Shah Assistant Editor Live History India is a first-of-its-kind digital platform aimed at helping you Rediscover India's great history and cultural legacy, do write to them at contactus@livehistoryindia.com www.livehistoryindia.com

We would like to thank all those who contributed by words, deeds and prayers for this publication; copyright holders have been identified where possible and we apologize for any inadvertent omissions.